EPIC
DRIVES
of the
WORLD

Explore the planet's most thrilling road trips

CONTENTS

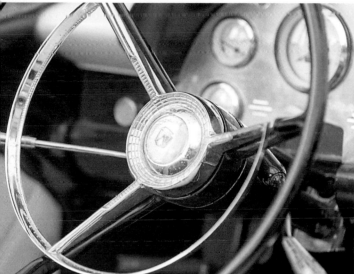

Easy   Harder   Epic

INTRODUCTION

Epic road trips are a source of stories and happy memories for years to come. And, on one occasion, they sparked the idea of Lonely Planet itself. When Tony and Maureen Wheeler set out from England to drive to Afghanistan in 1972 and then journey onward to Australia, they didn't realise that at the end of the trip their experiences and insights would be the basis for Lonely Planet's first guidebooks.

They were far from the first people to drive halfway around the world. In 1968 a group of six British grandmothers bought two second-hand Land Rovers, packed some supplies in Tupperware and drove from London to Australia, passing through Turkey, Iran and India via the Khyber Pass. Go all the way back to 1903 and H. Nelson Jackson, Sewall K. Crocker and their dog Bud took 63 days to drive across the USA from New York to San Francisco.

No matter who you are – youthful or more mature, solo or with a family in tow – the open road is irresistible to travellers.

This book is intended to offer fresh inspiration for your next road trip. We asked our global network of travel writers for their suggestions and selected 50 of the best drives the world has to offer. Their stories cover almost every corner of the world. The classic routes are well represented with the likes of Route 66 and the Pacific Coast Highway in the US, the Great Ocean Road in Australia, and Iceland's Ring Road. Coastlines are a magnet to the roaming motorist – our authors cruise along the coasts of Norway, Ireland, the Cote d'Azur, the Adriatic, the Baltic and beyond. The adventurous won't be disappointed: we feature drives in Vietnam, Bhutan and Nepal, we cross the Kalahari, and Tony Wheeler introduces the Gibb River Road in Western Australia's Kimberley region. There are also easy-going excursions, for instance around Scotland's Isle of Skye, that are no less beautiful or memorable.

We've tried not to discriminate against any driver: we have routes written and ridden by motorcyclists and even a tour of Northern California by electric vehicle. A few of these drives take a day but others can be enjoyed over a weekend, a week or more. Most of the

drives that made the grade are recognised routes – from the Going-to-the-Sun Road across the Rockies in Montana to the Wild Atlantic Way in Ireland – with regular signposts to minimise the chance of going wrong. A few, especially those in the more remote reaches of Australia, Asia and South America, require some logistical planning, a degree of mechanical experience (at least check that you're carrying a spare wheel and a jack!) and a more intrepid attitude. With the sophisticated mapping apps available today, we've avoided providing turn-by-turn directions. The most important role of these tales from the road is to inspire you to pack an overnight bag and hop behind the wheel to explore somewhere new.

Road trips can be a way of linking together a string of highlights, such as southern Utah's unbeatable series of national parks, making a musical pilgrimage or simply cruising through beautiful scenery, stopping where you please. What they have in common is that the road tripper is always independent. Want to take a detour (and we suggest some gems) or stay an extra day? Go right ahead. It's all about the journey. Driving a car need not be a mode of transport that insulates you from your surroundings: if you stop regularly, explore, encounter local people and their culture, you'll have as rich and rewarding an experience as you could hope for.

HOW TO USE THIS BOOK

The main stories in each regional chapter feature first-hand accounts of fantastic drives in that continent. Each includes a factbox to start the planning of a trip – when is the best time of year, how to get there, where to stay. But beyond that, these stories should spark other ideas. We've started that process with the 'more like this' section following each story, which offers other ideas along a similar theme, not necessarily on the same continent. Drives are colour coded according to difficulty, which takes into account not just how long, remote and challenging they are but the logistics and local conditions. The index collects different types of drive for a variety of interests

Clockwise from left: a South African service station on the Panorama Route; a classic Ford Galaxy on the Pacific Coast Highway (also below). Previous page: exploring the east coast of New Zealand in a VW campervan

THE SELF-DRIVE SAFARI

Set off on a road trip beneath the big skies of Zambia, roaming among big game by day and pitching under the stars at night.

Rules 47 to 54 of the Zambian Highway Code concern animals. They offer considered advice, such as 'Do not carry animals on vehicle rooftops' and 'Be careful around larger game animals (which) may charge your vehicle, causing damage and endangering your life.' Where most safari-goers travel in the company of a knowledgeable guide – on hand to deal with this type of situation – on a self-drive safari you are your own guide, driver, navigator, cook, first-aider and engineer. There are few places better for such an adventure than Zambia: among the most sparsely inhabited countries in Africa, with remote swathes of forest and grassland bisected by arrow-straight highways that stretch to the horizon.

I'm setting out on one such highway, the Great East Rd, with photographer Phil Lee Harvey. We are bound for the wilderness country of South Luangwa National Park, ready to drive unsupervised among the big beasts of the African bush. Soon the chaotic traffic jams of the capital Lusaka retreat behind us. Potholes appear in the road: these are big craters that jolt the car and send loose items airborne.

The potholes are all the more difficult to dodge when you're distracted by a landscape of such exquisite loveliness. At first, low forested hills rise on all sides, growing taller as the road skirts the border with Mozambique, before lapsing into infinite green plains on the cusp of the Luangwa Valley. Homecoming schoolchildren shuffle along the roadside, bound for villages where bonfire smoke swirls about thatched roofs.

When we arrive at the market town of Chipata, people sell us groundnuts through the car window. A police officer flags us down at a checkpoint for a symposium on the English footballer Wayne Rooney. Mostly we are alone on the road, although every now and then big freight trucks from Malawi, Congo and Zimbabwe barge past (seemingly unsure whether Zambians drive on the left or on the right side of the road).

The dark of the night descends swiftly, and soon the headlights pick the shapes of sleeping villages out of the gloom. An owl swoops into the glare of the beams. It is many hours before we arrive at the gates of the national park, and the last hiccups of tarmac give way to rusty-brown earth.

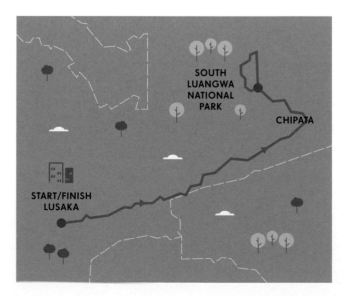

SOUTH LUANGWA NATIONAL PARK

CHIPATA

START/FINISH LUSAKA

Clockwise from top: elephants crossing in an orderly fashion; a female leopard in South Luangwa; the sun goes down on the banks of the Luangwa; piloting the 4WD through the park. Previous page: under the starry canopy of a Zambian campsite

Like any highway, the bush tracks of South Luangwa National Park have their own set of rules. For instance, when attempting a three-point turn on a riverbank, you should check the rear-view mirror for oncoming hippos. Above all, however, you should be respectful to other road users. Soon after arriving in the park I have to do an emergency stop as a young bull elephant barges onto the road. It becomes clear he is the white-van man of the Luangwa traffic system, honking angrily at our vehicle and anything else hoping to overtake him. Keeping a sensible following distance are a convoy of giraffes, heads gently bobbing above the treeline.

Finding your way around requires skill in South Luangwa's labyrinth of tangled foliage and oxbow lakes. It means that even self-drivers are advised to sometimes park up at lodges and enlist the services of a guide. We enlist Yona Banda, a local who has honed a Superman-like ability to spot animals at long range. With Yona at the wheel, we soon happen upon a herd of 40 more elephants crossing the Luangwa River – their trunks raised like periscopes as they wade through the current. Not long after, he scouts a group of 14 lions and cubs, all watching intently on a riverbank as one of their pride swims across the water, three crocodiles in pursuit. Transfixed by the plight of their comrade, the lions don't seem to register our vehicle, coming close enough that their whiskers brush the car door.

We are the only visitors at our bush campsite, arriving as the dying sun slips beneath the canopies of sycamores and tamarind trees. We pitch up our vehicle's built-on roof tents (complete with mattresses and soft pillows), shaking 500 miles (804km) of dust off the outer sheet. Logs are chopped, sausages grilled, beers clinked, stories shared. Finally, the last embers of the fire crackle and die, and it is time to climb the ladder up to our rooftop beds.

At this point, tales laughed over by the warm glow of the fire acquire a new, sinister resonance in darkness. Polytetrafluoroethylene-coated polycotton rip-stop fabric can repel rain, sleet and snow, but its all-season outdoor performance specifications do not extend to withstanding a sharp feline claw. Lying inside the tent at night, you soon realise that only a few millimetres of fabric separate you from all the animals you have seen on the road, and that for all you know, all the elephants, lions and crocodiles you've spotted could be inches outside (perhaps forming an orderly queue at the bottom of the ladder).

It takes about 45 minutes for the human eye to fully reach maximum sensitivity in darkness. Poking my head out the tent into the inky blackness, it takes 10 minutes before I spot bats flitting through the patch of sky around Orion's Belt; another 15 before I spy baboons stirring in the high branches of nearby fig trees. It takes a full nine hours, however, before I climb out of my tent in the slanting morning sunshine and see that the footprints of a leopard have crossed the tracks of our vehicle on the far edge of camp. It's often said that safari is one long drama – and in moments like these it is easy to feel like a cast member with just a tiny role in a production that has been playing for millennia. **OS**

SOUTH LUANGWA'S WILDLIFE

Alongside elephants, giraffes, lions and leopards, South Luangwa is famous for its buffalo herds, which are dramatic when they gather in the dry season. There's also a stunning variety of 'plains game', including bushbucks, waterbucks, impalas, kudu and puku. Luangwa has a population of wild dogs, one of Africa's rarest animals. About 400 species of birdlife have been recorded in the park.

Opposite: elephants and impala at dawn in South Luangwa

DIRECTIONS

Start/End // Lusaka.
Distance // The drive from Lusaka to the Mfuwe Gate, the main entrance to the park, via the Great East Rd, is around 435 miles (700km) one way.
Getting there // Zambia is increasingly well connected, with direct flights to destinations inside and outside Africa.
What to take // Clothes suitable for safari don't need to be specialised or expensive. It's colour that matters: nothing bright that can easily be spotted by wildlife (white is the worst offender) and no black or very dark colours, which will attract tsetse flies. Go with greens and light browns and a combination of shorts for very hot days and long, lightweight trousers for walking in the bush. Also bring binoculars, a wide-brimmed hat, sunglasses, high-ankle walking shoes and a small torch.

*Opposite: the Grand Teton mountains
are reflected in the Snake River in
Wyoming's Grand Teton National Park*

MORE LIKE THIS
WILDLIFE WATCHING

GIPPSLAND & WILSONS PROMONTORY, AUSTRALIA

Traversing one of Australia's most underrated corners, this journey southeast and east of Melbourne takes in the wild landscapes of Phillip Island and Wilsons Prom, and engaging rural towns such as Inverloch, Koonwarra and Port Albert, before almost falling off the map in the ghost town of Walhalla on the way back to Melbourne. Phillip Island hosts the sunset arrival of the penguins at Penguin Parade, one of Australia's great wildlife spectacles, and also claims the country's largest colony of fur seals, as well as the Koala Conservation Centre. Wilsons Promontory National Park, meanwhile, sits at Australia's southernmost tip and its dense woodland shelters a rich portfolio of native Australian wildlife. As you make your way past Port Albert to Walhalla, you'll certainly want to stop at Ninety Mile Beach, an isolated strip of sand backed by dunes that is exactly what it says on the tin.

Start // Phillip Island
End // Walhalla
Distance // 308 miles (495km)

KAIKOURA COAST, NEW ZEALAND

This stretch of State Highway 1 is a relatively quick and convenient route between the South Island's two major traveller gateways, Picton and Christchurch, but it also boasts several of its major highlights. The beautiful Marlborough Sounds and Blenheim's world-class wineries can hardly be missed, but hidden, low-key and up-and-coming attractions also abound. The main draw for wildlife watchers will be the Kaikoura peninsula, where a walkway from the town offers the chance to see shearwaters, petrels, albatross and other seabirds, plus seals lazing around at Point Kean, seemingly oblivious to the attention of hordes of human gawpers. Several species of whale and dolphin (including sperm whales and even blue whales) either live in the Kaikoura area or swing by, which explains the popularity of the marine tours, especially Whale Watch Kaikoura. Your other key chance to spot beasts comes at Willowbank Wildlife Reserve in Christchurch, which provides a rare opportunity to view kiwi.

Start // Picton
End // Christchurch
Distance // 219 miles (352km)

GRAND TETON TO YELLOWSTONE, WYOMING, USA

Yellowstone is nature's tour de force. Its unique supervolcano features half the world's geysers, the country's largest high-altitude lake and a mass of blue-ribbon rivers and waterfalls. To the south, Grand Teton National Park complements with craggy peaks, peaceful waterways and sublime alpine terrain. Wildlife spotting can start at Jackson, where elk, bison and bighorn sheep congregate in winter at the National Elk Refuge, and grizzly sightings are not uncommon as soon as you head out onto the Moose-Wilson back road. The wet lowlands at Oxbow Bend provide a scenic spot to view moose, elk, bald eagles and other birds, while bear (or bison) jams are sometimes an issue from Yellowstone Lake on. Beyond Grand Canyon of the Yellowstone, head east towards Lamar Valley, dubbed the 'Serengeti of North America' for its herds of bison, elk and the occasional grizzly or coyote. It's also the place to spot wolves, particularly in spring.

Start // Jackson
End // Mammoth
Distance // 250 miles (402km)

CRUISING CLARENCE DRIVE

Less than an hour from Cape Town, this spectacular coastal road hangs over the Atlantic Ocean, with ancient mountains providing an equally impressive backdrop.

In a country blessed with bucolic vineyard-dotted lanes, meandering mountain passes, roads that wind through wildlife reserves, and long, straight highways cutting across the seemingly endless expanse of the semi-desert, it's tough to single out just one road trip. Yet Clarence Drive, about an hour east of Cape Town, often makes it onto drivers' lists of most scenic road, not just in South Africa, but in the world.

It might be a slight exaggeration to say that driving this road changed my life, but it did, in some small way, contribute to my decision to settle in South Africa. It all starts in Gordon's Bay, a low-key seaside spot tucked away in a corner of False Bay. Most people pass by on their way from Cape Town to destinations east, but swerving off the N2 highway at Gordon's Bay provides a magnificent alternative way to reach the 'whale capital' of Hermanus, or indeed a marvellous day trip in its own right. You could cover the 60km (37-mile) stretch from Gordon's Bay to just past Kleinmond in around an hour, but there is so much to see, and you are going to want to take photographs. Lots of photographs.

Strictly speaking, the road doesn't become Clarence Drive until the darling little hamlet of Rooiels, but most people would agree that the most spectacular stretch begins just above the yacht harbour in Gordon's Bay. Here the going is slow – not so much for the back-to-back bends (although there are said to be 77 of them along the whole route) but because, if you're anything like me, you're going to have to stop every 500m or so to grab a snap of the vast ocean blue from a slightly different angle. Luckily, lookout points abound, giving you the chance to imagine False Bay as 16th-century sailors would have seen it. To be fair, though,

they probably weren't as enraptured as today's traveller is. The bay was more of a bane to some – its name comes from the fact that early explorers thought they had passed the craggy rocks of the Cape of Good Hope and were entering Table Bay. Imagine their disappointment when they veered inland only to realise the notoriously choppy cape was still ahead and that they weren't quite on the home stretch to Europe just yet.

The deceptive headland was actually Hangklip, a leaning peak in Pringle Bay marking the easternmost point of False Bay. Pretty Pringle Bay is one of those envy-inducing towns that makes you

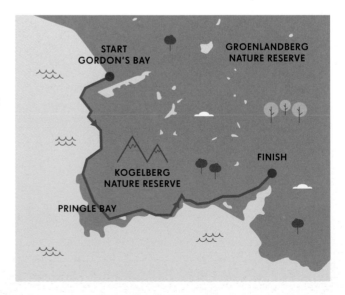

Clockwise from below: a cape sugarbird in the Harold Porter National Botanical Garden; Clarence Road carves around the bay; sugarbush blossoms (protea) in the botanical garden. Previous page: the rugged and wonderful Cape coastline

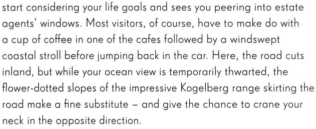

start considering your life goals and sees you peering into estate agents' windows. Most visitors, of course, have to make do with a cup of coffee in one of the cafes followed by a windswept coastal stroll before jumping back in the car. Here, the road cuts inland, but while your ocean view is temporarily thwarted, the flower-dotted slopes of the impressive Kogelberg range skirting the road make a fine substitute – and give the chance to crane your neck in the opposite direction.

But the coast is never far away and just outside Betty's Bay there's a chance to meet a few of the ocean-dwelling locals. Stony Point's penguin population is far less famous than those that inhabit Simon's Town, on the other side of False Bay, but they are no less entertaining, and here you're likely to have the colony pretty much to yourself.

Actually, there's a lot of quiet time available along this route. To call Betty's Bay sleepy might be clichéd, but it's also undeniably true. Houses here are either of the retirement variety or else second homes for wealthy weekending Capetonians – and you can see why. Sandwiched between the mountains of the Kogelberg Nature Reserve and the Atlantic Ocean is a collection of spacious, individually designed homes, a chocolatier and a potter's studio, worth the drive just for a ceramic souvenir. It is here that, on my first jaunt along Clarence Drive, I made pipe dreams for an oceanfront retirement. Most people drive right on by, but we always stop to stock up on road-trip sustenance (namely, chocolates from GaBoLi) before jumping back into the

"The road again hits the craggy coast, but with False Bay behind you, it's now the mountains that are the star"

car – if you're similarly tempted, ask about the fynbos-filled truffle, featuring plants endemic to the region.

You've hardly got into third gear when you reach the Harold Porter National Botanical Garden, a highlight of the route. Leg-stretching opportunities range from gentle strolls among the fynbos vegetation, to clambering hikes past waterfalls into the rolling mountains. Once you can tear yourself away, the road here once again hits the craggy coastline, but with False Bay behind you, it's now the mountains that are the star. Look out for a dirt road just before the town of Kleinmond, and if you have a day or two to spare, veer off to visit the Kogelberg, part of a World Heritage site, thanks to its abundance of endemic flora. This is where you ditch the car and pull on the hiking boots for an hour or eight.

From Kleinmond you can retrace your steps, continue to Hermanus – whale town extraordinaire (from June to November) or head north to join the N2 as it meanders through apple country and descends Sir Lowry's Pass, giving epic views across the Cape Flats and all the way to Cape Town. It's not in the same league as the coastal road, but it's not an ugly way to get back to the city. As I said, glorious drives are not in short supply in South Africa. **LC**

WHALE WATCHING

Although Hermanus is the most celebrated spot for whale watching in South Africa, in calving season (June to November) you stand a good chance of seeing Southern Right Whales all along this stretch of coast. Take a pair of binoculars and keep an eye out for noses, fins and tails poking out of the bay. If you're out of luck, continue to Hermanus where the world's only whale crier points out sightings to eager visitors.

DIRECTIONS

Start // Gordon's Bay
End // Rte 43 between Bot River & Fisherhaven
Distance // 37 miles (60km)
Getting there // Fly to Cape Town, approx 37 miles (60km) from the start of the drive.
When to drive // The route is sublime year-round, though try to go mid-week if possible – Cape Town dwellers often use Clarence Drive as a weekend escape.
Where to stay // Camp at Kogel Bay Holiday Resort or book an Eco Cabin at Kogelberg Nature Reserve.
Where to eat // Eat a picnic in the Harold Porter National Botanical Garden or pick a seafood spot in Betty's Bay.
More drives // To extend the coastal drive from Cape Town, opt for Rte 310 out of Muizenberg.
Further info // www.kleinmondtourism.co.za

Cruising Clarence Drive

Opposite: a quiver tree in the Goegap
Nature Reserve, Namaqualand

MORE LIKE THIS
SOUTH AFRICAN DRIVES

SANI PASS

The only road connecting KwaZulu-Natal and Lesotho is a truly epic mountain pass. Rising to 2876 metres over a series of steep switchbacks, this is not a drive for the faint-hearted. Things start gently until the border post. From here, local law dictates that only 4WD vehicles can continue into Lesotho, and with good reason – tight bends, loose gravel, streams traversing the road and potholes galore all add to the excitement. If you're lucky enough to drive the pass on a clear day, the views are predictably magnificent. Enjoy with a pint at Africa's highest pub, found atop the pass. If you're not continuing into Lesotho, the downward journey is nail-biting and passengers will find themselves hitting imaginary brakes around the tighter corners.
Start // Himeville
End // Sani Top
Distance // 24 miles (38km)

NAMAQUALAND FLOWER ROUTE

For most of the year, the N7 highway is a dreary drive, but every August the barren, russet landscape briefly bursts into Technicolor with the arrival of the spring flowers. Start in the miniscule hamlet of Nieuwoudtville then join the N7 as it ventures north in one long, fairly flat, fairly straight line. Although wildflowers can be seen along the road, your destination is the off-the-beaten-track Namaqua National Park, where veritable blankets of orange, white, purple and yellow daisies take over the normally desolate hills. Further north, Springbok's Goegap Nature Reserve offers the chance to hike, drive or cycle among the flowers.
Start // Nieuwoudtville
End // Springbok
Distance // 193 miles (310km)

ROUTE 62

While Route 62 can be driven in three hours, you can easily turn this trip into a week-long adventure. Kicking off with the short but pretty Cogmanskloof Pass, the road cuts through Montagu, overlooked by the Langeberg range. Here the road widens and becomes the wonderfully named Wildehondskloofhoogte Pass (Wild Dog Ravine Heights Pass), winding alongside fruit orchards, vineyards and artsy towns. After Barrydale, things get dramatic again on the Huisrivier Pass, which snakes through rugged mountains sprinkled with green shrubbery. Best of all, Route 62 is known as South Africa's longest wine route – stop to sample robust reds and the renowned local port. Just make sure there's a teetotaller to take the wheel while you enjoy the changing landscape of the Little Karoo.
Start // Ashton
End // Oudtshoorn
Distance // 155 miles (250km)

CROSSING THE KALAHARI IN BOTSWANA

To drive the Central Kalahari Game Reserve is to traverse one of the Earth's remote and silent spaces, where black-maned lions rule over ancient river valleys.

Entering the great reserves of Africa always feels like crossing a threshold into an entirely different world where anything might just be possible. And so it was that, feeling a little like Alice in Wonderland or the children who climb the Magic Faraway Tree in search of adventures, I left behind the paved road and drove out onto the sands of Botswana's Central Kalahari Game Reserve.

This is one of Africa's largest protected areas, but it encloses within its boundaries barely a fraction of the Kalahari, the largest unbroken stretch of sand on the planet. Ever since I first arrived in the Kalahari years before, I have dreamed of this journey, of a crossing from north to south, less out of a desire to conquer one of Africa's great deserts than to leave behind well-trammelled trails in search of desert silences and the wildlife of its remote reaches.

Ahead of me lay a week of off-road driving, deep-wilderness camping and days without seeing another human being. Oh, and a puff adder. On the sandy trail in from Rakops my path was blocked by one of the most slow-moving yet fearsome snakes in all of Africa. Going too fast (I was yet to slow my pace to a patient desert rhythm), I swerved to avoid it – to kill a creature, any creature, before my adventure has even begun, would surely be an ill-starred omen. I reversed to get a closer look. It flicked its head at me in anger. I nodded in respect and continued on my way.

Soon I reached Deception Valley, one of the fossilised dry river valleys that define the Central Kalahari – it is one of the great ironies of this arid, sometimes desolate place that it owes its topography to water. As the sun neared the horizon, the golden grasses swayed to a cooling breeze of late afternoon, and gemsbok – the painted oryx of the Kalahari – and springbok

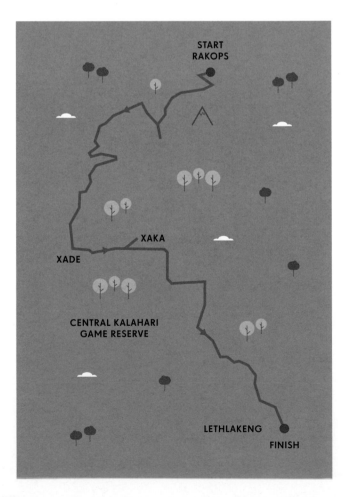

© Mark Eveleigh | Alamy

"I followed, as close as I dared, as a black-maned male lion strode along the valley, king of all he surveyed"

raised their heads, wary of the intrusion and watchful for night predators. Elsewhere, islands of acacias, where Mark and Delia Owens once made their home in that classic of desert exploration, *Cry of the Kalahari*, and salt pans became beautiful in the softening light. Where the Kalahari had at midday possessed all the charm of an over-exposed photograph, it now radiated magic in the descent towards darkness. From my campsite high on a sand dune haired with thin Kalahari vegetation, I watched as stars lit up the night sky, so far from the polluting sounds and lights of the city.

In the night, lions roared, and at dawn I followed, as close as I dared, as a black-maned Kalahari male lion strode along the valley, king of all he surveyed. Later, in a day spent driving another ancient valley, Passarge, I saw not another member of my species, and instead shared the trail with cheetah and honey badger, with bat-eared foxes and the world's heaviest flying bird, the kori bustard, with giraffe and ostrich, as jackals lurked just beyond reach, watching for opportunity.

Out on the salt pans in the west of the reserve, as shadows lengthened, an aardwolf ran like the night devil it so resembles and not once looked over its shoulder. Extravagantly horned kudu imagined itself unseen in a thorn thicket. And another lone cheetah, on the fringes of Piper Pan, set off on the hunt, an apparition of feline grace and elegance.

Vehicles were few, and they became even fewer the further south I travelled. Beyond Xade Gate, deep into the former homeland of the San indigenous peoples, there was no-one and the sand became deeper. Isolated campsites were silent, save for occasional gusts of wind and the night roars of lions close to the waterhole at Xaka. By the time I arrived at Bape campsite, on a rise above the dry river of Quoxo, I wondered what strange and silent land I had strayed into, so silent was the afternoon and night, and so powerful the sense of having left behind the world.

And then, at Mothomelo, still some distance north of the Tropic of Capricorn and with my fuel running low, in an unlikely glade of green and pleasant trees, a community of San people quietly approached my vehicle. One of the last remaining San communities still living in the Central Kalahari Game Reserve, the people of Mothomelo were reticent, like so many desert peoples, and the encounter felt like the briefest of meetings between two different worlds. We smiled often, and with no shared language other than mutual goodwill, we soon went our separate ways.

Much too soon, signs of the modern world, few at first, began to intrude – vehicle tracks in the sand, distant communication towers – until they were impossible to ignore. South of Gaugama, I crossed into the Khutse Game Reserve, the Central Kalahari's southern appendage. As I went I began slowly to reconcile myself with my return to the world. By the time I moved beyond the Tropic of Capricorn, any lingering regrets that the journey was coming to an end had given way to the joy of an adventure fulfilled. Even so, I knew it would not be long before I once again began to long for the roar of lions and the silences of Kalahari nights. **AH**

THE SAN

Although the Central Kalahari Game Reserve was originally set up to protect the San, they were forced to leave by Botswana's government in 1997, which claimed the reason was to protect wildlife and enable the government to provide services for San communities. Critics argued the move was because diamonds had been discovered in the reserve. Whatever the reason, the San won a court challenge in 2006 and were allowed to return.

Clockwise from left: the San are indigenous to the Kalahari; ever-watchful gemsbok; settling in for the night in the Reserve. Previous page: tackling the Kalahari terrain in a 4WD

DIRECTIONS

Start // Rakops
End // Lethlakeng
Distance // 746 miles (1200km)
Getting there // Maun airport (130 miles/210km northwest of Rakops) has flights to Johannesburg as well as domestic connections with Gaborone and Kasane.
Where to stay // There are two luxury lodges in the reserve – Kalahari Plains Camp and Tau Pan Camp – but you'll spend most nights camping.
What to take // A 4WD vehicle equipped with camping equipment. The nearest petrol stations are at Rakops and Lethlakeng. Also carry at least three full jerrycans of additional fuel – sandy tracks mean you'll use up a lot.
More info // To arrange vehicle hire, campsite bookings and a satellite phone, contact www.drivebotswana.com.

*Opposite: the Atacama Desert
in Chile forms part of the
Dakkar Rally's new route*

MORE LIKE THIS
DESERT DRIVES

TANAMI TRACK, AUSTRALIA

Australia's Outback has endless ways
to cross the desert, but the Tanami is a
classic. Beginning 12 miles (20km) north
of Alice Springs in Australia's Red Centre,
it's paved only for the first 198 miles
(315km), as far as the Tilmouth Roadhouse.
Thereafter, the reasonably well-maintained
gravel track (which is sometimes
impassable after rain and should only
be attempted in a 4WD) passes through
remote indigenous communities, such as
Yuendemu, and hundreds of kilometres
of desert terrain, passing isolated desert
massifs and cattle stations en route. It
begins in the Northern Territory and ends
in Western Australia, and is best driven
from June to September.
Start // Alice Springs
End // Halls Creek
Distance // 643 miles (1035km)

NAMIB DESERT, NAMIBIA

You could drive the paved road between
the two coastal Namibian towns of Lüderitz
and Walvis Bay, but the more direct route,
across Sperrgebiet National Park and
the dune fields of the Namib Desert is
far more adventurous. Coastways Tours
Lüderitz (www.coastways.com.na) offers
guided expeditions across this otherwise
inaccessible route. This is one of the most
beautiful and challenging desert routes on
the planet, crossing as it does the world's
oldest desert and with very few passable
tracks. Where the dunes meet the Atlantic
Ocean at Sandwich Bay is one of Africa's
most beautiful corners. It's a six-day epic
and one of the most dramatic desert
crossings in the world.
Start // Lüderitz
End // Walvis Bay
Distance // 466 miles (750km)

DAKAR RALLY, SOUTH AMERICA

Since concerns over terrorism and conflicts
in North Africa caused the race to be shifted
to South America in 2008, the Dakar has
taken in Argentina, Chile's Atacama Desert
and the salt pans of Bolivia, although the
route changes every year. The race itself is
strictly for professionals only but the route
can be driven at other times by anyone
with a reliable vehicle, plenty of time and
a strong sense of adventure. Full route
descriptions are available online, allowing
drivers to pick and choose the routes
that best suit their time and vehicles. The
sections that most capture the spirit of the
trans-Saharan crossing that defined the old
Paris-Dakar Rally (the Sahara remains off-
limits) are those in the Atacama Desert, the
driest desert on Earth.
Start/End // Buenos Aires
Distance // 5776 miles (9295km)

FIT FOR A KING: JEBEL HAFEET

It's one of the world's best driving roads and not by accident; it was built for an emir who wanted maximum fun driving up to his palace.

Coming into land at Abu Dhabi airport during the night, the thought momentarily crosses my mind that the aircraft is being guided in by the seemingly endless yellow dotted lines that crisscross the blackness of the desert below. But no, these lines are just roads – roads with street lighting for hundreds of kilometres of nothingness. I guess this is one of the perks of having as much energy as you want from the oil and gas that flow from the ground here in the United Arab Emirates.

Next morning I'm out on those roads, heading for the border city of Al Ain where the ruling dynasty of Abu Dhabi comes from. Sheik Zayed still has a palace out there, although the capital of the Emirate is now in Abu Dhabi itself. I imagine he actually has more than one palace in Al Ain, but one of them is just outside town on the mountain and that's the one I'm headed for. Or rather the road that leads to it.

It's not very often that you get a chance to ride what many have called the world's best motorcycle (and driving) road, and I'm a bit breathless in expectation, although that would be partly from the 40°C (104°F) heat. I am also a bit confused, which is why I end up back at the airport instead of on the Al Ain road. This is all my fault; the Arabic/English signposting

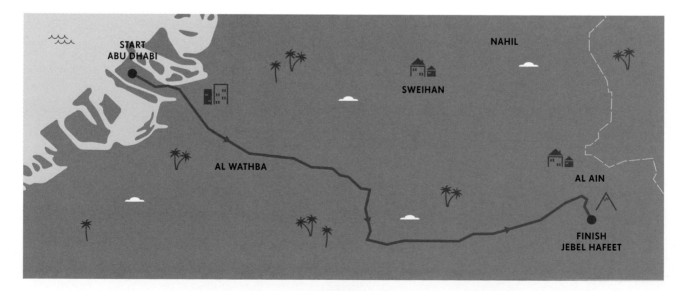

is relatively good. I turn the big beast of a BMW K 1300 S around again and find the correct turn.

The signposting informs me that there is a 120km/h (74½mph) speed limit, but when he handed the bike over to me this morning, the bloke from the motorcycle hire company told me that the radar cameras give 20km/h (12mph) leeway. And seeing that this hire company will be wearing any radar camera speeding fines I accumulate on my borrowed bike, I'm prepared to believe him.

One thing you don't need to worry about on the six-lane freeway is trucks as they have their own freeway off to the north. You can just see them thundering through the desert. However, you do need to worry about the local drivers who whistle past at 200km/h (124mph) and then suddenly slam on the brakes as soon as a speed camera looms.

I stop for fuel, and one of the drivers who is filling up a 4WD saunters over and says, 'What are you doing here?' It turns out that he is a subscriber to my magazine, *Australian Motorcyclist*, and one of the 92% of the population of Abu Dhabi who are not native. He grins. 'You're a brave man. My bike is safely back in Adelaide; the traffic's a bit too aggressive here for me. Not to mention the camels,' he adds. 'The fences don't mean anything to those buggers.'

Suitably warned, I continue at near enough to 200km/h (124mph) except when I see a speed camera, where I join the locals in their crazed braking manoeuvres. I am having fun.

> *"The German company that built this marvellous road did a superb job, the corners are occasionally tight but the surface is near enough to perfect"*

Already. Al Ain comes into view, and I turn off to the Green Mubazzarah, an oasis at the foot of the mountain. Alongside is the beginning of the Jebel Hafeet road; a 'mere' 11.7km (7 mile) snake of beautifully designed, outstandingly flat and smooth tar. It has between 21 and 60 corners, depending on whom you believe, and I swallow hard before I turn the throttle and release the clutch to liberate the big BMW's 173 horsepower. Whoops – the rear tyre leaves a black line on the road; this bike does not have such soft luxuries as traction control. And we're off.

I snick the bike into second gear, then up into third. BMW motorcycle gearboxes sometimes come in for criticism, but this one certainly cooperates when you really make it work hard. Despite thinking that I would count the corners, I forget about them almost as soon as the first one looms. The German company that built this marvellous road did a superb job; the corners are occasionally tight, but the radius is always consistent and the surface is near enough to perfect. The Mini Club of Dubai comes here on weekends to run hill

climbs, but I can't imagine that this road would be nearly as much fun on four wheels.

Swinging from side to side is exhilarating and I push the bike harder and harder, so confident that my heartbeat stays slow and steady. Until a small truck comes the other way around a curve in my lane. It's the first vehicle I've seen on the mountain, and its sudden arrival right in my cornering line gives my heart all the workout anybody could ask for. He's not changing lanes for me, and braking is pointless, so I take advantage of the sticky tyres and get out of his way and back onto my line. A quick nervous laugh and I'm back into it.

I pass the exit to the hotel and soon afterwards I roll out into a large parking lot, near the top of the mountain. The smallish-looking palace is a little higher, and I suspect that strange motorcyclists from Australia are probably not among their usual guests. No biggie. I roll back down the road to the hotel and check in. My room has expansive views of the vast desert, and once it's dark I'll sit at the floor-to-ceiling window with a gin and tonic and admire those yellow dotted lines heading for the horizon. But for now I'm only interested in getting back out onto that road, and nothing else.

I ride the Jebel Hafeet road again, down and then up and then down again. I time my runs, though I'm not going to reveal my time here because I'm hardly a gun. But I sure felt like one. Is this the best motorcycle road in the world? Who cares. It's the best for now. **PT**

OFF THE ROAD

Keep in mind that you are in Arabia, the heart of the Muslim world. There are ways to get around Muhammad's prohibition of alcohol while respecting it in spirit – by staying in a Western-owned and -run hotel, for instance. But you may need to scour the bazaars of Al Ain to find yourself a suitably demure swimming costume, perhaps a pair of voluminous board shorts which, when worn with a t-shirt, will pass scrutiny in the hotel pool.

From left: negotiating the switchbacks of the Al Ain Road; the Al Wahda district of downtown Abu Dhabi. Previous page: the Remah Desert, Al Ain

DIRECTIONS

Start/End // Abu Dhabi
Distance // 108 miles (175km) to the Green Mubazzarah, 7 miles (11.7km) to the top of Jebel Hafeet
Getting there // Fly in to either Abu Dhabi or Dubai.
When to drive // It's always hot. But choose winter if you can. Temperatures are likely to be below 30°C (86°F) and the chance of precipitation is only 10%.
Where to stay // The Mercure Grand on the mountain.
What to take // A hot weather riding suit. BMW's Venting Suit combines netting with nano-crystal heat reflection.
Formalities // Visas are available online.
Vehicle hire // Motorcycle and car rental is available in both Dubai and Abu Dhabi, but easier in the former.
Detours // It's not exactly a detour, but the ride down from Dubai is only about 93 miles (150km).

*Opposite: overlooking a tranquil
Alpine lake towards Switzerland's
fearsome Matterhorn*

MORE LIKE THIS
STATEMENT DRIVES

ROUTE DE TOURINI, FRANCE

Often listed as one of the most dangerous
roads in the world, the Route is nothing
of the kind – if you are careful. But not
everyone is careful, especially the drivers
of the Monte Carlo Rally, whose supercars
have knocked the ends off the typical French
stone balustrades that guard the drop to
the valley. Thirty-four hairpins take you up
1604 metres to the top of the pass, where
three hotels wait to help you calm your
pulse. The Hôtel Les Trois Vallées has walls
full of photos from the Monte Carlo Rally;
while there is a warning that the road may
close in winter, this doesn't seem to apply to
rallyists whose cars are often depicted up to
the windows in snow. Unfortunately, you'll
have little chance to enjoy the outstanding
scenery along this section of the D2566,
because if you don't pay constant attention
to the road it will justify its reputation in the
most unfortunate manner.

Start // Sospel
End // Col de Turini
Distance // 15 miles (25km)

DEATH VALLEY, CALIFORNIA, USA

So named for good reason, Death Valley
is a punishing, barren place, harsh, hot
and lifeless, littered with ghost towns
and abandoned mines that tell of the
human struggle to survive here. Yet a drive
through this National Park also reveals
a place spectacularly alive with natural
wonders: 'singing' sand dunes, water-
sculpted canyons, mysteriously itinerant
desert boulders, volcanic craters and
palm-shaded oases. From the expansive
salt pans of Badwater to the bizarre stately
desert home of Scotty's Castle (closed for
renovations at time of writing), this journey
– as the World's tallest thermometer at
Baker will show – is likely a rather warm
one, so stock up with plenty of water and
make sure your car has reliable air-con.

Start // Baker, San Bernadino County
End // Scotty's Castle
Distance // 380 miles (610km)

THE SWISS ALPS

The Alps are both a blessing and a
burden when it comes to tripping around
Switzerland. The soul-stirring views are
stupendous, but you have to go over,
around or through one mountain to reach
the next. Starting in Arosa and finishing in
Zermatt, this drive itself is one long feast
of scenery, via thrilling hairpins and past
lovely lakes, mountain-clinging countryside
and rugged wilderness, but exceptional
stop-offs include Andermatt in Uri canton,
which is at the crossroads of four major
Alpine passes and thus a terrific base for
hiking and cycling. And you'll need to get
out of the car for the real jaw-droppers: the
cable-cars to the 360-degree, 200-peak
panorama from the 2970m Schilthorn, and
likewise from Fiesch to properly view the 14-
mile (23km) swirl of ice that is the Aletsch
Glacier. And then, to finish, there's the
train ride from Täsch into car-free Zermatt,
which presents your first magical close-up
of the one-of-a-kind Matterhorn.

Start // Arosa
End // Zermatt
Distance // 382 miles (612km)

PASSING OVER
THE PANORAMA ROUTE

*Tracing a path up and over South Africa's Drakensburg Escarpment, this is a
journey with an abundance of geological wonders and gold-rush sites en route.*

The Panorama Route starts not with a bang but a whimper. As the buildings of Hoedspruit disappear in the rear-view window, the prospect at the end of the car bonnet seems initially uninspiring: a landscape flat and featureless under low cloud. Things soon pick up. Fields of orange, mango and avocado flash by, and signposts to private game reserves make a detour compelling.

I resist, though – the clouds lift and I'm encouraged on by a glimpse of the route to come: the dark peaks of the Drakensburg Escarpment loom ahead, towering over the plains of Mpulamunga. At its base, the Panorama Route gets interesting. The road zigzags up through the rocks, the milky brown waters of the Olifants River churning its way downstream. My ears pop as I near the summit.

Emerging through Abel Erasmus Pass, I arrive at a plateau as flat as the plains below. Donkeys and long-horned cows nibble at the grass verges, nonchalant to passing cars. Alarmingly long-toothed baboons stake out roadside stalls selling jewellery, clay pots and fruit, pondering a smash-and-grab.

The Three Rondavels is where the Panorama Route begins to earn its stripes. It marks the starting point of a canyon 16 miles (26km) long and 400m deep, the third largest in the world. When I arrive, the mist entirely obscures the view, drifting and tumbling over the canyon's sides in ghostly fashion. Patience, it seems, is a virtue on the route. Soon, the first panorama is unveiled: the granite pinnacles of the Three Rondavels rise up from the valley floor, the dark green slug of the Blyde River winding around them.

Back in the car, I continue over the plateau on a road that follows the canyon. I plough in and out of low clouds, the cliff face and the prospect of a plunge to the valley floor to my left occasionally

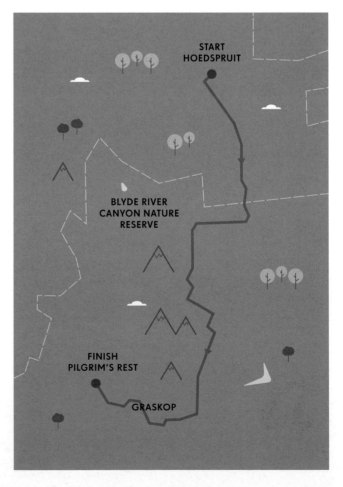

"On a really clear day at God's Window you can see the beaches of Mozambique, 93 miles away"

obscured, and emerge into patches of sunlight, the pink flowers of the roadside jacaranda trees dazzling in the afternoon sun.

Every couple of miles there is a stop, another view to wonder at. At Bourke's Luck Potholes (named after one Thomas Bourke whose schemes to make his fortune prospecting for gold here ended in ignominious failure), a series of cascades tumble over smooth, orange rocks. Anorak-clad visitors toss coins into deep pools for good luck – perhaps fruitlessly given the site's namesake.

The waterfalls gain in superlatives as I head south: rainbows form at the base of the Berlin Falls (45 metres) and Lisbon Falls (90 metres), while at Pinnacle Rock, water spills off the cliff-face and into the trees below, looping its way round a spike of quartzite that rises 30 metres from the valley floor.

The view at God's Window is, aptly, the most spectacular. Noting the signs to 'Please keep God's Window clean', I make my way to the viewpoint along a rain-sodden path. The sides of the canyon, steeped in ferns and aloe vera, plummet to the forest floor, mist hovering over the canopy. Among the trees lurk klipspringers, bush babies, kudu, perhaps a leopard or two. On a really clear day, you can see the beaches of Mozambique, 93 miles (150km) away.

Beyond the town of Graskop, where most visitors along the route park their cars and motorbikes for pancakes, biltong and souvenir fridge magnets, the attractions of the Panorama Route take on a more cultural bent. There is one final waterfall – the single plume of water that makes up Mac Mac Falls, named after the Scottish gold prospectors who flooded the area when the metal was first discovered in the 1850s. A mile downstream, the waters form a series of natural bathing pools.

The road from here winds over low hills, through pine and eucalyptus forests, and passes a spot that changed the region's – and South Africa's – fortunes forever. One day in 1873, Alec 'Wheelbarrow' Patterson struck gold at Lone Peach Tree Creek. Within months, a gold rush had started – the surrounding fields were soon home to 1500 chancers, all hoping to make it big.

The town of Pilgrim's Rest grew up around the mines as the birthplace of South Africa's gold-mining industry. By 1876, it was home to tin-roofed saloons, banks, post offices and liquor stores, and the requisite band of charlatans, thieves and smugglers that follows the first sniff of new money. Though the mines are largely gone, the town stands much the same today, a living monument to a time when this small settlement in the province of Mpulamunga was the centre of all South Africa. There's the old garage that used to service vehicles making the run down to Johannesburg in the south, general dealerships, shops selling fool's gold, maps and antique bottles. Vervet monkeys stroll down the street, and hadeda ibis sail overhead, their distinctive cry floating in the air.

From Pilgrim's Rest, the road continues south, through the hills to Robber's Pass, where gold-runners were often availed of their riches en route to Johannesburg. Here's where I end the trip, with a beer in the old bar of the Royal Hotel, faded pictures both of fortune-seekers and gold-robbers on the walls keeping me company. **AC**

KRUGER'S GAME

An hour's drive east of Pilgrim's Rest lies one of the world's greatest wildlife reserves: Kruger National Park. You've a good chance of encountering the Big Five (buffalo, lion, leopard, elephant and rhino) within its 7000 sq km, as well as cheetahs, hippos and packs of the rare African wild dog. Plentiful, cheap accommodation options in the park make the excursion from the Panorama Route even easier to justify (www.sanparks.org).

Clockwise from left: a local store in Pilgrim's Rest; a vervet monkey with youngster at Pilgrim's Rest; the Panorama Route lives up to its name. Previous page: cloud covers Blyde River Canyon

DIRECTIONS

Start // Hoedspruit, Limpopo province
End // Pilgrim's Rest, Mpumalanga province
Distance // 130 miles (209km)
Getting there // East Gate airport, just outside Hoedspruit, has regular flights from Johannesburg and Cape Town.
Car hire // Avis has an office at East Gate airport, and there are other local hire companies in Hoedspruit itself.
Where to stay // Forever Resort Blyde River Canyon (www.foreverblydecanyon.co.za) for the start of your trip, has views out over the canyon from its grounds; at journey's end, Pilgrim's Rest Royal Hotel is full of gold-rush-era charm.
Where to eat // Graskop has options, including top-class pancakes at Harrie's; in Pilgrim's Rest, try the Vine for bobotie, South Africa's national dish of spicy minced meat.
More info // www.southafrica.net

Opposite: the Dolomite peaks loom
over the village of Santa Maddalena

MORE LIKE THIS
WONDROUS VISTAS

GRANDE STRADA DELLE DOLOMITI, ITALY

One of the world's most beautiful mountain ranges, the Dolomites (Dolomiti) range across the South Tyrol, Alto Adige and Veneto, combining Austrian and Italian influences with the local Ladin culture. On this magnificent road trip (*grande strada*), your hosts may wear Lederhosen, cure ham in their chimneys and use sleighs to travel from village to village. More recently, a new generation of eco-chic hotels, cutting-edge spas and Michelin-starred restaurants have started grabbing the headlines, but overall these mountain peaks remain very low key. Along this vista-rich 120-mile (193km) drive, the finest views include the sculpted ridges and buttress towers of the Fanes plateau rocks, which architect Le Corbusier called 'the most beautiful architecture in the world', and the staggering stretch of road between Ortisei and Siusi. And if the alpine majesty of the Dolomites ever starts to make you giddy, you can easily make the descent towards sea-level for a splendid break at Lake Garda or Venice.

Start // Bolzano
End // Alpe di Siusi
Distance // 121 miles (195km)

SEA TO SKY HIGHWAY, CANADA

Drive out of North Vancouver and straight into the wild west coast. This short expedition reveals the essence of British Columbia's shores with its majestic sea and mountain views. Woven along this highway are chances to get active (picturesque Whistler is a world-famous ski resort), watch wildlife (bald eagles feast on salmon at Brackendale; grizzlies and cougars inhabit the Tantalus mountains), glimpse the region's rich Native American culture (Squamish Lil'wat Cultural Centre is a trove of song, design and cookery) and prove your bravery by standing on the viewing platform over the precipitous Brandywine Falls. Near Howe Sound, keep an eye out for the Stawamus Chief, at 700m the world's largest freestanding granite monolith. A sacred place to the Squamish, and nesting ground to peregrine falcons, only experienced climbers should attempt to scale it. Between Squamish and Whistler along Highway 99, you'll also find plenty of freshly roasted, organic coffee to enjoy. How much more 'BC' can you get?

Start // Horseshoe Bay, BC
End // Whistler, BC
Distance // 82 miles (132km)

THE GREAT OUTDOORS, SPAIN

Starting up high in the Sierra Nevada, this outdoorsy itinerary swings west and south through a mesmerising patchwork of dramatically contrasting Andalucian landscapes. First you'll tackle Las Alpujarras' twisting mountain roads and the Sierra Nevada's highest peaks (the whitewashed village of Capileira is perched at 1436m), before stopping at the bizarre and beautiful El Torcal rock formations. Then you'll fly across the Sevillan countryside into Parc Nacional de Donana, a raw, natural world brimming with wildlife – 360 bird species and 37 types of mammal to be exact – finally tackling some classic Costa de la Luz driving, back to Seville and south down the A4, to cruise past Tarifa's white-sand surfer beaches, a Moroccan-flavoured haven of outdoor fun. This is an adventure-filled drive that uncovers a stash of history, architecture and cuisine as varied as its backdrop.

Start // Capileira
End // Tarifa
Distance // 492 miles (792km)

MARRAKESH TO TAROUDANNT

Hewn out of Morocco's High Atlas, this incredibly scenic but challenging drive weaves from the souks of Marrakesh to the tranquil villages of the Souss Valley.

The Tizi n'Test is one of those roads that really makes you wince as you veer round blind corners while clinging on just that little bit tighter to your steering wheel. At its peak it's got relentless hairpin bends, steep, unguarded drops and, in some places, is barely the width of a car. Blunt rocks hang low over the road and it's prone to washouts, rock slides and sudden changes in weather. But none of that is what makes it so memorable. It's the view. One superb, breathtaking panorama that plays out before you from the summit and gets seared into your memory forever.

I'd been over the pass on a hair-raising drive on a public bus and then again in a taxi, squashed in beside Berber women and sacks of grain. But I wanted to stop and soak up the remarkable views, spend time walking in the mountains, visit the village markets and explore the kasbahs en route. So here I was, back in Marrakesh meandering the labyrinthine laneways of the souks, as beguiled by their timeless charm as I was on my first visit.

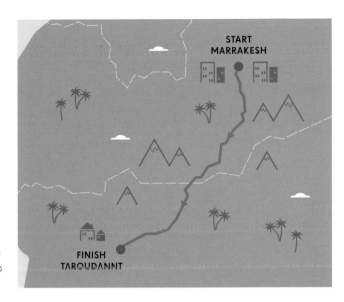

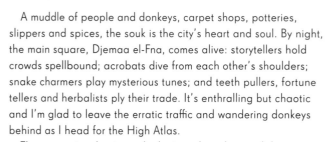

A muddle of people and donkeys, carpet shops, potteries, slippers and spices, the souk is the city's heart and soul. By night, the main square, Djemaa el-Fna, comes alive: storytellers hold crowds spellbound; acrobats dive from each other's shoulders; snake charmers play mysterious tunes; and teeth pullers, fortune tellers and herbalists ply their trade. It's enthralling but chaotic and I'm glad to leave the erratic traffic and wandering donkeys behind as I head for the High Atlas.

The mountains dominate the horizon, brooding and dramatic. At their foot is Asni, a fruit-growing area set against a backdrop of wooded hills. It's a scenic spot where the almond trees are in bloom, and goats, old men and small boys wander the streets. We stay the night in a traditional riad, eating dinner cross-legged on the floor and are woken by the call to prayer the following morning. Outside, the village is almost unrecognisable. It's market day: livestock wander by, stalls are piled high with fruit and vegetables, and the butchers fan flies off the meat. It's a gloriously authentic, ramshackle affair.

Beyond Asni the scenery becomes increasingly dramatic and the road gets more unnerving, as drivers weave between lanes, happily overtaking in the face of oncoming traffic and honking mercilessly at anyone who gets in their way.

We're soon surrounded by spectacular mountains and the most incredible gorges and canyons. Jebel Toubkal (4167 metres), North Africa's highest peak, appears on the horizon. We pull up in the pretty village of Ouirgane, which is set in a lush valley

"We wind round hairpin bends, the road dropping rapidly and revealing another magnificent view with every turn"

where pine forests meet red earth hills. It's a good base for hiking, mountain biking and horse riding, and we decide to spend a day in the mountains. Our guide does not show up so we hike far into the hills until we reach a waterfall where we find an extended Berber family on an annual outing to wash their rugs and blankets. The washing done, they're sitting around chatting and we swap stories, take an icy plunge and then pile into the back of one of their small trucks for a lift back to the road.

The road was only blasted out of the mountains by the French in the late 1920s and it's easy to see why. Remote and inaccessible, it was the perfect base for the Almohad Empire that lorded over the tribes of West Africa right up until the 13th century. Crumbling kasbahs perch on the edge of rocky outcrops and in tiny Tin Mal we ramble around a 12th-century mosque that more resembles a fortress than a place of worship. Its rose-coloured walls hide arrays of decorative arches and walkways and a tranquil great hall.

From here-on the driving gets tougher, the road more tortuous, yet each hairpin bend reveals yet another spectacular mountain view as we make our way to the top of the Tizi n'Test at 2092

CLOCK THE KASBAH

A stronghold of the Almohads in the 12th century, the Tizi n'Test held a strategic position on the route to the fertile Souss Valley. The kasbahs here date from the 19th century when the pass was controlled by the powerful Goundafi clan. Two of the most impressive are the ruined Talat N'Yaccoub Kasbah, 2 miles (3km) north of Tin Mal, and the privately owned Agadir N'Gouj, a few kilometres south of the town.

From left: a Marrakesh souk; the driver's hair-raising view; snake charming at Djemaa el-Fna; the perilous Tizi n'Test. Previous page: the Atlas Mountains form a striking backdrop to Marrakesh

DIRECTIONS

Start // Marrakesh
End // Taroudannt
Distance // 141 miles (227km)
Getting there // Fly to Marrakesh and hire a car.
When to drive // Mid-April to mid-June or September to October. Summer can be oppressively hot. In winter, the pass can close due to snow, landslides or washouts.
How to drive // Drive in daylight, for safety reasons and for the views. But if you want to relish the scenery then best leave the driving to someone else.
What to take // A full tank of fuel, plenty of water, a phrasebook if you don't speak French or Arabic, hiking boots and, above all, a camera.
Hazards // Sudden weather changes, crazy drivers, stray donkeys, herds of goats, camels and overzealous hawkers.

metres. It's not Morocco's highest pass but it is certainly its most dramatic. The edge of the road abruptly gives way to steep cliffs, rugged gorges lead off into mountain spurs, and low overhangs make it obvious just what a mammoth feat of engineering this was. The aggressive tailgating dissipates at last, as the road narrows and vehicles swerve to avoid rocky debris. Driving requires absolute concentration.

And then there it is. The view. A sweeping, expansive panorama that lays out the whole of the Souss Valley before us. The High Atlas cradle us to the left and right, the Anti Atlas guard the rear and the road coils below us like a snake as it tumbles down the mountainside to the valley floor. It's mesmerising and humbling all at the same time.

As we begin our descent we wind round hairpin bends, the road dropping rapidly and revealing another magnificent view with every turn. We make our way to Taroudannt, a busy market town enclosed by mud red walls. Framed by a backdrop of snow-capped peaks, the 15th-century ramparts are magnificent. Inside them the Taroudannt people are friendly, laid-back and totally unconcerned by tourism.

We wander through the souks and avenues lined with orange trees, hibiscus and bougainvillea, pick up a picnic of olives, oranges, bread and almonds and eat it on the ramparts as the sun sets. It's wonderfully low key. Families pass on an evening stroll, the clip-clop of horses' hooves rings in the air and the hustle of Marrakesh seems a million miles away. **EOC**

*Opposite from top: chamois perch
near the Grimsel Pass in Switzerland;
the Sc-390 snakes through Brazil's
Serra do Rio Rastro mountains*

MORE LIKE THIS
HAIRPIN HEAVEN

SUSTEN-GRIMSEL-FURKA
LOOP, SWITZERLAND

Taking in three Alpine passes, the Susten-Grimsel-Furka loop offers switchbacks, chicanes and vertigo-inducing drops. You'll pass lush forests, glaciers, reservoirs, barren mountaintops and sweeping panoramas of the peaks. A wide road with manageable gradients, the Susten Pass eases you into things before the more challenging terrain of Grimsel where the climbs are relentless, the grades steep and the switchbacks awkward. It's closed from October to May, due to heavy snowfall. Then there's Furka, a narrow road with no guard rail, steep drops and hairpin bends, made famous as the scene of James Bond's car chase in *Goldfinger*. Check the forecast before you set out.
Start/End // Andermatt
Distance // 75 miles (121km)

CIRQUE DE COMBE
LAVAL, FRANCE

One of France's most spectacular balcony roads, the Cirque de Combe Laval is carved into the vast karst landscape of the Royans in the Rhône-Alpes of the southeast. Surrounded by towering peaks, it is a national heritage site protected for its incredible landscape. Construction of the road began in 1861 with the intention of bringing timber out of the area more easily, but it was not until 1898 that the route was complete. The dizzying heights, low overhangs, limited passing places and perilous drop on the other side of a low stone wall make this a route only for good drivers with a head for heights. The views and the sheer thrill of driving such a perilous route make it worthwhile, however.
Start // Vassieux-en-Vercorsr
End // Pont-en-Royans
Distance // 28 miles (45km)

SERRA DO RIO
DO RASTRO, BRAZIL

Built in 1903, the serpentine SC-390 winds its way up the Serra do Rio Rastro mountain range in southern Brazil. The route begins gently, weaving through lush valleys dotted with colourful houses and distinctly European villages, but once past the town of Lauro Müller the incline gets steeper, the road clinging to the side of the valley as it passes canyons, waterfalls and forests. The scenery is spectacular and huge windmills generate electricity to keep the treacherous bends lit at night, but even by day you should drive cautiously, as trucks and buses need the full width of the road to get round the bends. São Joaquim, at the end of the route, is one of Brazil's coldest spots but a fruit-growing region known for its wines.
Start // Tubarão
End // São Joaquim
Distance // 83 miles (134km)

TAKE THE HIGHWAY TO HANA IN HAWAII

Buckle up for an exhilarating spin through Maui's wild, tropical garden, where a narrow road twists past splashy waterfalls, hidden pools and lava-rock shores.

A skirmish between nature and civilisation plays out daily on the rear side of Haleakala, the hulking volcano that anchors eastern Maui. And nature has the edge. Rainstorms flicker across slopes tangled with tropical greenery. Waterfalls explode from heavenly heights. Mudslides teeter on the edge of seaside cliffs. And waves crash against jagged black lava. The Road to Hana ribbons along the rumpled coastline here, a lonely strip of pavement working hard to prove that it has all been tamed.

Five hundred years ago the grand King's Highway circled the entire island, built as a trade route during the reign of King Pi'ilani. Today only fragments of this great road are visible along the coastline, where the frequent rains and unforgiving sunshine take their toll on manmade structures. Nineteenth-century churches, constructed from lava-rock and missionary zeal, still dot the landscape, but weak roofs and dwindling populations have taken their toll. And mobile phone service? Hmm. Maybe here. Maybe there. But overall, not so much.

They say there are 54 bridges (mostly one-lane) and more than 600 curves along the Road to Hana, which connects the surf town of Haiku with the sleepy community of Hana. Every time that I drive the route, it feels as if I'm writing a new adventure. Who knows what lies ahead? A road-blocking mudslide? Downed

trees? Or maybe today it's all sunshine and rainbows – a tropical paradise too unbelievable even for postcards.

The drive has become much more crowded in recent years, with rented jeeps and convertible Mustangs angling hard for parking spots beside the flashiest waterfalls. Don't let the fear of

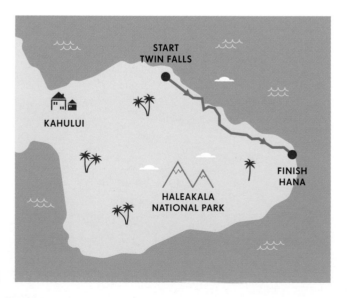

missing out elevate your stress levels. If there's no parking at the waterfall ahead, then catch the next one. The road isn't lacking in cascades. Otherwise, chill out and enjoy the wait. Remember, you're on the Road to Hana, man.

If I'm after a short morning hike and a quick swim, I like to take the trail to Twin Falls, where some particularly photogenic cascades tumble down into a lovely pool. From here, on the eastern fringes of Haiku, the drive begins to get much wilder, with a bamboo forest, colourful eucalyptus trees and thick tangles of green giving a little taste of the wilder scenes ahead.

Organic farms are tucked here and there behind the greenery. The only signs of their existence are lonely fruit stands selling coconuts, pineapples, mango and apple bananas. Many are manned by college grads and gap-year students participating in Worldwide Opportunities on Organic Farms (WWOOF) programs. They work the fields in exchange for room and board. One girl confided that she lived in a tent pitched just behind the stand. I'm not sure if she was WWOOOFing it, but it did sound like an adventure.

Nature is definitely in charge along the Waikamoi Nature Trail. This 1-mile (1.6km) easy loop descends into a thick tropical forest, passing a mossy sign near the trailhead that reads 'Quiet. Trees at work'. I always start this walk thinking I'll be rewarded with a sweeping view of the forest and sea from the trail's summit. But nope, the view is always overgrown and the trail clogged with thick mud and slick roots. My sneakers are trashed every time.

"The loop descends into a thick tropical forest, passing a mossy sign that reads 'Quiet. Trees at Work'"

About halfway to Hana, waves smash against swaths of black lava along the Ke'anae Peninsula, a flat strip of fertile land jutting into the sea. The scene is dramatic, sometimes foreboding, but my camera can never capture its intensity. I've always felt more comfortable inside Ke'anae Congregational Church. Just steps from the shore, this 1860 lava-rock church, with its open doors and guest book, evaporates my stress. As does the fresh banana bread from Aunt Sandy's snack stand just a short drive up the road.

The waterfalls along the highway are far from shy and retiring, and photogenic cascades tumble just upstream from most of those 54 bridges. Upper Waikani Falls, also known as Three Bears Falls, is a triple waterfall that is always game for a photograph. At Pua'a Ka'a Falls I've marvelled at a young daredevil catapulting from a cliff-top into the adjacent pool. More recently, I admired a painter who was serenely catching the scene from a covered picnic table, while raindrops were plunking all around them.

My mood always turns more contemplative at the Pi'ilanihale Heiau, a 413ft-long (126 metres) lava-rock platform recognised

Hikers should carve out a few hours for the Pipiwai Trail in Haleakala National Park. It's a 4-mile (6.4km) round trip with the path climbing beside the 'Ohe'o Gulch streambed, passing the bridal-veil Makahiku Falls before twisting through a thick bamboo forest. The final reward is the Waimoku Falls, a thin cascade dropping down a sheer 400ft granite wall. The trailhead is 10 miles (16km) south of Hana on Hwy 360.

From left: hugging the coast on the road to Hana; mango from a fruit stand; eucalyptus line the trail to Twin Falls; a Maui creek meets the Pacific Ocean. Previous page: rounding the curves of Honomanu Bay

today as the largest *heiau* (temple) in the whole of Polynesia. There's a solemnity and mysteriousness about the massive structure, which rises sternly above the sea. Archaeologists think its construction began in the 13th century. The well-manicured Kahanu Garden surrounds the base of the mighty *heiau* like a dainty tropical leash – restraining stories and secrets from the days of ancient Maui chieftains.

Civilisation may have got the upper hand in Kahanu Garden, but the same cannot be said of Wai'anapanapa State Park further down the road. On my last visit here a construction team was upgrading the coastal walkway with new pavements, new overlooks and new stairs. But these nods to order won't be able to tame the place. The surf at the black-sand beach is prone to riptides. The lava caves are threatened by falling rocks. And that fickle trailside blowhole could surely blast a hiker high into the sky. For adventurers, there be dragons here.

At the end of this rainbow of a drive is Hana, where the alohas are warm. A vestige of old Hawaii, this small community is a place to 'talk story' (chat) with locals, relax on crescents of golden sand and tuck into the hyper-local fare. In fact, Hana is so low-key and quiet that honeymooners have been known to vacate the town after only a single night, more than a little spooked by all the tranquillity. But the rest of us? It pays to stay a few days. Wander around. Talk story. You'll see. Civilisation is precious in these wild parts, so embrace it while you can. Tomorrow is another adventure. **AB**

DIRECTIONS

Start // Twin Falls
End // Hana
Distance // 32 miles (52km), but with a maximum speed limit of 25mph (40km/h), give yourself a good few hours
Getting there // Hana is 52 miles (84km) east of Kahului Airport, where you can rent a car. Convertibles and 4x4s are popular, but compact cars squeeze more easily into tight roadside pull-offs. The Road to Hana starts as Hwy 36 turns into Hwy 360 at mile marker 16, where the markers restart at zero. Fill up with fuel in Kahului or Paia before the off.
When to drive // With a tropical setting, the Road to Hana is drivable all year. Start your drive by 8am to avoid the crowds. If you have time, spend at least one night in Hana – on the drive back, you can stop by the waterfalls you missed.
Road rules // Pull over when you can to let residents pass.

Opposite: offering golden sands (top) and widescreen vistas such as Nualolo Valley (bottom), the island of Kaua'i also serves up its own epic drive

MORE LIKE THIS
HAWAIIAN DRIVES

WAIMEA CANYON DRIVE, KAUA'I

These islands may be small but they present some immense scenery for road tripping. On Kaua'i, of all its unique wonders, none can touch Waimea Canyon for grandeur. A gargantuan chasm of ancient lava rock 10 miles long and more than 3500ft deep in places, it is nicknamed the 'Grand Canyon of the Pacific' for good reason. Drives here on a clear day are phenomenal. A paved road follows the entire length of the canyon, climbing from the coast 19 miles (31km) to Pu'u o Kila lookout point. Along the way, the Garden Isle gives a rollicking display of its tropical attributes: a rippling rust-red valley, lush moss-green foliage and streaming waterfalls. Waipo'o Falls drop Rapunzel-like over a height of 800ft (244 metres) and can be spied from numerous points along the drive.
Start // Waimea
End // Pu'u o Kila Lookout
Distance // 19 miles (31km)

O'AHU'S WINDWARD COAST

Amble down O'ahu's lushest, most verdant coast on this drive where turquoise waters and light-sand beaches share the dramatic backdrop of misty cliffs in the Ko'olau Range. Begin the drive in Honolulu, on the opposite coast, and slice your way through the range on the equally scenic Pali Hwy to Kailua. If it's been raining heavily, every fold and crevice in the jagged cliffs will have a fairytale waterfall streaming down it. Then take it slow on a serpentine cruise up the coast past untamed beaches, small farms, jungly hiking trails and lava-rock fishponds. Pull over at Kualoa Ranch for a tour of famous TV and movie locations, as seen in *Lost* and *Jurassic Park*. At the end of the drive you'll be rewarded with the shrimp trucks of Kahuku, where you can chow down on a plate of fresh crustaceans stir-fried with garlic and butter.
Start // Honolulu
End // Kahuku
Distance // 38 miles (61km)

CHAIN OF CRATERS ROAD, THE BIG ISLAND

For some serious Hawaiian lava action through the windscreen, the Chain of Craters Rd is the one. Winding 20 miles (32km) through the heart of the steaming Hawai'i Volcanoes National Park, it is the most surreal and scenic drive on Hawai'i, the Big Island. The road sits on the slopes of Kilauea, the Earth's youngest and most active volcano and the predominant view is of the black stuff itself – mile upon mile of hardened lava. The end of the route is dictated by the lava itself; fresh flows have repeatedly oozed over the last section of paving. The best time to take photographs of this unique landscape is in the early morning and late afternoon when the sunlight slants off the lava.
Start // Crater Rim Road
End // Holei Sea Arch
Distance // 40-mile (64km) round trip

JUST FOR KICKS: ROUTE 66

The Mother Road knows America best: Route 66 covers more than 2400 miles (1500km), eight states and nearly a century of red, white and blue moments.

I finish the 2448-mile (3940km) drive before I've even begun. 'End' reads the Route 66 sign on Jackson Blvd, Chicago. I circle the block, searching for a plain brown square, an arrow pointing west. 'Begin' urges a sign on Adams St. I bounce in my car seat and do as I am told.

Route 66, the legendary highway connecting Chicago to Los Angeles, dates from 1926, but only 80% of the original road still exists – hence the navigational confusion. It has also been realigned several times, before being decommissioned in 1985 and replaced with five different interstates. Because of its patchwork condition, I find myself flitting between old and new segments, smooth and

bumpy. With so many attractions – monumental and kitschy, natural and plastic – along the route, I fall woefully behind schedule.

'Route 66 time is different,' Jerry McClanahan, a cartographer and artist, tells me at his gallery in Chandler, Oklahoma. 'If it's quick, you're not doing Route 66.'

Over the decades, the road has attracted American dreamers. In the early 20th century, they piled into jalopies to escape the Dust Bowl and find work during the Great Depression. In WWII, soldiers followed the road in the name of duty. In the mid-century, liberated motorists embraced car culture, and later counterculture. Now, nostalgia-seekers like myself board Route 66 to travel back in time.

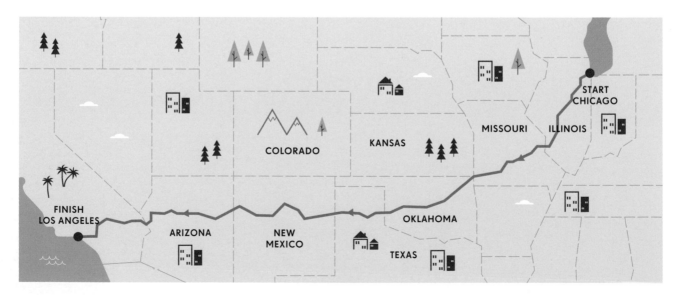

I meet Jim Jones, a living remnant of the road. At the Route 66 Association Hall of Fame & Museum in Pontiac, Illinois, he reminisces about the highway that defined his youth.

'I was seven years old and pumping gas,' he says of a 1940 photo of himself and his brother in his hometown. 'Odell had 13 gas stations and 951 people. Dad made a good living.'

In 1947, the Jones clan drove the entire route, camping along the way. Sixty-six years later, Jim repeated the trip, staying in hotels. I ask him how the road had changed over the years.

'It's more of a history-oriented highway today,' he says. 'People drive it for the nostalgia.'

In Adrian, Texas, the midway point of Route 66, I nearly kiss the sign informing travellers that Chicago and LA are an equidistant 1139 miles (1833km) away. I cross the empty street to the Midpoint Café and ask the owner's daughter if the restaurant honours the halfway achievement. 'Eat a piece of ugly pie,' she says.

Her father joins me at the counter. He plucks some old postcards from a rack to illustrate Adrian's former self as a robust railroad town. The community once supported five cafes open 24/7; today, the sole surviving restaurant closes at 4pm.

'Route 66 was the lifeblood of the town, because of all the traffic,' says another customer, Finis Brown, the town mayor. 'It still is.' He explains how Adrian was experiencing a slight upswing – the population increased from 159 in 2000 to 166 in 2010.

One of most exhilarating sections is the 159 miles (256km) of uninterrupted road in western Arizona. I brake only for wild ferrets and Angel Delgadillo. Angel's reputation precedes him by more

REBRANDING WILLIAMS

Williams was the final town to be bypassed by the interstate, but the Arizona outpost didn't die. Instead, it rebounded as the Gateway to the Grand Canyon. The Grand Canyon Railway runs train services to the South Rim of the national park. The town also plays up its Wild West character with shoot-out performances. For a traffic-free ride, the Route 66 Zipline transports passengers in a flying car that reaches speeds of up to 30mph (48km/h).

Clockwise from top: riding the Route into California; the lifeguard post at Santa Monica Pier where the journey ends; you know you're on the right road in Winslow, Arizona. Previous page: roadside in the robust Route 66 town of Seligman, Arizona

than 1700 miles (2736km). When your nickname is 'the Godfather of Route 66,' you amass a vast fan base. The barber, who was born in 1927, grew up with his Mexican parents and eight siblings in a modest home on Route 66 in Seligman, Arizona.

'The people in the cars looked so down and out,' he said of the Dust Bowl migrants. 'We'd say, "Here comes a poor Okie. He's only got one mattress. Here come rich Okies. They have two mattresses."'

The date that makes Angel shudder is 22 September 1978, when the interstate south of town opened, killing the town's livelihood.

'They turned off the lights on Main Street,' he lamented.

In February 1987, Angel organised a meeting seeking historic designation for the 89 miles (143km) of road from Seligman to Kingman. The group urged lawmakers to post historic signs, which would help preserve the road. Angel's perseverance paid off, and his victory inspired other communities to embrace the cause as well.

'Seligman has the distinction of being the town where Route 66 got its rebirth,' he says. 'We helped save a little bit of America.'

Route 66 originally terminated on Broadway and Seventh St in downtown LA. Two weeks after leaving Chicago, I roll up to the intersection, park and excitedly jump up and down on the pavement outside Clifton's Cafeteria. I ask a bystander if there was a historical marker I could high-five. The restaurant's owner points to a small blue sign: 'Original terminus of Route 66 (1926–1939).'

On Santa Monica Pier, the last of the three finales, I approach Ian Bowen, who is tucked inside a Route 66 kiosk. He shakes my hand, 'Congratulations.' Several minutes later, a couple from North Dakota receive the same reception.

While standing in line to snap a picture of the 'End of the Trail' sign, I compare notes with the Dakotans. Much to our delight, we had both taken a wrong turn in Chicago. In our photos, we flash knowing smiles that we had done Route 66 right. **AS**

"'Route 66 time is different,' Jerry McClanahan tells me. 'If it's quick, you're not doing Route 66'"

DIRECTIONS

Start // Chicago
End // Los Angeles
Distance // 2448 miles (3940km) and eight states
Getting there // Pick up your rental car from Chicago's O'Hare or Midway airports or, if you are driving west to east, Los Angeles International Airport.

When to drive // Late spring, summer and early autumn are best. In summer, book lodgings in advance as many of the vintage motels sell out. Also be aware that some attractions and shops keep small-town hours, even during peak months.

Maps // Most GPS units and mapping apps ignore Route 66 and kick drivers on to the interstates or major highways. Jerry McClanahan's *EZ66 Guide for Travelers* is invaluable. The author plots every turn along the route with sightseeing and dining suggestions, historical snippets and more.

Hot tip // Don't let your fuel gauge fall below half, especially in the Southwest, where gas stations are sparse.

Opposite, clockwise from top:
sunrise over Key West; the
former Cape Cod home of artist
and bat enthusiast Edward
Gorey; refreshment options off
the Overseas Hwy

MORE LIKE THIS
CLASSIC US DRIVES

OVERSEAS HIGHWAY, FLORIDA

The 113-mile (182km) Overseas Hwy ribbons
through the Florida Keys, from Key Largo to
Key West, the country's southernmost city.
The All-American Road features 42 spans,
including the famous Seven Mile Bridge
(cue *True Lies*). In many spots along the
route, you'll feel like a bug gliding on the
water. Look left for the Atlantic, right for
the Gulf of Mexico and up for pelicans,
osprey and great white herons. Follow the
mile-markers to such Keysian attractions
as John Pennekamp Coral Reef and Bahia
Honda state parks, which offer stellar
diving. For dryer wildlife, the National Key
Deer Refuge is home to the smallest North
American deer, while at the Turtle Hospital,
patients await their return to sea. When
you're out of road, exit the car and enter
a bar. Order a Key West classic, the key
lime margarita. If you're travelling during
hurricane season, remember that there's
only one way in, and out, of Key West.
Start // Key Largo
End // Key West
Distance // 113 miles (182km)

KANCAMAGUS HIGHWAY, NEW HAMPSHIRE

The Kancamagus Hwy – 'the Kanc' for
short – delves into nature and doesn't
return to civilisation for a glorious 34 miles
(56km). Opened in 1959, the American
Scenic Byway starts at the junction of
Route 16 in Conway and meanders through
the White Mountains before finishing in
Lincoln. You'll trade restaurants, hotels,
service stations and mobile phone
coverage for views of the Swift River, hiking
trails of varying endurance levels and
possibly a moose sighting. The Russell-
Colbath House, the only original structure
remaining from the town of Passaconaway,
peeks at New England life in the 1800s. In
the warmer months, cool off in the spray
of Sabbaday Falls; in autumn, soak up the
colours from the Kancamagus Pass (870m).
Some spots require a parking pass, which
you can purchase on-site at a kiosk (US$3
for the day), ranger station or visitor centre.
Start // Conway
End // Lincoln
Distance // 34 miles (56km)

ROUTE 6, MASSACHUSETTS

Rte 6 started modestly, as a jaunt from
eastern Massachusetts to Brewster,
New York State. By 1937, the highway
stretched to Long Beach, California,
and, for a spell, held the honour of the
longest transcontinental highway in the
country – total mileage: 3652 (5877km).
Realignments and re-numberings removed
the road from its podium. However, in
the Bay State, you can still drive the
Grand Army of the Republic Highway (its
more reverential name) from its original
departure point in Provincetown, along
Cape Cod, over the Sagamore Bridge
and to the border with Rhode Island. The
road passes through historic beach towns,
such as Yarmouth Port (one spine-tingling
attraction: the Edward Gorey House) and
Sandwich, the oldest on the Cape. Rte
6 also partly parallels the nearly 40-mile
(64km) Cape Cod National Seashore. In
the summer, beachgoers jam the road.
Start // Provincetown, Massachusetts
End // Providence, Rhode Island
Distance // 119 miles (192km)

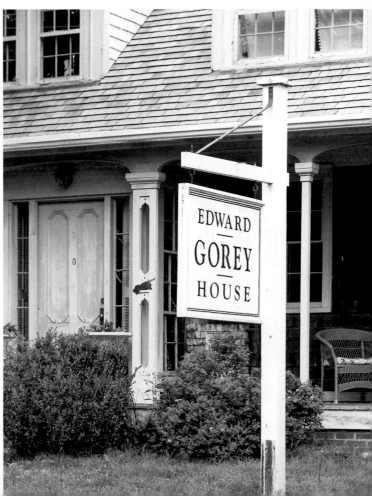

COOL RUNNINGS: CANADA'S ICEFIELDS PARKWAY

Snowcapped peaks, glinting glaciers, azure lakes and more wildlife than your average safari – the road from Lake Louise to Jasper is hard to top for scenic splendour.

'm only half an hour into my road trip into the Canadian Rockies, and I've already come to a screeching halt. A moose has parked himself on the asphalt. Antlers speckled with dew, breath clouding in the autumn air, he's rooted in the middle of the highway, chewing on some grass while he checks the view. I've been waiting 10 minutes. He hasn't budged an inch.

I honk my horn. The moose doesn't seem bothered. I try revving the engine. The moose just keeps on chewing. I lean my head out and holler for him to shift his hide, haul ass, vamoose. Nothing. I ponder the wisdom of manhandling him out of the way, but since the moose outweighs me by 700lb and his antlers look capable of turning me into a plate of short ribs, I decide against it. If Mr Moose feels like standing in the road a while – well, I'll just have to wait.

Happily, the Icefields Parkway is possibly the best place on the planet to find yourself in a traffic jam, moose-based or otherwise. Not that there's much traffic. Stretching for 113 epic miles (230km) between Lake Louise and Jasper, this wild, mountain-framed road

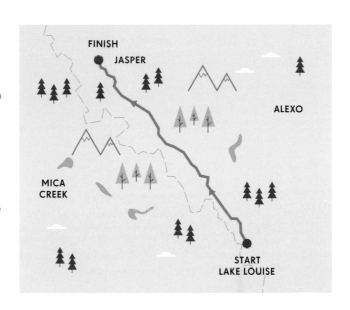

FINISH
JASPER

ALEXO

MICA
CREEK

START
LAKE LOUISE

*"At times, the highway feels
more like a safari park.
Only here, the wildlife is
just that — wild"*

is one of the most beautiful drives on Earth. From vast ice fields to plunging valleys, glacial lakes to serrated peaks, it packs more scenery into the drive than any road I've ever driven.

'Having some trouble, sir?' drawls a mustachioed park ranger, as his 4x4 slows to a halt alongside my car. 'Let's see if we can't get things moving.' The ranger nudges his jeep forward, flanking the moose. The animal reluctantly trudges off into the grass, leaving the highway clear. 'Sometimes all it takes is a little persuasion. Safe driving!' the ranger smiles as he rolls off into the distance.

It's the first of many memorable wildlife encounters on the Icefields Parkway. Near Bow Lake, sipping coffee at the old hostelry of Num-Ti-Jah Lodge, I watch a pair of eagles soaring overhead as they search for prey. Further north, from the trail over Parker Ridge, I spy a family of mountain goats picking their way along the canyon walls, like a troupe of acrobats dressed in fur coats. When I stop for lunch at the Saskatchewan River Crossing, I listen to the peeps of pikas and the whistles of marmots. And once, near the Athabasca Falls, about 25 miles (32km) south of Jasper, I spy a mother black bear and two cubs foraging for berries in the wildflower meadows. Sometimes, the Icefields Parkway feels more like a safari park than a public highway, only here, the wildlife is just that – wild.

But while the animals are fascinating, it's the scenery that makes the Parkway special. Based along the route of an old packhorse trail established by First Nations people and fur traders, the road was completed in 1940 to join Banff and Jasper national parks. It's a thread of civilisation fringed by sprawling wilderness. Craggy peaks spike the skyline to east and west, and beyond lies wild backcountry barely changed since the days when Stoney, Kootenay and Blackfeet tribes called this land home. Waterfalls thunder down rock walls. Lakes sparkle electric blue. Then there are the glaciers that gave the road its name: more than 100, glinting like gems in the mountainside.

Sadly, climate change now threatens these icy wonders. Even the mightiest have shrunk dramatically in size over recent decades. At the Athabasca Glacier, about halfway along the Parkway, I stop at the Icefield Centre, and take a 90-minute trip onto the glacier itself in an all-terrain snowcat. It's a thrilling detour as the vehicle bumps and jolts over the ice, grinding its way onto the vast Columbia Icefield – at 125 sq miles (325 sq km), the largest expanse of ice in the Rockies. At the top, passengers snap selfies surrounded by a boundless sea of ice: frozen in waves, cracked by crevasses, glinting like glass and tinted with a rainbow of icy colours. It's sobering to think that one day even this great glacier might melt into memory.

But for now, there are more natural wonders to explore ahead: a hike along the craggy ravine of Sunwapta Canyon, a detour to see the thunderous crash of the Athabasca Falls, an afternoon picnic with a view of the pyramid-shaped Mt Fryatt. It's well after dark when I finally pull into Jasper, and I've only travelled 143 miles (230km), but I head to bed happy in the knowledge that I've driven some of North America's most spectacular scenery.

Tomorrow, I think I might just hop back in the car, pull a U-turn and do it all over again. **OB**

SEEKING YOGI

Bears are top of the must-see list, but they're tricky to spot. The best time is between June and August, when they forage in preparation for hibernation. Look out for them in bushy meadows, avalanche corridors and near railway tracks. Grizzlies are larger, and distinguishable by their dish-shaped face and neck hump. Black bears, despite their name, can be brown, red and cinnamon. Keep a respectful distance and stay inside your car if you spot a bear.

Clockwise from left: all-terrain snow couches take visitors onto the icefields; caution – grizzly crossing; the Canadian Rockies provide stunning scenery Previous page: the slowly receding Athabasca Glacier

DIRECTIONS

Start // Lake Louise
End // Jasper Town
Distance // 143 miles (230km)
Getting there // Calgary International Airport is a two-hour drive from Lake Louise. The nearest international airport to Jasper is in Edmonton, a four-hour drive.
When to drive // Late autumn to avoid summer traffic.
What to take // Binoculars for wildlife spotting, hiking boots for trails, food and drink for roadside picnics.
Where to stay // Simpson's Num-Ti-Jah Lodge (www.sntj.ca); The Crossing Resort (www.thecrossingresort.com).
Further information // www.icefieldsparkway.com; www.travelalberta.com
Car hire // Major rental firms can be found in both Banff and Jasper.

Opposite from top: the Alaskan
Highway crossing the Yukon;
Scotland's magical Great Glen

MORE LIKE THIS
WILDERNESS DRIVES

TROLLSTIGEN, NORWAY

Norway has no shortage of stunning roads, but none can compare to the legendary Troll's Path in terms of scenery. This twisting, snaking mountain road runs between the towns of Åndalsnes and Valldal, and is famous for its steep incline (more than 10% in places) and 11 hairpin bends, each sporting its own name, like Dronningen (the Queen) and Bispen (the Bishop). The road is closed from October to mid-May due to snowfall, so summer is the only time to see it – even then, due to the elevation, mist can obscure the view, so it's worth saving for a clear day. The best time of all is after a period of heavy rain, when waterfalls cascade down from the mountainsides. Troll sightings aren't guaranteed, however.
Start // Åndalsnes
End // Valldal
Distance // 55 miles (89km)

GREAT GLEN, SCOTLAND

With their sweeping valleys, mist-draped lakes and stark mountains, the Scottish Highlands are a driver's paradise, and the road that runs from Glasgow through the Great Glen is arguably the most memorable of them all. Officially the A82, it cuts through some of Scotland's most iconic scenery: along its 174-mile (280km) route, you'll pass the shores of Loch Lomond, the beautiful valley of Glen Coe, Britain's highest peak, Ben Nevis, and the moody battlements of Urquhart Castle – not to mention the mysterious waters of Loch Ness. Take your time, and don't forget binoculars – you never know, Nessie might just decide it's time to put in an appearance...
Start // Glasgow
End // Inverness
Distance // 174 miles (280km)

ALASKAN HIGHWAY

If it's true wilderness you want, head north – way north. At nearly 1400 miles (2232km) long, the Alaskan Hwy is one of the longest roads in North America, running all the way from Dawson Creek in British Columbia to Delta Junction in Alaska. It was built during WWII to connect the rest of the US with Alaska, and for years still had long stretches of gravel road, although it's now paved along its entire length. It's a very different prospect to most American road trips – you won't find any motels or malls, and gas stations are few and far between, but what you get in exchange is wilderness and wildlife in abundance. This is one road trip that really does deserve to be called epic, in every sense of the word.
Start // Dawson Creek, BC
End // Delta Junction, Alaska
Distance // 1387 miles (2232km)

THE SALAR
DE UYUNI

A sea of salt, vibrantly coloured lakes, weird rock formations, steaming fumaroles and floating islands all await in the hauntingly surreal landscape of southwest Bolivia.

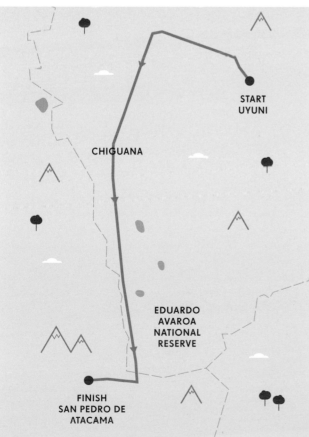

START
UYUNI

CHIGUANA

EDUARDO
AVAROA
NATIONAL
RESERVE

FINISH
SAN PEDRO DE
ATACAMA

Dazzlingly white and near featureless, the Salar de Uyuni is the world's largest salt pan. It covers an unfathomably large chunk of Bolivia's most remote highlands and is all that remains of ancient Lago Minchín. It has no roads, no services and no landmarks for navigation, making it a surreal and otherworldly place to travel. In the wrong conditions it's also dangerous. From December to April a pool of water covers the surface turning it into a vast mirror that magically reflects the sky but also causes openings in the crust that can collapse under the weight of a vehicle.

Car rental companies refuse to let you take their vehicles here, so joining a tour or hiring a guide with a 4WD is practically the only option for exploration. That's not a bad thing, however: the scenery is so mesmerising and the experience so immersive you'll be glad to leave the driving to someone else.

An expedition across the *salar* begins in the small town of Uyuni in southwestern Bolivia. It sits at an altitude of 3653 metres and is surrounded by scorched desert and jagged mountains. Tour operators prowl the streets, each of them offering a special trip (the usual route), a reduced rate (the standard cost) and a promise of rain.

The tour takes from three to four days, crossing some of the 4633 sq miles (12,000 sq km) of the *salar* and continuing through the Atacama Desert to San Pedro de Atacama in Chile. Upon leaving Uyuni, a bumpy, rutted desert road leads out to the edge of the salt pan where a rough ramp extends across the thin veil of salt by the edge of the *salar*. Even experienced local drivers

have been known to become stuck at this point. It doesn't take us long before we're surrounded by an eerie glow, though. The immense blanket of white stretches as far as the eye can see in every direction, mountains float above the distant horizon and the glare is almost unbearable.

The salt is split into interlocking geometrical shapes and is so flat that NASA calibrates its satellite sensors here. A floating spot on the horizon turns out to be Isla del Pescado, a volcanic outcrop covered in towering, 400-year-old cacti. Vicuñas (the smallest member of the camel family) roam through the scrub, and from the top I get my first proper glimpse of the *salar*, endlessly white and enigmatic. The immense cacti are silhouetted against the sea of white, with jagged peaks and snow-capped volcanoes dwarfed in the distance. It's unlike anything I have ever seen and feels like a million miles from anywhere.

We set off again and head for the far side of the *salar*, crossing mile after mile of nothingness. An ominous silence descends as we drive though a patch of pooled water. My heart drops as I feel the wheels sinking into the slush. We are soon up to the axles in water, tense and fearful, but eventually lurch out onto the shore.

Herds of llamas and vicuñas startle and scatter as we pull up in a tiny village of adobe houses.

This is the Atacama Desert, the driest in the world, and by morning every drop of moisture has been sucked from my skin. We drive on past spectacular mountain ranges and smoking volcanoes through a region that is completely uninhabited and untouched. We gain elevation steadily and at Laguna Chiguana see rare James's flamingos huddled together against a backdrop of turquoise water, sweeping dunes and brooding mountains. Next up is the so-called Dalí Desert, where bizarre, free-standing rock columns litter the valley floor. The most magnificent, the Árbol de Piedra (stone tree), is a sculptural form scooped out into smooth curves and sharp edges by the sheer force of nature.

We haven't encountered another soul all day and by evening pull up at Laguna Colorada, a large pool of what looks like toxic tomato soup surrounded by white dunes of salt. Harmless minerals and algae colour the water, the dunes are borax, and set against a backdrop of black mountains and immense blue sky. It is mesmerising. The sun is just beginning to set and it is bitterly cold. We are now at an elevation of over 4000 metres and even

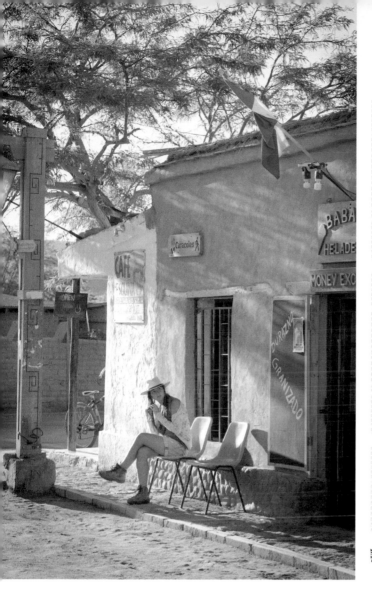

As ancient Lago Minchín receded and dried out, it left behind a shallow pool of water rich in precious minerals. The Salar de Uyuni is estimated to be the world's largest reserve of lithium, an ultra-light metal used in smartphone and electric car batteries. Until now, extraction has been on a relatively small scale, but there are plans to dramatically increase output from 2018, though the process poses environmental concerns for this fragile environment.

Left to right: the Atacama Desert is the world's driest; a well-earned rest in San Pedro de Atacama, Chile, the final stop. Previous page, left to right: a 4WD atop the surreally beautiful salar; sunrise on the salt pans

DIRECTIONS

Start // Uyuni, Bolivia
End // San Pedro de Atacama, Chile
Distance // 310 miles (500km)
Getting there // Fly into La Paz then head (by air/bus) to Oruro, then train.
When to drive // May to November for access to all areas. From December to April parts of the *salar* will be impassable, but pooling water creates a mirror effect.
Self driving // Only possible in your own 4WD. Take local advice seriously. Follow other vehicles across the *salar* and bring food, fuel, water and plenty of spares.
Tour operators // Choose wisely and ask about guides' experience, training, vehicle condition and equipment.
Hot tip // Tours run in both directions but are significantly cheaper from Uyuni.

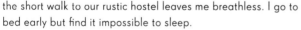

the short walk to our rustic hostel leaves me breathless. I go to bed early but find it impossible to sleep.

We rise before dawn on the final day of the trip, tired and bleary eyed, as we set off for the Sol de Mañana geothermal field. As the sun rises, we pile out onto a steaming landscape that looks as if it could be the set of a 1970s science-fiction film. Mud pots splutter and boil, billowing clouds of vapour rise out of the ground, fumaroles hiss, and a thick whiff of sulphur hangs in the air. We are at an elevation of 5000 metres but it feels as if we are entering the very belly of the Earth.

We have one more stop before crossing the border, Laguna Verde, a vivid turquoise lake that changes colour as the wind disturbs sediments in the water. Behind it, the perfect cone of Volcán Licancábur rises sharply into the sky, the last of our Bolivian landmarks. We cross the border, a ramshackle trailer and a post in the ground, and switch to a luxury mini bus and immaculately paved roads. The scenery is no less spectacular, and San Pedro promises good food, hot showers and cosy beds but, unfortunately, none of the adventure. This is one trip I can't imagine I'll ever forget. **EOC**

Opposite from top: the rains draw wildlife to Namibia's Etosha Pan; the baobab trees of the Makgadikgadi Pans, Botswana

MORE LIKE THIS
SALT PAN DRIVES

BONNEVILLE FLATS, UTAH, USA

Motorheads can get a slice of racing history on the Bonneville Salt Flats on the Utah–Nevada border. Numerous land speed records have been set here and you can get your own taste of the mesmerising surroundings by taking a drive across the 30,000 acres of salt. The flats are graded for racing so don't get any ideas about setting your own records – pressure ridges and standing water can result in a very different end to your drive – but the otherworldly surroundings and shimmering mirages make a drive here a surreal experience. In recent years, surface conditions have been deteriorating, so stay well away from the edges where you can easily get stuck in the mud. If at all possible, try to follow the tracks of other vehicles and avoid pools of water. Don't forget to wash your car thoroughly once you are back on the road.
Start/End // Wendover, Utah
Distance // 25 miles (40km)

ETOSHA PAN, NAMIBIA

Vast, ghostly and incredibly beautiful, the Etosha Pan covers 1853 sq miles (4800 sq km) of northern Namibia. The 'great white place' in the language of the local Ovambo tribe, it is the remains of a huge lake that dried up thousands of years ago and is now protected as a national park. You can't drive on the pan itself but there's a well maintained system of roads skirting the southern edge of the salt flats offering majestic views of the white, shimmering expanse of salt as well as access to the grasslands and waterholes that attract large numbers of lions, leopards, elephants, giraffes and rhinos. From November to April, a pool of water covers the pan and attracts hundreds of thousands of flamingos.
Start // Nehale Iya Mpingana Gate, Etosha National Park
End // Anderson Gate, Etosha National Park
Distance // 120 miles (193km)

MAKGADIKGADI PANS, BOTSWANA

A remnant of an African superlake, the Makgadikgadi Pans is a region of three large salt pans interspersed with rich grassland, palm islands, rocky outcrops and isolated dunes. The main salt flats can be visited from Maun in a 4WD, via a route which passes glistening salt crust, cracked earth, ancient fossil beds, giant umbrella acacias and towering baobab trees. The region has been inhabited since the Stone Age and it's worth getting out of the car to take a walk with local bush people and learn about how they track animals and find water in this arid landscape. As you travel the Makgadikgadi Pans, dusty whirlwinds spin across the road but in the wet season (between November and March), the place is transformed into a lush wetland that attracts thousands of birds as well as herds of zebras and wildebeest, which are often pursued by lions.
Start/End // Maun
Distance // 300 miles (483km)

DRIVING DOWN BRAZIL'S COSTA VERDE

Lush rainforest, postcard-perfect beaches, pristine colonial villages, wild tropical islands – the Costa Verde cradles paradise along the most scenic stretch of Brazil's transcoastal highway.

With the urban sprawl of Rio de Janeiro firmly in the rearview mirror, the lush coastline along the storied BR-101 comes into focus just outside Itaguaí, the last bastion of civilisation before concrete blocks and snarling traffic yield to mountainous rainforest tumbling down into the sand and sea below. This is Brazil's Costa Verde, best seen on the winding, coast-hugging segment of the BR-101 – the country's longest highway – between Rio de Janeiro and Santos, the main port for the metropolis of São Paulo, 52 miles (83km) inland.

Though a tiny 345 mile (555km) blip of the 2980 mile (4800km) BR-101 that spoons the Brazilian coast from the northwestern state of Rio Grande do Norte to São José do Norte in the southernmost state of Rio Grande do Sul, the stretch between Rio and Santos packs a tropical wallop that will leave you punch-drunk on paradise.

On the left of my rented Fiat Palio, the clear cerulean waters of the Atlantic; on the right, the Serra do Mar mountain range that dominates the rugged coast, carpeted in a shade of tropical green that beautifully clashes with the bright blue sea. There are beaches round every turn that don't get so much as a second glance from Brazilians, but would be dream getaways in less blessed countries. Wait, what are these signs that say, 'Fiscalização Eletrônica de Velocidade' every few miles? Who cares! Destination: Paraty!

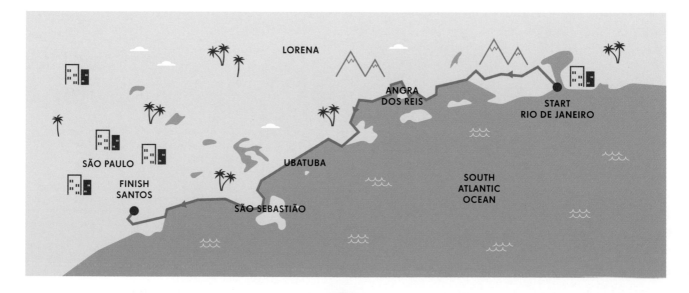

I speed through Angra dos Reis, an 80-mile (129km) stretch of coastline two hours north of Paraty. Angra is mostly used as the jumping off point for Ilha Grande, a vast island Eden that's both a backpacker haven and a playground for the rich and famous (who party on yachts in the surrounding seas). It's also infamous for village-destroying mudslides, so best avoid this drive in the rainiest months between January and April.

The Unesco World Heritage-listed village of Paraty, 150 miles (240km) or so into the drive, is the perfect pit stop. I turn off the BR-101 and park up as no vehicles are allowed in the historic centre. Paraty, a living museum of seaside Portuguese colonial homes with multi-hued trim and latticed windows, and centuries-old churches set against a backdrop of steep, jungled mountains, is a cinematic place best suited for two feet. Pure fairy-tale, its centre is one of the most staunchly preserved patches of colonial history in Brazil.

Besides its photogenic setting, Paraty is one of two spots in Brazil famous for producing *cachaça*, the country's homegrown firewater distilled from sugar cane (and the main ingredient in Brazil's national cocktail, the *caipirinha*, jovially combined with limes and sugar). Well, I'm no longer driving – don't mind if I do!

As the road twists and turns out of Paraty the next morning, yet another series of beaches induce jaw-dropping hysterics in the foreground, the spray from yet another waterfall splashes the windows from the rock walls on the passenger side. I cross into São Paulo state on my way towards Ubatuba, a 60-mile (100km) stretch of the *Litoral Paulista* (Paulista Coast), home to 84 wild beaches and regarded as the surf capital of São Paulo.

I set my satnav for a small fishing village called Picinguaba, not much more than a few ramshackle beach abodes where fishermen have tucked themselves in for centuries clinging to a hillside that gives way to a 3km-wide beach and idyllic bay. But it's home to Pousada Picinguaba, a refuge that is one of Brazil's most charming inns, a beach fantasy come to life with no TV, no internet and no air-con. My biggest worry here? What I'll choose for dinner and which boozy bevy of tropical goodness I'll order to wash it down.

From Picinguaba, it's another 73 miles (117km) to São Sebastião, the gateway to another gorgeous island, Ilhabela. São Sebastião is one of the few towns on the Paulista coast that has preserved a portion of its colonial centre, and is worth a look if you're carrying on by ferry to Ilhabela, a 15-minute channel crossing away.

Maresias, Juqueí and Guarujá – summer beach getaways for São Paulo's bold and beautiful – follow as the coast winds up in Santos, a pleasant port city best known for Pelé, who played his formative years for Santos FC. I dump the car and grab a taxi to Museu Pelé, the museum in his honour. As the taxi speeds through town, I notice that sign again – "*Fiscalização Eletrônica de Velocidade*" – followed by an abrupt application of the brakes by the taxi driver. It dawns on me: it's announcing an upcoming speed camera...

I realise I must have sped through dozens of them between Rio and here. How many speeding tickets will be forwarded on to me by the rental car company? I'm going to need another *caipirinha*! **KR**

TAKE A BREATHER

If you feel like breaking up the drive in a place with no cars, look no further than Ilha Grande, one of Brazil's most unspoilt tropical islands. Located 13 miles (21km) off the Costa Verde and reachable via ferry from Angra dos Reis or Mangaratiba, this 75 sq mile (193 sq km) paradise is home to fiercely preserved Atlantic rainforest, over 93 miles (150kms) of hiking trails and the sun-toasted sands of Lopes Mendes, a storybook beach.

Opposite: the pretty village of Paraty is a Unesco World Heritage site. Previous page: running the Ubatuba stretch on the Rio to Santos road

DIRECTIONS

Start // Rio de Janeiro
End // Santos
Distance // 345 miles (555km)
Getting there // Fly into São Paulo or Rio de Janeiro.
Where to stay // Pousada da Ouro (www.pousadadoouro. com.br) is a small inn in Paraty with colonial charm and an interior garden and pool. Pousada Picinguaba (www. picinguaba.com) is a 10-room inn, home to fiercely curated artwork, rustic furniture and a pool overlooking the bay.
Where to eat // At Paraty's Banana da Terra (www. restaurantebananadaterra.com.br), the flambeed shrimp on black rice, or grilled fish with mashed *mandioquinha* and shaved hearts of palm are outstanding. Cantinho da Lagoa at Prumirim Beach near Ubatuba is a glorified sand shack producing sophisticated Brazilian beach cuisine.

*Opposite: a view of Venice's
Campanile San Marco (tip:
best not bring the wheels here)*

MORE LIKE THIS
WATERY ROUTES

A VENETIAN SOJOURN, ITALY

Pinch yourself, and you might expect to wake from this dream of pink palaces, teal waters and golden domes. Instead, you're in the Veneto, where gondoliers call and water laps at your feet. Scan the coastline and you might spot signs of modern life – beach resorts, malls, traffic. But look closer and you'll catch the waft of fresh espresso from Piazza San Marco's 250-year-old cafes, faded villas on the Brenta Riviera and masterpieces everywhere: Titians in Venice, Palladios in Vicenza and Giottos in Padua. You'll obviously be starting the trip around Venice and Murano by boat, but once on the road you'll be able to access the country retreats of fashionable Venetians in Brenta Riviera, see European architecture change course in Vicenza and prep your camera for Asolo, known as the 'town of 100 vistas' for its panoramic hillside location.

Start // Venice
End // Treviso
Distance // 115 miles (186km)

HAIDA GWAII ADVENTURE, BC, CANADA

Far-flung and isolated, the lush Haida Gwaii ('Islands of Beauty') are steeped in superlatives – most stunning scenery, tastiest seafood and most accessible First Nations culture. This rugged northwestern archipelago maintains its pioneering spirit but you'll be welcomed to what feels like the edge of the earth with a warm, hearty greeting. You'll be arriving from mainland Prince Rupert on a BC Ferry, so arrange a hire car from Skidegate in advance. Check out the First Nations highlight Haida Heritage Centre before a journey that sticks to Highway 16 all the way to Rose Spit and the dense, treed Naikoon Provincial Park fronted by 60 miles of white sand beach. In-between, stop at the Bottle and Jug Works at Tlell, the forest trail to the Yakoun River at Port Clements, and Masset, with its disused military base, First Nations' village and maritime museum.

Start // Skidegate
End // Rose Spit
Distance // 85 miles (137km)

THE GRACEFUL ITALIAN LAKES

Formed at the end of the ice age, and a popular holiday spot since Roman times, the Italian lakes have an enduring natural beauty. At Lake Maggiore, the palaces of the Borromean Islands lie like a fleet of vessels in the gulf, their grand ballrooms and shell-encrusted grottoes once host to Napoleon, while the siren call of Lake Como draws Hollywood movie stars to its discreet forested slopes. Your drive first clings to Maggiore's shores, from the resort town of Stresa to the dreamy village of Cannobio, before you retrace the pretty 22km to Verbania to board the cross-lake ferry to Laveno. Head on to Lake Como and the elegant town of Como itself, still Europe's most important producer of silk products. After a spectacular drive northeast you'll find it impossible not to be charmed by the waterfront towns of Bellagio, Tremezzo and Varenna, before heading off again down the other 'leg' of Lake Como.

Start // Stresa
End // Bergamo
Distance // 128 miles (206km)

ROUNDING QUÉBEC'S LA GASPÉSIE LOOP

Trailblazing fishermen and fleeing colonialists gave the Gaspésie its complex cultural character, and it was its dense forests, rich seas and prolific wildlife that drew them here.

Even if you speak French, the dialect spoken on the Gaspé Peninsula – or the Gaspésie as it is also known – is almost unintelligible. A throwback to 17th-century France with a colonial overtone, it bewilders visitors and sets locals apart, even from their Québécois neighbours. But then again, the Gaspé is a place apart. An isolated peninsula on the edge of the Americas, it is surrounded by exceptionally rich seas.

These seas attracted the attentions of Basque and Portuguese fishermen before the French arrived in 1534. Not long after, the precocious Gaspé became a cosmopolitan hub with settlers from France and the Channel Islands followed by the English, Scottish and Irish. A roaring trade in fur and fish linked this isolated outpost to Europe, the Caribbean and South America, and a hybrid culture evolved combining the settlers' language, traditions and musics.

The looped Rte 132 skirts the perimeter of the now sparsely populated Gaspé. The seaboard is marked by striking rock formations, pebble beaches and dense forests that stop abruptly on the crest of rugged cliffs. Inland, it's remote and untouched, with wild rivers and forested mountains making it perfect for hiking, mountain biking, white-water rafting, fishing, skiing and snow-shoeing.

This combination of heritage, nature and adventure is what makes the Gaspé so alluring. As you drive, you'll be constantly tempted to

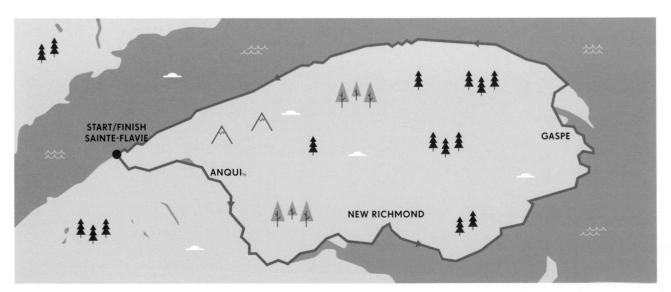

"I was constantly tempted to stop and hike, take a boat trip, kayak, go whale watching or linger over a long lunch"

stop and hike, take a boat trip, hop in a kayak, go whale-watching or linger over long lunches of succulent lobster and smoky eel.

I start out gently with a tranquil drive east from Québec City, passing the charming villages of the Bas-St-Laurent. But by the time I make it to Ste-Flavie, things have become a little less genteel, a little more provincial and, with every passing mile, a lot more wild.

As I drive east the landscape becomes more rugged – windblown cottages cling to rocky headlands and striated cliffs tumble to the sea. Along the northern coast I spot Marcel Gagnon's army of rough wooden figures emerging from the water at Ste-Flavie and then the 133 turbines of one of Canada's largest wind farms at Cap-Chat.

I detour inland to the Parc National de la Gaspésie, a wild, densely forested place, home to some of Quebec's highest peaks, and miles of glorious hiking trails. Alpine meadows and lush valleys give way to the fantastically named Chic-Choc and McGerrigle Mountains, which host the region's only herd of woodland caribou.

Back on the coast, sinewy cliffs round the head of the peninsula to Forillon National Park, where mountains plunge directly to the sea, forest blankets the slopes, whales bask in the water and harbour seals dot the rocks. At Grande-Grave beach there's a restored fishing village giving a glimpse of how late-19th-century settlers lived.

It was here, at the tip of the peninsula, that Breton explorer Jacques Cartier landed in the 16th century. The land was known to the indigenous Mi'kmaq people as *gespeg*, meaning 'end'. Cartier knocked a wooden cross into the ground, claimed it for France and began a period of great upheaval. The history of the Mi'kmaq is poignantly illustrated at the Site d'Interpretation de la Culture Micmac de Gespeg where a reconstructed 17th-century village and summer camp offers a chance to learn about their culture.

I take the undulating road that winds on around craggy headland until I reach the pretty village of Percé, where the Rocher Percé (Pierced Rock) rises out of the sea. This huge hunk of limestone is the Gaspé's most famous landmark and has a colossal rock arch at one end. Beyond the rock is Île Bonaventure, North America's largest migratory bird refuge. More than 250,000 sea birds nest here, most of them raucous northern gannets.

The landscape changes as I round the head of the peninsula to Chaleur Bay. It's a region of picturesque villages and beaches set against a backdrop of red cliffs and forested mountains. The sheltered location drew a jumble of settlers, and local culture is a vibrant mix of influences held together by a shared love of the sea. Herring, lobster and salmon fisheries keep the economy alive and a host of sites unveils the history of the fishermen. Further west, at Miguasha National Park things go much further back. The cliffs here are rich with fossils, many dating from the Devonian period.

As the road turns inland back to Ste-Flavie it winds along the lush Matapédia Valley where covered bridges and heritage homes nestle in verdant forest surrounding lakes and salmon fisheries. Anglers come here in droves. It seems at every turn I'm reminded of the abundant natural resources on the Gaspé; it's easy to see why the peninsula attracted so many early settlers. I know I'll be back. **EOC**

ACADIAN SONG AND DANCE

The Acadians were descendants of emigrants from France who settled on the eastern seaboard of Canada. They were exiled by the British in the 18th century, some fleeing as far south as Louisiana – the Cajuns – others taking refuge in New Brunswick and the Gaspé. Their language, culture and music evolved in a unique way. A great place to see it in action is the Théâtre de Vieille Forge in Petite Vallée.

Clockwise from left: the restored 19th-century village at Grande-Grave; the sublime peninsula at Forillon National Park. Previous page: steer clear, literally, of the region's many moose; skirting the Gaspésie seaboard on Rte 132

DIRECTIONS

Start/End // Ste-Flavie
Distance // 550 miles (885km)
Getting there // Head east from Québec City along the southern shore of the St Lawrence River.
When to drive // Spring and autumn for bird watching; summer for live music and kayaking with whales; autumn for salmon fishing; winter for snow sports.
Good to know // Moose are common here and can do severe damage to your car. They're especially active at dawn and dusk in autumn. Black bears are also regularly seen, keep your food and cooking utensils well away from your tent if you're camping.
Side trip // For a brush with the wilderness, head inland on Rte 299 through the Chic-Choc Mountains.
More info // www.tourisme-gaspesie.com

*Opposite: following the route
of the gold rush through
Yukon's Klondike Highway*

MORE LIKE THIS
PIONEERING DRIVES

KLONDIKE HIGHWAY, YUKON

Climbing steeply out of Skagway, the
Klondike Hwy rises over the infamous White
Pass that proved the undoing of many
would-be prospectors in the Klondike Gold
Rush. It's a tough, lonely but breathtaking
drive following in their footsteps all the
way to Dawson in the Yukon. The road
passes through large tracts of wilderness
where desolate mountains loom over steely
lakes and abandoned roadhouses, cabins,
dredges and tailings hark back to the glory
days. There are few modern communities
along the route. Places to stop include
amiable Carcross with its historic general
store and surreal sand dunes, Whitehorse,
the thriving capital of the Yukon, and finally
bohemian Dawson, a throwback to the gold
rush era. False-fronted wooden houses line
Dawson's dirt roads, colourful characters
still pan for gold in the remaining claims
and you can party the night away with
dancing girls and honky-tonk tunes at
Diamond Tooth Gertie's Gambling Hall.
Start // Skagway, Alaska
End // Dawson, Yukon
Distance // 444 miles (715km)

VIKING TRAIL, NEWFOUNDLAND

Tracing a historic route through one of
the most remote corners of Canada, the
Viking Trail links ancient native burial
grounds, the oldest European settlements
in North America and relics of French
and British occupation along a route
lined with stunning scenery. Icebergs float
majestically past monumental sea stacks,
towering fjords are gouged out of some of
the world's oldest mountains and salmon
the size of small children leap up the rivers.
It's an incredible drive along a windswept
coast where wooded valleys give way
to sheltered coves, ancient volcanic
formations and landscapes scarred by
colossal glaciers. En route you'll pass
5000-year-old burial grounds at Port au
Choix, Unesco-protected fjords and, at
the very tip of northwest Newfoundland, a
Viking settlement established five centuries
before Jacques Cartier or Christopher
Columbus 'discovered' the new world.
Start // Deer Lake, Newfoundland
End // St Anthony, Newfoundland
Distance // 304 miles (489km)

STEWART-CASSIAR HIGHWAY, BRITISH COLUMBIA

Cut out of the dense forest that surrounds
the towering mountains of northern British
Columbia, the Stewart-Cassiar Hwy was
only completed in the 1970s. It joined the
trails that gold prospectors, loggers and
miners had used to explore the area and
winds through some of the wildest and most
isolated territory in BC. Driving the route
offers pioneer history and aboriginal culture
aplenty all set against a backdrop of
magnificent lakes and snow-capped peaks.
Expect grizzly and black bears, caribou and
moose, ghost towns and lava fields, and
tiny, doggedly determined communities.
Take a detour to the historic mining town of
Stewart or to Gold Rush remnant Telegraph
Creek and you'll get history by the bucket
load as well as more spectacular scenery.
Start // Kitwanga Junction
End // Watson Lake, Yukon
Distance // 450 miles (740km)

CROSSING THE CARRETERA AUSTRAL

Chile's Southern Highway snakes its way south for 770 miles (1240km) through a remote land of mountains, lakes, forests, fjords and tiny settlements.

The ferry makes its steady way through the fjord, the green hills on either side obscured by a curtain of mist and drizzle. I started out at dawn from Puerto Montt, the Chilean Lake District's busy port town, speeding along the freshly paved road to make the three ferry crossings that would bring me to the start of my long drive south.

The ferry finally deposits me at Caleta Gonzalo, the gateway to the southern half of Parque Pumalín, an immense protected area that is part of the legacy of US conservationist Doug Tompkins. Well-kept trails branch off from either side of the gravel road, and I decide to stretch my legs along a short trail that loops through a grove of millennia-old *alerce* (Patagonian cypress) trees. I feel dwarfed by these giants and the enormous *nalca* (Chilean rhubarb) leaves that erupt from the dripping vegetation around me.

In the half-ruined town of Chaitén I call on my friend Nicolas, an American who was one of the few hardy residents who refused to leave when the Chaitén volcano erupted in 2008, burying half the town in a cocktail of mud and ash. Essential services have long been restored, but those abandoned, dilapidated houses are a stark contrast to the sunny little rodeo town I first visited a year before the eruption. 'We're surviving,' Nicolas tells me.

A beautifully paved road sweeps southeast through the valley, passing through the village of El Amarillo, the jumping off point for Parque Pumalín's southernmost trails, including a stunning hike to the base of a glacier from what is possibly the world's prettiest campsite. I continue onwards to where the Carretera Austral forks at the village of Villa Santa Lucia, and take a detour towards the Argentinian border, skirting the glacial Yelcho lake and following the Futaleufú river upstream to its eponymous picture-perfect village.

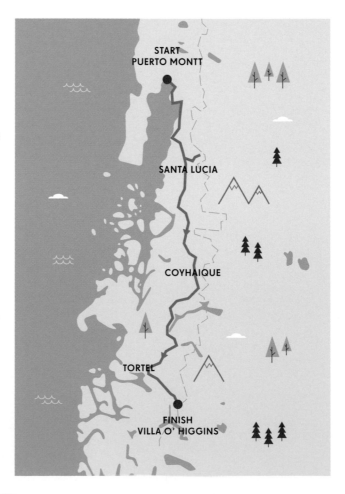

START
PUERTO MONTT

SANTA LUCÍA

COYHAIQUE

TORTEL

FINISH
VILLA O' HIGGINS

© Christian Handl | Getty Images

Morning finds me geared up with the rest of the rafting team, then drenched in icy spray and paddling frantically through the surging rapids of the aquamarine Futaleufú – one of the world's top white-water rafting rivers – to the shouted instructions of our guide.

That adrenalin burst is followed by a tranquil drive back to the Southern Hwy, and south once more, past La Junta, a former *estancia* (ranch) turned market town. The Carretera Austral was built in the 1970s as part of Pinochet's move to tame and populate Chile's southern wilderness. Nearing the fjordside village of Puyuhuapi I wait in a queue of a dozen cars. The rains the night before have predictably brought a landslide onto the road, and the last of it is being cleared. That taming is obviously an ongoing process.

It's early evening by the time I pull up in front of Casa Ludwig, an alpine homestead run by the descendant of one of Puyuhuapi's German founders who set up a textiles factory here in the 1930s. A soak in the thermal pool overlooking the placid waters of Ventisquero Sound, followed by a simple dinner of fresh fish grilled at a family-run eatery by the water, then it's feet up by the roaring fire at Casa Ludwig, and the company and tales of my fellow travellers – it's the perfect antidote to the day's excitement.

The most challenging part is still to come. The next day's drive is along a potholed, narrow, bumpy stretch of road that skirts the edge of the fjord. I pass secluded, high-end fishing lodges before turning inland and climbing to Queulat Pass. The road's narrow, serpentine curves are liberally strewn with jutting rocks, crisscrossed by shallow streams and cratered with enormous potholes. In spite of that, this is among the most beautiful parts of the Carretera Austral: the

PATAGONIA PARK

Eleven miles (18km) north of Cochrane, a detour takes you to beautiful Patagonia Park – a former *estancia* home to guanaco, pumas, flamingo and huemul. The 266-sq-mile (690-sq-km) valley was bought in 2004 by Conservacion Patagonica, which protects land and wildlife. With campgrounds, trails and a restaurant, this regenerated wilderness is to form part of the future 927-sq-mile (2400-sq-km) Patagonia National Park.

Clockwise from top: stopping off to explore dense Chilean forest; a hanging glacier at Queulat National Park; a river bisects the landscape. Previous page: a rugged but picturesque gravel stretch of the Carretera Austral

narrow road is hemmed in by unruly vegetation and glacier-fringed mountains rise in front of me, glistening with ribbons of waterfalls.

The potholes turn into a stretch of paving and I breathe a sigh of relief. The land is immediately less remote, as craggy peaks give way to rolling farmland and, finally, the Southern Hwy's metropolis: the pioneer town of Coyhaique, where a comfy bed and a meal await me in the web of streets radiating from the pentagonal main square.

South of Coyhaique, a good gravel road traverses wide valleys overlooked by snow-tipped peaks. There's little in the way of human habitation here. I pass through tiny settlements – this is all pioneer country – with occasional sightings of sheep-herding *huasos* (cowboys) on horseback. South of Lago General Carrera – Chile's great inland sea – I pass the turnoff for Patagonia Park, the region's newest protected area, before rolling into the former ranching town of Cochrane. I make the most of it: this is the last chance to fuel up, eat a good steak and get a good night's sleep before the last, long, lonely stretch to the very end of the road.

The next day, a quick detour along the Río Cochrane takes me west to Tortel, to visit a friend. This unique fishing village is strikingly positioned between two icefields. There are no roads – just cypress-wood houses clinging to the hillside, connected by boardwalks, and the smell of freshly cut wood in the air.

Back on the Carretera Austral, a final ferry crossing awaits at Puerto Yungay. The road that follows is the bane of long-distance cyclists: a bumpy washboard with narrow hairpin bends and a sheer drop to one side. It promises the untimely demise of any driver showing less than constant vigilance.

Then the land flattens out and I find myself at my final destination: a neat grid of streets huddling against towering mountains – the pioneer outpost of Villa O'Higgins. My reward? *Cordero al palo* – delicious Patagonian lamb barbecued over a wood fire. **AK**

"The narrow road is hemmed in by unruly vegetation and glacier-fringed mountains rise in front of me"

DIRECTIONS

Start // Puerto Montt
End // Villa O'Higgins
Distance // 770 miles (1240km)

Getting there // You can hire a car in Puerto Montt, drive all the way south and then back up, or fly into Coyhaique's Balmaceda Airport, rent a car in Coyhaique and then use the town as a base for driving north and south.

When to drive // Between October and April. Give yourself plenty of time, as some sections of the road are susceptible to landslides.

What to drive // A 4WD is not necessary but a vehicle with high clearance is essential.

What to take // Petrol stations are found in most towns, but take a spare tyre, a jack, sleeping bag, food and water in case of breakdown.

Hot tip // Make advance reservations for ferries if travelling in peak season.

Opposite: making the south-eastern approach to Uluru on foot

MORE LIKE THIS
METTLE-TESTING TRIPS

DEMPSTER HIGHWAY, CANADA

If you're looking for another drive of comparable magnitude and challenge, Canada's Dempster Hwy fits the bill. This hard-packed, gravel road branches off the North Klondike Hwy near Dawson City, Yukon, and swings north through pristine wilderness for 457 miles (736km) before ending in Inuvik, the northernmost town of any size in Canada's Northwest Territories, way beyond the Arctic Circle. From 2018, it should be possible to drive all the way to Tuktoyaktuk, a tiny settlement on the shores of the Arctic Ocean, 75 miles (120km) north of Inuvik. It's a gorgeous, lonely drive that passes through dense forest (you may spot grizzly bears), past snow-tipped mountains and finally through vast expanses of flat tundra. There are two tiny settlements near Inuvik – Fort McPherson and Tsiigehtchic, where you have to take a car ferry.
Start // Dawson City
End // Inuvik
Distance // 457 miles (736km)
Top tip // Rent a 4WD, take two spare tyres, and fill up on petrol. Bring emergency supplies in case you break down as there is practically no phone reception here.

HIGHWAY 500, MALAYSIA

If you have never seen homemade water-cooled brakes on trucks, get ready for a treat up in the Crocker Range overlooking Sabah's capital, Kota Kinabalu. The brakes on the trucks are simply not up to the descent, so the drivers rig up plastic pipes, which dribble a regular supply of cooling water onto the brake drums. From Kota Kinabalu, the road starts innocuously enough, curving gently through golf courses and farming villages. That changes when it reaches the range, and the road begins the tortuous tight corners and hairpins that will take it to its 1800-metre ridge-line. Vibrant jungle is interspersed with small villages, many of them boasting a basic restaurant and all of them home to dogs that just love sleeping on the warm roadway. The prime tourist attraction of this route is surely one of the smelliest in the world: it is the Rafflesia Information Centre, devoted to the world's largest and most pungent flower.
Start // Kota Kinabalu
End // Tambunan
Distance // 47 miles (75km)

ULURU & THE RED CENTRE, AUSTRALIA

Tackle this outback adventure between April and August as the rest of the year is fiercely hot. Your departure point, Uluru, is an extraordinary, soulful place utterly unlike anywhere else on the planet. Nearby, the 36 domed rocks at Kata Tjuta and Kings Canyon's yawning chasm leave spellbound all who visit. Using Alice Springs as your most easterly point, and somewhere to wash off the dust and sleep between clean sheets, make a beeline to the steep-sided rocky waterhole of Ellery Creek Big Hole, and swim in its icy-cold water if you're brave. This is one of several standout stop-offs – be sure to visit Standley Chasm and Ormiston Gorge – in the West MacDonnell Ranges, which capture the essence of the Red Centre: red earth, red rocks and ghostly gums in a spiritually charged landscape.
Start // Uluru (Ayers Rock)
End // Tyler Pass Lookout
Distance // 761 miles (1224km)

THROUGH THE CALCHAQUÍ VALLEYS

With its multicoloured mountainscapes and high-altitude vineyards, Argentina's Valles Calchaquíes circuit offers intrepid oenophiles the perfect wine pairing: adventure.

Wh-en adobe walls vibrate to the sound of trembling guitars, the air smells of sizzling steaks and your tongue tastes of greasy empanadas and jammy malbec you'll know you've finally made it to a *peña*. These music halls, famed for their *zamba* folk singers and meaty comfort foods, are the big draw luring local Argentines to Salta, a city in the northwestern corner of this triangular nation where it bumps up against the dusty frontiers of Chile and Bolivia. I found this *peña* by accident, like a foreigner entering Nashville and stumbling into a honky-tonk unawares. That's because I've come to this forgotten corner of Argentina precisely to leave this city in my rear-view mirror. Yet, I'm finding that extremely hard to do.

Salta means 'the beautiful one' in the language of the indigenous Aymara people. Spanish-speaking Argentines call it 'Salta la Linda', or 'Salta the beautiful'. With its bubblegum-pink cathedral, soaring neoclassical architecture and lively curb-side cafes, it's not hard to see why. This time-capsule of a city sprung

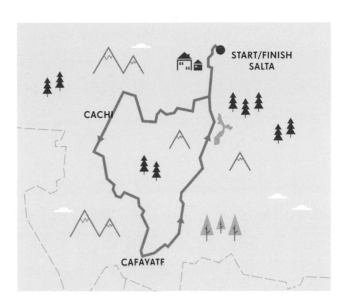

START/FINISH
SALTA

CACHI

CAFAYATE

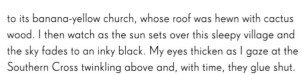

up on the outer fringes of the Inca Empire during the height of the Spanish conquest and would go on to become a vital cog of commerce nearly halfway between Lima and Buenos Aires.

After a long night at the *peña* and a lazy morning spent revelling in Salta's storied history at the institutions on Plaza 9 de Julio (including a treasure-filled archaeology museum), I set off on the pockmarked roads out of town. It's here my real adventure begins as I ride into the sun-baked nether regions of greater Salta Province.

The plan is to spend three days winding through the windswept Valles Calchaquíes of the Andean foothills, crossing through three vastly different ravines before looping back to Salta.

The first ravine, Quebrada de Escoipe, is surely the work of Mother Nature's abstract-expressionist friend, its mountains are multicoloured thanks to the oxidation of minerals such as sulphur (yellow), iron (red) and copper (green) over thousands of years. After crossing this surreal landscape I zigzag my way to the top of Bishop's Slope, a 3400m-high overlook where visitors seek the blessing of Archangel Raphael (patron saint of travellers) at a chapel built in his honour.

At the thatched stall by the chapel I purchase road snacks (llama sausage and goat's cheese) and continue onwards into the rust-red hills of Parque Nacional los Cardones. This reserve is a photographer's dream – cartoonish cacti appear on the horizon like an army of green ghosts wandering through a desert plain.

When I reach the adobe homes and time-forgotten streets of Cachi, I cut my engine for the evening and stroll through the village

"Cafayate is home to some of the highest vineyards in the world, a landscape of soaring mountains and emerald vines"

to its banana-yellow church, whose roof was hewn with cactus wood. I then watch as the sun sets over this sleepy village and the sky fades to an inky black. My eyes thicken as I gaze at the Southern Cross twinkling above and, with time, they glue shut.

The following morning I set out into the cool air of the Andean foothills and forge onward past the archaeological ruins of a pre-Inca city called La Paya into the Quebrada de las Flechas (Ravine of Arrows). It's a landscape not unlike the badlands of North America with a menagerie of misshapen rocks and beguiling formations that can make you question whether the Earth hasn't tilted just a little bit off its axis.

With massive condors soaring up above and hiking trails snaking off into the distance, it's a place I could linger for hours. But I know that on the far side of this spectacular geological rift lies an even more appetising treat: the vineyards of Cafayate.

Cafayate is Argentina's second wine centre after Mendoza, but it's a place that's much more down to earth and approachable than its ritzier neighbour to the south. While Mendoza prizes big bold bottles of malbec, Cafayate is a region dominated by the more demure torrontés, a white wine grape that grows exceptionally well

WINES WITH ALTITUDE

The high-altitude vineyards of Salta lie between 1700m and 3111m, giving the wines power, structure and minerality. Torrontés is the most widely planted grape, but you'll also find bottles of malbec markedly different from those further south in Mendoza, where vines are below 1500m. The altitude creates stressful conditions – such as higher solar radiation and dramatic shifts in temperature – that give the grapes more concentrated flavours.

From left: Torrontés grapes on the vine; and in the barrel; the altar at Cathedral of Salta; the winding road to Cachi. Previous page: curious rock formations mark the Ravine of Arrows

DIRECTIONS

Start/End // Salta
Distance // 325 miles (523km)
Getting there // Salta's airport has direct flights from Buenos Aires and Lima. You can bus in from most big cities in Argentina, as well as San Pedro de Atacama in Chile.
When to drive // Night-time temperatures can dip to near freezing in the dry winter months (Jun-Aug), while summer (Dec-Mar) is rainier and hotter. Heavy summer rains can cause flooding and make some roads impassable.
Where to stay // La Merced del Alto (lamerceddelalto. com) is an elegant adobe-built *estancia* just outside Cachi. Patios de Cafayate Wine Hotel (www.patiosdecafayate. com) puts you right in the middle of Cafayate's vineyards.
Detours // Explore the light installations of American artist James Turrell at his museum on the Colomé wine estate.

in these cold, windswept valleys. Torrontés has a deceptively sweet nose (like a riesling) that belies its dry finish. As such, it goes down like grape juice when you're basking in Cafayate's afternoon sun.

Cafayate is home to some of the highest altitude vineyards in the world, so to sip and swirl your way through this quite literally breathtaking landscape of soaring mountains and emerald vines is a rare experience. The town itself – with its Andean handicraft markets and family-run bodegas – has a refreshing authenticity.

I leave the rolling vines behind on my last day in Santa Province as I enter yet another magnificent landscape: the fossil-rich Quebrada de las Conchas (Ravine of the Shells). The remnants of an ancient lakebed, it is rife with otherworldly rock formations such as the Garganta del Diablo (Devil's Throat) and Anfiteatro (Amphitheatre). The latter is the site of a prehistoric waterfall with solid rock that now takes on blanket-like folds and improbable swirls. Its walls are also riddled with holes, which reveal themselves to be the homes of burrowing parrots.

My final leg skirts past a ghost town called Alemania and an artificial lake, Cabra Corral, that's become a popular weekend retreat for Salteños. Green fields of tobacco then give way to a smattering of increasingly substantial villages.

Soon the adobe walls are vibrating once again, the air is thick with sizzling steaks and my tongue is purple with malbec. I have made it back to the city of Salta and I have stumbled – though very much on purpose this time – into the all-absorbing atmosphere of the *peña*. **MJ**

*Opposite: a typically serene
scene in the wineries of
Bannockburn, New Zealand*

MORE LIKE THIS
WINE ROUTES

CENTRAL OTAGO, NEW ZEALAND

Travel the valley-hugging roads between
Queenstown and Wanaka and you'll
stumble upon one of New Zealand's most
under-appreciated wine regions: Central
Otago. As the southern-most wine region
in the world, Central Otago's vineyards
specialise in cool-climate grapes such as
pinot noir and riesling. To get the most out
of your trip, leave Queenstown and link up
with Hwy 6 into the Gibbston Valley, where
vineyards fight for space between rugged
mountains and the Kawarau River gorge.
Continue to the wineries of Bannockburn
before curving north on Hwy 8 along the
east coast of Lake Dunstan where you'll
find the vineyards of Bendigo. Finish with
a stay in the resort town of Wanaka.
Start // Queenstown
End // Wanaka
Distance // 80 miles (128km)

VAL D'ORCIA, ITALY

The World Heritage-listed landscapes
of Val d'Orcia have featured in many
Hollywood films from *Gladiator* to *The
English Patient*. These patchwork hills
and verdant valleys are the Tuscany of
dreams, home to Renaissance villages
such as Pienza and walled medieval
cities like Montalcino. At the vineyards
near Montalcino you can pair the distinct
Brunello sangiovese with choice items from
the local larder such as chestnuts and
truffles. A road trip through Val d'Orcia
might run from the medieval hill town
of Montepulciano to the vineyards of
Montalcino. Then head south down SR2 to
the quaint village of Castiglione d'Orcia,
before ending at Radicofani fortress.
Start // Montepulciano
End // Radifocani
Distance // 56 miles (90km)

WILLAMETTE VALLEY, USA

Pinot noir is the grape that put Oregon
on the wine map when a bottle from Eyrie
Vineyards outshone its French rivals at the
1979 'Wine Olympics'. The US state has
since grown a reputation for its pinot gris
and riesling, too. See for yourself on a road
trip through Oregon's Willamette Valley.
This 150-mile (240km) basin is the state's
agricultural heartland and you can use its
main thoroughfares, I-5 and 99W, to dip
in and out for wine tastings. Both roads
run between the coast and the Cascade
mountain range, from the hipster haven of
Portland down to the buzzing college town
of Eugene. Along the way ride past fields
and farm stands, hopyards and vineyards,
winding rivers and bubbling hot springs.
Start // Portland
End // Eugene
Distance // 112 miles (180km)

© Radius Images | Getty Images

SOUTHERN UTAH NATIONAL PARK CIRCUIT

Cut a swath through southern Utah's canyonlands, taking in parts of eight states, national scenic byways and close to a dozen protected areas.

'This is the most beautiful place on Earth.'
So begins *Desert Solitaire* (1968), Edward Abbey's account of a summer spent in the canyonlands of southern Utah, and I couldn't agree with him more. It is a land where the scorched red earth does impossible things, and each bend in the road produces a jaw-dropping moment. Yet writing about road trips in the context of Abbey is conflicting. The pugnacious environmentalist rued the very existence of roads in his spiritual home and muse. To truly experience the canyonlands, he wrote, get out of the car and 'walk, better yet crawl, on hands and knees, over the sandstone and through the thornbush and cactus.'

I sympathise with Abbey's point of view. But exploring deserts on hands and knees involves more time than most of us have. So I drive. Often. Always am I sure to set aside plenty of time for hikes in the area's magnificent wilderness. Abbey would approve.

On a recent trip I set my sights on the three heavy hitters of Utah's national parks: Arches, Bryce and Zion. I had visited each individually, but never together in one glorious swoop. The drive was the icing on the cake: 475 mouth-watering miles (764km) along the scenic byways of southern Utah. The route has no name, but is rather an agglomeration of several famous drives, many with names that will be familiar to US road-trip aficionados – Trail of the

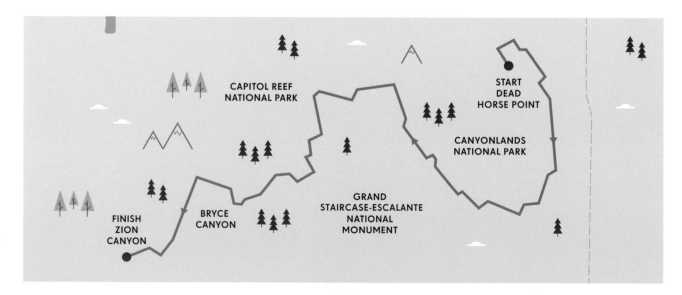

"Wind, frost, rain and rivers have been slicing and dicing the ruddy sandstone into fantastic shapes for eons"

Ancients, Bicentennial Scenic Byway and the mind-blowing Hwy 12 (dubbed, rather awkwardly, 'A Journey Through Time Scenic Byway').

The building block of the American Southwest's stupendous canyons, arches, mesas and grottoes is sandstone, a malleable substance formed by the hardening of sand dunes over time. Wind, frost, rain and rivers – most notably the Colorado – have been slicing and dicing the ruddy sandstone into fantastic shapes for eons, and will continue to do so for eons more.

The most famous product of this is the Grand Canyon, just south of the Utah border in Arizona. A couple of hundred miles (about 300km) up the Colorado River from the Grand Canyon's north rim is Dead Horse Point, which overlooks Canyonlands National Park at the confluence the Colorado and Green rivers. After a morning spent hiking in nearby Arches National Park, where Abbey was a ranger in the 1950s, our road trip begins. The massive abyss beneath Dead Horse Point plays tricks with one's sense of space. To the east, the snow-draped La Sal Mountains lord over the canyon's burgundy-toned eastern rim. This is southern Utah: serene, brutal, inspiring.

From Dead Horse Point, we follow the Trail of the Ancients due south and then west towards our next hiking stops, Natural Bridges National Monument and Capitol Reef National Park. Abbey loved the summer here, but it's not the best time to visit. For one thing, the national parks are overrun with RVs, as Abbey long-ago predicted would happen. Summer is also unbearably hot. March is about perfect: cool and crisp for those day hikes, and not too crowded.

We leave the Trail of the Ancients behind at Natural Bridges and follow the Bicentennial Scenic Byway through Capitol Reef, then pick up Hwy 12 in Torrey and drive south to Bryce Canyon. This entire stretch is mesmerising, the road snaking into snowy pine forest and down into dusty red desert, skirting huge mesas. There are myriad potential side trips, many bearing cheeky names like Cheesebox Canyon, Kodachrome Basin, Moss Back Butte and Dirty Devil River.

By the time we reach Bryce Canyon National Park we think we've lost the ability to be impressed. We haven't. Erosion has sculpted the crumbly earth into fields of colourful totem-pole-like formations called hoodoos that change colour by the hour. Our hike is under sunny skies but there's a nip in the air – at over 8000ft, Bryce is the highest of these national parks. On our way back to the car, a snow squall moves in. We watch as the hoodoos, their tops dusted white, transmogrify into the distinguished old men of the high Utah desert.

Leaving the snow behind us, we descend towards Zion National Park, 80 miles (128km) west and a couple of thousand feet lower. We opt for a half-day hike to Observation Point, 2100ft above the Zion Canyon floor. There are several slot canyons – giant alleyways cut into the sandstone – to negotiate along the way, and from the top we can look straight down to the valley, where the Virgin River dances among Zion's imposing cliffs.

From Zion we have ample opportunities to extend our road trip. It's only two hours to the Grand Canyon or five to Death Valley. Alas, this time we head home, leaving Abbey's Country to continue its intricate pas de deux with time. **GB**

HOLE-IN-THE-ROCK

Predecessor to the scenic byways of southwestern Utah, the Hole-in-the-Rock Rte was a wagon road, from Escalante (along present-day Hwy 12) to Bluff, built by Mormon settlers in the late 1800s. The route, in use for a year, crossed the Colorado via an actual hole in the rock, a steep notch in a 1200ft cliff. Ropes and oxen lowered wagons down the notch, which can be visited by road from Escalante or boat from Lake Powell.

Clockwise from left: Native American art in Utah's caves; extraordinary sandstone formations; snowy slopes in Bryce Canyon National Park. Previous page: the Watchman peak in Zion National Park

DIRECTIONS

Start // Dead Horse Point State Park
End // Zion National Park
Distance // 475 miles (764km)
Getting there // Dead Horse Point is near Moab, accessible by air or by road from Salt Lake City, 230 miles (370km) northeast. Zion is 160 miles (257km) from Las Vegas.
When to drive // Low season rules: go October to March.
Where to stay // Zion Lodge (www.zionlodge.com; reserve months in advance) in Zion Canyon; Gonzo Inn (www.gonzoinn.com) on the main drag in Moab; Capitol Reef Inn & Cafe (www.capitolreefinn.com) in Torrey.
Climate // It's seriously cold at night in the desert from October to April. Days are mild outside of summer's heat.
Hot tip // Some of the best side trips are accessible via unsealed roads, so hiring a 4WD makes sense.

Clockwise from top: the lure of the
Florida Keys, from beach; to bar;
towering trees of Kings Canyon
National Park, California

MORE LIKE THIS
AUTHORS' ITINERARIES

JOHN MUIR'S COUNTRY:
SIERRA NEVADA

What the canyonlands were to Edward Abbey, the Sierras were to John Muir a couple of generations earlier. The legendary conservationist and Sierra Club founder was also one of the early American travel writers, producing volumes on his excursions into this wild mountain range near the California–Nevada border. This trip takes in a trio of Californian national parks from north to south: Yosemite, Kings Canyon and Sequoia. You'll see the expected big trees, big cliffs and big waterfalls, along with lesser-known gems like the Kings Canyon Scenic Byway (Hwy 180) – 50 miles (80km) of alpine eye candy, culminating in the dramatic descent into Kings Canyon. This is high-altitude driving: in the cold months many roads close and snow-chains are mandatory. It goes without saying that there are huge hiking opportunities along this route, including the John Muir Trail.
Start // Yosemite National Park
End // Sequoia National Park
Distance // 260 miles (418km)

STEPHEN KING'S COUNTRY: MAINE

Stephen King has two homes in Maine, and many of his gritty horror stories are set in the state. From Portland, take maritime US Rte 1 'downeast' to Ellsworth, then detour south and loop around the Acadia Scenic Byway, one of 31 All-American Roads. The coastal route brings you past icons (the LL Bean store, the Bath Iron Works), natural wonders (the entire coastline), man-made marvels (the 1827 Pemaquid lighthouse, Bucksport's Penobscot Narrows Bridge), picturesque harbors (Camden, Bar Harbor) and unexpected artist havens (Portland, Belfast, Rockland). Get out of the car and hike in the Camden Hills or Acadia National Park. Or take a car ferry to explore the Fox Islands or Deer Isle. End up in pleasant Bangor, King's part-time residence and gateway to Maine's wild north. Crowds thin and the foliage is spectacular in the autumn; be ready for inclement weather at any time of year.
Start // Portland
End // Bangor
Distance // Approx 300 miles (482km)

JIMMY BUFFETT'S COUNTRY:
THE FLORIDA KEYS

It's tempting to call the Florida Keys Hemingway's country, but the author only lived in Key West for eight years and the area didn't inspire his books. Tennessee Williams lived in Key West for decades, and Thomas McGuane caroused there with other authors in the 1970s and set his signature novel, *Ninety-Two in the Shade*, in Key West. Ultimately, however, the Keys are Jimmy Buffett territory. The 'Margaritaville' crooner got his start in Key West and has written countless songs and several best-selling short-story collections about the Keys. Perhaps it's the drive to Key West that inspires so many artists and writers. The Florida Keys Scenic Highway, a prestigious All-American Road, traverses a magnificent seascape as it hops, one bridge at a time, among the Keys' myriad islands. Hurricanes are a threat from July to November, so check the radar to ensure you aren't driving into one.
Start // Key Largo
End // Key West
Distance // 110 miles (177km)

AROUND THE WHITE MOUNTAINS

This loop through New Hampshire is a dramatic tug-of-war for drivers: majestic mountains lure you forward while gorges, waterfalls and one grand hotel demand immediate detours.

As a lifelong hiker, I find a drive through the White Mountains to be an exquisite form of torture. Just steps from the road, unfurling through the hardwood forest, is a network of trails that I will never have time to conquer. The trailheads are like mountain sirens, calling out promises of roaring streams, tumbling cascades, alpine huts, windswept summits and valley vistas that roll to the horizon. But there is no way that I can hike them all.

The Kancamagus Hwy (NH 112) ribbons west from the town of Conway, and is where my road trip begins. This 34.5-mile (55.5km) National Scenic Byway is beloved by leaf-peepers in autumn, when the foliage blazes yellow, gold, orange and red. But I prefer to drive 'the Kanc' during the spring, when the Saco River, unleashed from the frozen winter, roars to life and the trees begin to shake off their chill. And the wildlife? Let's just say things are getting frisky out there.

My first stop is the US Forest Service ranger office, which is

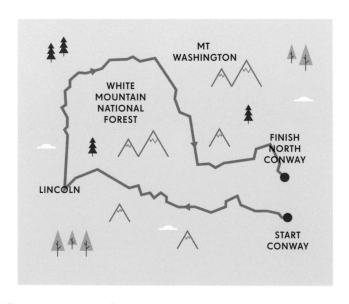

just to the west of town, where I pull in for a recreation parking pass (a total of $3 for the day), a list of roadside trails and a few minutes of chitchat with the ranger about the adventures that await ahead. From here, the byway rolls west into the White Mountain National Forest. This vast expanse of hardwoods and conifers soon surrounds me like a big green hug, its grip loosened only by the exuberant Swift River, which splashes alongside the road just beyond my window.

The byway was named after Kancamagus ('The Fearless One'), chief of the Pennacook Native American people who inhabited the area in the late 15th century. Though the Pennacook were largely peaceful, ongoing aggressions by the English drove the chieftain to bloody conflicts with the invaders. The tribes eventually scattered, and Kancamagus moved north, but the thick forest here still feels wild, like a territorial outpost that was never quite tamed.

This elemental sense of wildness is on full display at the Rocky Gorge Scenic Area, where the Swift River drops through a corridor of granite. My favourite spot for photographs is the graceful footbridge a short walk east from the parking area. Look upstream at the tumbling waters then take your shot

Like most hikers, I'm drawn to trails that end with a payoff, a big 'wow' that replenishes the spirit – or at least earns my physical burn. The 0.3-mile (0.5km) hike to Sabbaday Falls meets these criteria. The trail ends at a compact gorge waterfall, which powers through granite bedrock then cascades into lovely pools. The trail is an easy streamside stroll and wheelchair-accessible.

From here the byway roller-coasters up to the Kancagamus Pass (elevation 2855ft), where overlooks give panoramic mountain views. The road then drops into the town of Lincoln, where the White Mountains Visitor Center welcomes road trippers with coffee, a large fake moose and a forest ranger desk. Just beyond is North Woodstock and the Woodstock Inn, Station & Brewery; the patio here is my preferred spot for a post-drive sandwich and brew.

Steep mountains flank I-93, an easy-going interstate that flows north for eight scenic miles (13km) through Franconia Notch State Park. The roadside attractions here include the Flume Gorge, a cascade-filled corridor of granite whose mossy walls reach heights of 70ft to 90ft. A few miles north, the Cannon Mountain Aerial Tramway whisks guests to a lofty viewpoint.

Just north, US 3 rolls through the town of Twin Mountain then joins US 302 for a spin through Bretton Woods, the photogenic centrepiece of the Presidential Range, the highest mountain range in the White Mountains. And while it's true that I brake for mountains, I slam to a surprised halt for the Mount Washington Hotel, a red-capped wonder shimmering at the base of Mount Washington. Yep, this beauty never fails to catch me off-guard when it bursts onto the horizon.

In 1944, the hotel hosted the Bretton Woods Conference, which created the World Bank and stabilised the global economy at the close of WWII. The world leaders in attendance hoped to avoid the devastating economic failures that followed WWI.

I like to wander the hallways off the lobby, where I stare at black-and-white photos of the property and wonder about the lives of long-ago guests and staff. For mid-trip inspiration, I stop a moment on the back veranda to soak up the impressive view of mighty Mount Washington, the tallest mountain in New England.

This stretch of US 302 is also a conduit to adventure. In summer, the Mount Washington Cog Railway and its coal-fired steam locomotive carries passengers to the mountain's 6288ft summit. Layer up for this chilly trip. Summit temperatures hover around 7°C (45°F) in summer, and it's windy up there.

South of the resort, you might find me dozing in an Adirondack chair on the front lawn of the Appalachian Mountain Club (AMC) Highland Center, which is a convenient launch pad to the trails crisscrossing the Presidential Range. Reasons to stop? Trail information, a hearty meal and an endless supply of adventure-loving guests. Also known as my people. The lodge-style dorm rooms are a convenient place to rest up and check your gear before tackling a hut-to-hut hike on the nearby Appalachian Trail.

Back on US 302, you might glimpse the Conway Scenic Railroad Notch Train as it chugs into the depot just south of the Highland Center. The train begins its leafy journey in North Conway, a friendly mountain town packed tight with indie motels, cozy breakfast joints and outlet stores. My favourite last stop is the convivial Moat Mountain Smokehouse & Brewery Co, where the Czech-style lager, the ½lb burger and the spicy Cajun fries are always a good idea. **AB**

HUT-TO-HUT HIKING

The Appalachian Mountain Club (www.outdoors.org) runs eight overnight huts along the Appalachian Trail in the White Mountains. It's a day's hike between each dorm-style hut, in use for more than 125 years and complete with bunks, pillows and blankets. From summer to early autumn, a dinner and breakfast are included with your booking. A seasonal 'croo' cooks the meals and shares info about the region.

Left to right: across Big Lake to Mount Washington; Crawford Depot serves the Conway Scenic Railroad Notch Train. Previous page: rainbow foliage runs the length of Kancamagus Hwy

DIRECTIONS

Start // Conway
End // North Conway
Distance // 92 miles (148km)
Getting there // Boston Logan International Airport is a 2.5-hour drive from Conway.
When to drive // Autumn draws crowds for the colourful foliage display, which peaks between late September and mid-October. Summer is an idyllic time for hiking. Spring temperatures can be fickle, and many attractions are closed, but there may be lighter crowds.
What to bring // If you plan to hike, pack layers of non-cotton clothing, a windbreaker or rain jacket, and sturdy shoes. You may want hiking poles for the more steep and rocky trails.
More info // www.visitwhitemountains.com

*Opposite: an evening out on New
Orleans' legendary Bourbon Street*

MORE LIKE THIS
AMERICAN DRIVES

CROOKED ROAD, VIRGINIA

During America's colonial era, European
settlers in the Appalachian region
began playing their fiddles alongside
banjos brought over by African slaves.
The Bristol Radio Sessions brought this
old-time mountain music to the masses in
1927. Today, the Crooked Road Heritage
Music Trail celebrates old-time music and
bluegrass, swinging past music jams,
bluegrass museums and down-home
restaurants on a journey through the Blue
Ridge Mountains of southwestern Virginia.
You'll find live music along the trail most
nights of the week, with lively crowds
dancing every Friday night at the Floyd
Country Store. Signs along the route are
emblazoned with banjos, and road-side
exhibits give information and recordings
of local musicians you can tune into on
your car radio. Don't miss the Carter Family
Fold, where Johnny Cash performed his
very last live show.
Start // Rocky Mount
End // Breaks Interstate Park
Distance // 330 miles (531km)
More info // www.myswva.org/tcr

CAJUN COUNTRY, LOUISIANA

Surrounded by brackish swamps, slow-
moving bayous and thick stands of bald
cypress, the drive west from New Orleans
through the Mississippi River Delta on US
90 is a soggy, sometimes eerie, adventure.
On overcast days you might find yourself
believing the legend of the swamp-dwelling
rougarou, a red-eyed werewolf who
snatches up naughty children. But never
fear, this moody landscape is the stomping
ground of Louisiana's Cajun community,
beloved for their upbeat music, hearty
food and swamp tours – where alligator
sightings are virtually guaranteed. Cajuns
are the descendants of French-Canadian
refugees, originally called Acadians, who
migrated to southern Louisiana in the late
1700s from Canada's maritime provinces.
A classic road trip stops by the Tabasco
factory on Avery Island then pulls up to
a crawfish joint in Breaux Bridge, with
a final stop at the Blue Moon Saloon
in Lafayette for raucous Cajun music
performances. Accordions, yelps and foot-
stomping should be expected.
Start // New Orleans
End // Lafayette
Distance // 170 miles (274km)

OLD WEST

There's no better place than central
Arizona to celebrate your inner cowboy
or cowgirl. From Wickenburg north to
Sedona and Flagstaff, the hard-charging
Hwy 89/89A rolls through a scrubby
landscape of deserts and mountains that
wears its Old West history on its dusty
sleeve. Cowboy museums and dude
ranches will try to lure you from your car
as you climb from the Sonoran Desert into
the Weaver Mountains, home to Prescott
and its rowdy Whiskey Row. Wyatt Earp
and Doc Holliday partied here in the
1870s. The artsy charms of Jerome – a
former mining town clinging to the side of
a mountain – soon gives way to the red
rocks of Sedona, where Pink Jeep Tours
(www.pinkjeeptours.com) tries to lasso
up customers for rides over the red rocks.
Lively Flagstaff channels the past at old
hotels and an ever-rocking log cabin,
better known as the Museum Club.
Start // Wickenburg
End // Flagstaff
Distance // 150 miles (241km)

THE PACIFIC COAST HIGHWAY

Follow America's west-coast route from Seattle to San Francisco to find free-spirited cities, Pacific vistas and forests of epic proportions.

Opened in 1926, US Highway 101 is laid along the First World's final frontier: 1540 miles of ancient wood and wild water, linking the Pacific coast from Washington state to California. It's a route and a region that has always attracted adventurers and rebels, and somehow, for all the RVs and visitor centres, the 101 still retains that sense of wilderness and opportunity.

Seattle seems a fitting point of departure: the northwest's dominant metropolis is also America's youngest, fastest-growing city. A city of geeks and freaks that gave us Jimi Hendrix, Kurt Cobain, Microsoft and Amazon, Seattle is switched-on, radical and proud of it (and a great place to sample a micro-brewed beer or three).

Leaving Seattle means a car ferry and a drive across the world's longest floating bridge, together sufficient to blow away any happy-hour cobwebs. At once the traffic thins and the trees close in, and after an hour or so at the rigorously enforced speed limit, you're into deepest, darkest Washington state: the Olympic Peninsula, a virgin enormity of forests and mountains that wasn't fully mapped until last century.

With a couple of hundred miles under your wheels, you will have grasped why licence plates hail Washington as the Evergreen State. After *Twilight*-heavy Forks, and an optional side trip to the Hoh Rainforest's Hall of Mosses – where every bough is eerily draped in cobwebby beards of hanging vegetation – Highway 101 swings southwest and soon hits the super-sized coastal scenery that will grace it for the bulk of its progress: a thousand-mile parade of lighthouse-topped bluffs and surf-sculpted sea stacks.

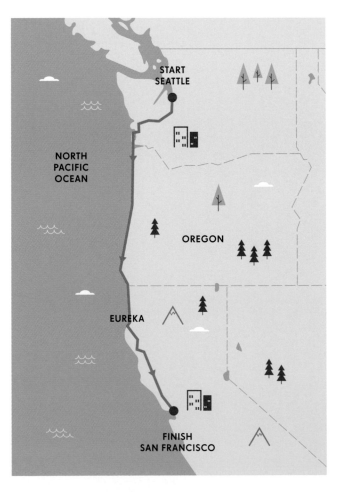

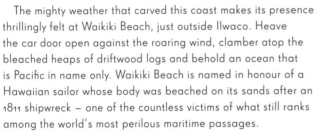

The mighty weather that carved this coast makes its presence thrillingly felt at Waikiki Beach, just outside Ilwaco. Heave the car door open against the roaring wind, clamber atop the bleached heaps of driftwood logs and behold an ocean that is Pacific in name only. Waikiki Beach is named in honour of a Hawaiian sailor whose body was beached on its sands after an 1811 shipwreck – one of the countless victims of what still ranks among the world's most perilous maritime passages.

Drive onwards into Oregon and the road is no longer yours alone, with RVs and long-distance cyclists joining the shiny lumber trucks whose payload leaves the roadside lined with drifts of red bark. Fish-canning ports give way to beach resorts, and the wildlife becomes ever-less retiring. A lively pod of grey whales may snort puffs of water into the clearing sky, and down in the surf below a viewpoint car park, some plump, sleek sea lions bark and loll recklessly in a spume-churned cove. Their well-fed presence pays tribute to a fecund ocean. Fish and chips is a regional institution, with even high-end salmon and halibut given the low-brow treatment.

Perched on a grassy headland and wedged between two magnificent state parks, Port Orford is a small working fishing port and the most westerly town in the lower 48 states. Boasting an artistic community, the ageless main street is home to glass-blowers and art galleries, and there's a restaurant where braised kale and butter lettuce have elbowed the coast's normally ubiquitous chowder clean off the menu.

> *"The 101 comes into its own as it approaches California – majestically engineered, a sinuous two-lane backdrop casually thrown along the jagged coast"*

The miles come easy now, and the 101 comes into its own as it approaches California – broad, smooth and majestically engineered, a sinuous two-lane blacktop almost casually thrown along the jagged, rearing coast. Under a big blue sky, the open road has never seemed so open – until it's quite abruptly closed, hemmed in by colossal ochre trunks.

This is the Redwood empire, the Prairie Creek Redwoods State Park, which was established in 1923 when the first stirrings of environmental panic kicked in. Fewer than five per cent of old-growth redwoods survived the logging onslaught, most of them felled in the age before chainsaws, when cutting one down might take a team of loggers a month.

The world's tallest tree – a 379-footer – and the oldest redwood, pre-dating the Roman Empire by half a millennium, both stand in this forest, their locations kept secret for their own good. There is no such thing as a small old-growth redwood, of course, and strolling among them feels like a tour of some overbearing art installation. A sepulchral quiet reigns. Most of the animal life is way up in the distant canopy. At ground

level, nothing survives without the redwoods' blessing: the odd spindly hemlock clinging gratefully to one for support, sword ferns suckling on the mulch of a fallen 'nest log' that will take several centuries to rot away.

The road flails about like a dying snake as it heads southwest back to the sea, twisting up through a farewell army of redwoods and the tourist trappings of a less-enlightened age: drive-through trees, chainsaw-carved representations of Big Foot and $5 take-away redwood seedlings.

Then the trees part and a very different California emerges, one that is drier, browner and balder, where the thin coastal vegetation is decorated with garish tufts of pampas grass. Seaside settlements soon begin to multiply, their names a reminder that this was Spanish-Mexican territory until the middle of the 19th century. Named by early Hispanic navigators, the small town of Mendocino became one of California's first outposts. One of the state's oldest churches is here, looking down a handsome main street that actually recalls New England, complete with grand wooden houses and fancy old water towers.

A couple of hours south, the traffic builds and quickens; the 101 morphs from homely travelling companion to faceless freeway. The Golden Gate Bridge makes a grand finale to an epic drive, the giant leap for mankind that ushered in America's automobile age. And perhaps, after 1000 glorious miles, it's time for another local brew, or two. **TM**

THE TWILIGHT ZONE

Until 2005, the town of Forks was little more than a speck on the Washington state map – then along came Stephenie Meyer's *Twilight* saga and suddenly several thousand pilgrims were pitching up here every year. From a festival timed around *Twilight* character Bella's birthday to *Twilight* tours, themed accommodation and the local pizza parlour's Love at First Bite menu, Forks draws *Twilight* fans like, well... like vampires to blood.

From left: the 101 rounds Oregon's Cape Sebastian; surfers and wildlife abound on route; the beach at Mendicino; the iconic Golden Gate signals journey's end. Previous page: dwarfed by giant redwoods on the Pacific Coast Hwy

DIRECTIONS

Start // Seattle
End // San Francisco
Distance // 1050 miles (1690km)
Getting there // Seattle and San Francisco are well served by domestic and international flights.
When to drive // Winter can be dreary, but may appeal to storm watchers; grey whales migrate north from March to June or south from November to February. July to September is dry and sunny, but be prepared for a busier drive.
Where to stay // Wildspring Guest Habitat (www.wildspring.com) in Port Orford for wooded serenity.
Where to eat // Bowpicker (www.bowpicker.com), a trawler-turned-chippie serves fish and chips at its battered best.
Hot tip // For a neon-and-jukebox roadhouse experience, stop by San Fran's It's Tops (www.itstopscoffeeshop.com).

*Opposite: better suited to city
streets than any road trip, a three-
wheeler parked up in Sicily*

MORE LIKE THIS
CLOSE TO THE SHORE

MODERN ART MEANDER, FRANCE

There's a particular kind of magic that
happens when you connect with a work
of art in the place it was created, and
Provence is where many 20th-century artists
found their greatest source of inspiration.
Cross this photogenic, good-time region
and discover its vivid, creative history along
the route, not only in the region's stellar
art museums, but also the bays, beaches,
fields, hilltop eyries, bars and bustling
boulevards where the modern masters
lived, worked and partied. Bathed in the
south of France's glorious ever-inspirational
light, and taking in some stretches of
gorgeous coast road, appreciate what
stimulated Cocteau in Menton, Chagall
and Matisse in Nice, Picasso in Antibes,
Cezanne in Aix-en-Provence and Van Gogh
in Arles. Permanent galleries and museums
dedicated to these artists, and many more
besides, are found in the fine towns and
cities lining this beautiful drive.
Start // Menton
End // St-Rémy de Provence
Distance // 211 miles (340km)

OKANAGAN VALLEY TOUR, CANADA

Filling up on sun-ripened fruit at roadside
stalls has long been a highlight of
travelling through the Okanagan in BC
on a hot summer day. Since the 1980s,
the region has widened its embrace of
the culinary world by striping its hillsides
with grapes. More than 100 vineyards
take advantage of the Okanagan's cool
winters and long summers. Icewine, made
from grapes frozen on the vine, is a unique
take-home tipple. And when you're done
soaking up the wine, you can soak up the
scenery at the countless beaches along
the way. This leisurely taste-tripping trawl
keeps you always within easy distance of
Okanagan Lake, heading out north on
Highway 97 from Mission Hill, crossing the
lake over the William R Bennett Bridge and
then turning south along Lakeshore Road
via a slight detour to Okanagan Lavender
Farm. End your tour by treating your driver
to something they can sample at Carmelis
Goat Cheese Artisan.
Start // Mission Hill
End // Carmelis
Distance // 22 miles (35km)

WONDERS OF ANCIENT SICILY

A Mediterranean crossroads for 25
centuries, Sicily is heir to an unparalleled
cultural legacy, from the temples of Magna
Graecia to Norman churches made
kaleidoscopic by Byzantine and Arab
craftsmen. This trip takes you from exotic,
palm-fanned Palermo to the baroque
splendours of Syracuse, once the largest
city in the ancient world, and lava-black
Catania. On the way, you'll also experience
Sicily's startlingly diverse landscape,
including bucolic farmland, smouldering
volcanoes and long stretches of aquamarine
coastline. Fifty miles (80km) along the
A29 from your start at Palermo, Segesta's
huge Greek temple is a magical site, while
further around the winding, undulating coast
road you'll arrive at the ruins of ancient
Akagras at Agrigento. Awaiting you at the
conclusion of this panoramic trip is the
perfect horseshoe-shaped Greek theatre
at Taormina, suspended between sea and
sky, with glorious views to brooding Mt Etna
through the broken columns.
Start // Palermo
End // Taormina
Distance // 368 miles (592km)

HAVANA TO VIÑALES

Cruise west from Havana in a classic car to discover the tobacco plantations and incredible limestone landscape of Cuba's Valle de Viñales.

The Malecon comes alive at sunset. This broad ribbon of cement curves around Havana's waterfront, and as the sun wanes, the sky turns pink and the road is washed in coppery gold light. Orderly rows of fishermen perch on the sea wall, chatting as they cast their lines and hoping for a haul of bonito tuna or red snapper. Locals sit in pairs, laughing and occasionally canoodling, while the sea breeze brings with it the sound of a three-piece jazz ensemble that's just started up along the way.

This stretch is considered the classic drive of Havana, tracing over four miles (7km) along the coast from the colonial centre of the Old Town to the business district of Vedado via a stately line-up of weather-faded houses from the 19th century and brutish Russian-style architecture.

It's here that the city meets the surging ocean. When a strong cold front hits this coast as it often does, waves hurl themselves against the sea wall and over, spraying dozens of feet in the air and flooding the road, but today the sea is calm and mild, lapping innocently at the dark rocks of the shore.

Unlike most great drives, where the highlight of the journey is glorious scenery passing by the windows, the best sights on the Malecon are on the road itself. Vintage 1950s American cars of all colours and kinds parade along its length. One second there is a dreamy round-nosed Buick in duck-egg blue; the next, a Chevrolet Bel Air convertible in brilliant red with silver fins followed by a royal purple Cadillac. They are so numerous and so perfect-looking, it could be a city-wide classic car rally.

The truth is, these vintage cars are not always a dream to drive. As I make my way along the waterfront behind the wheel of a 1955 Chevy – royal red and gold in colour – the gears show flashes of temperament, sticking and occasionally slipping, and the steering has so much give, each turn of the wheel is little more than a gentle suggestion. But there is an indefinable joy in driving one of these vehicles, and it's not just the warm, fusty smell that evokes the old girl's decades on the road or her soft leather bench-seats, so broad and comfortable it's like driving a sofa.

I make my way down the Malecon and turn onto the cobbled streets of Habana Vieja, Havana's Old Town. Left to crumble after the 1959 revolution, Havana is a time capsule, its formerly grand buildings broken and pocked with neglect. The Old Town dates back to the 16th century, and retains vestiges of its former

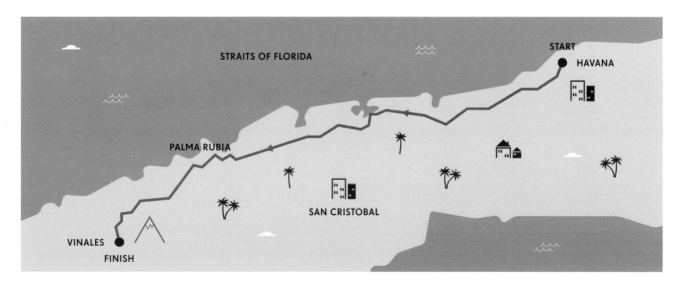

glory. Grand, palm-filled squares are surrounded by streets with imposing churches, houses painted in cheery pastel colours, and tiny kiosks selling freshly butchered meat or piles of fruits warmed by the sun.

Overhead, neighbours call to one another as they hang out washing in colourful strings from balconies; others gather on doorsteps to shoot the breeze, as often as not with fat Cuban cigars dangling from their fingers.

I wind my way through the Old Town, carefully avoiding street-sellers with their handcarts filled with peanuts or flowers or bread, and I tap my fingers on the wheel in time with the bursts of salsa music that float in through the windows.

From here, I head west into Havana's quieter, more residential suburbs, with wider streets and pretty, detached 1930s houses, and out onto the open road. My destination is Viñales, Cuba's agricultural heartland, around 110 miles (180km) from the city.

Havana disappears from the rear-vision mirror and the roadside spaces grow greener and more open until the landscape is filled to the horizon with broad fields and groves of waving palm trees. As the scenery changes, so do the cars. In Havana, many of the vehicles are beautifully maintained – often convertibles, they're buffed, perfected and primed to ferry visitors around the Old Town's sun-dappled streets. Out here on the highway are Cuba's real vintage cars – many of them old bangers, put to work transporting families or hauling trailers stacked with goods.

At the turnoff for Viñales, the road changes abruptly from smooth tarmac to coarse packed dirt, with corrugations and basin-sized potholes that make for a lurching, thumping drive. Out the window, pretty farm houses begin to dot the landscape, many with troupes of scratching, curious hens guarding front gardens.

The principal means of transport changes, too. In amongst the mix of old cars, juddering bicycles and carts filled with fresh local tomatoes and aubergines, are horses. Some have single riders on their backs; others are hauling goods on wooden carts that could have been in use a century ago, and *guarijos* (local farmers) all around sport wide-brimmed ponderosa cowboy hats woven from dried palm leaves.

Viñales is in the Pinar del Rio region, the western centre of Cuban agriculture, where much of the country's best fresh produce is grown in the fertile soil. By the roadside, coffee plantations and fields of yuccas and sweet potatoes give way to rows of young green tobacco plants, whose leaves will soon be dried and expertly rolled into the world's best cigars.

I pull up on the roadside at a viewpoint overlooking the Valle de Viñales. An expanse of red soil and waving crops stretches ahead, bordered with palms and backed by a rugged shelf of green-fringed limestone. In the middle distance, a farmer drives his ox through a field, turning over clumps of iron-rich clay, in a scene that's three hours' drive and a hundred years away from the modern bustle of Havana. **CL**

CAYO LEVISA

This Cuban key is a 35-minute journey by boat from Palma Rubia. It's a worthwhile trip: sugar-white sand and sapphire waters earmark Cayo Levisa as Pinar del Río's best beach. American writer Ernest Hemingway first 'discovered' the area in the early 1940s. These days Levisa attracts up to 100 visitors daily. You won't feel like an errant Robinson Crusoe here, you should find time (and space) for plenty of rest and relaxation.

Clockwise from left: in-car decoration; roadside companions; the limestone cliffs of the Valle de Viñales overlook tobacco plantations. Previous pages: driving Havana's Malecon and a central street scene

DIRECTIONS

Start // Havana
End // Viñales
Distance // 112 miles (180km)
Getting there // Havana receives direct international flights from Europe, Canada, Latin America and, at the time of writing, from several US cities, including Miami.
Car rental // Hiring a car in Cuba is fraught with pitfalls. There are state-owned rental companies at the airport but cars will need to be booked long in advance: prices are high, maintenance standards low. Seek up-to-date advice from Lonely Planet's Cuba guidebook. It's also possible to hire a private car and driver in Havana.
When to go // Peak times are Christmas, Easter, July and August – when it is also hot. An ideal time is from January to May, when it is warm but less crowded.

*Opposite: vines growing in
La Rioja, Spain*

MORE LIKE THIS
CULTURED CRUISES

CHATEAUX OF THE LOIRE, FRANCE

For centuries, France's great river has
been the backdrop for royal intrigue and
extravagant architecture. From warring
medieval counts to the kings and queens
of France, countless powerful figures
have left their mark on the Loire Valley.
Following a route roughly northeast from
Chinon to Chambord will take in nine of
the Loire's most iconic chateaux, running
the gamut from austere medieval fortresses
to ostentatious royal palaces at Langeais,
Villandry, Blois and Cheverny, as well
as the romantic, moat-ringed Azay-le-
Rideau – one of France's absolute gems
– the supremely graceful Chateau de
Chenonceau, the fortified 15th-century
Chateau Royal d'Amboise and the
over-the-top splendour of Chateau de
Chambord at your journey's end. Midway-
through, a circuitous detour on the A85
and D493 will take you off the beaten track
to four less-visited chateaux.
Start // Chinon
End // Chambord
Distance // 140 miles (225km)

LA RIOJA WINE REGION, SPAIN

La Rioja is home to the best wines in Spain
and on this short and sweet road trip along
unhurried back roads you'll enjoy gorgeous
vine-striped countryside and asleep-at-
noon villages of honey-coloured stone.
But the real interest is reserved for food
and drink: cutting-edge museums, bodega
tours and some of the best tapas in
Spain make this drive an essential for any
foodie. La Rioja's low-key capital Logrono
is your start and end point and, happily,
it boasts a monumentally good selection
of tapas bars. On your 100-mile (160km)
circuit away from here are monasteries,
walled towns and wine bodegas aplenty,
but don't miss the fascinating Dinastia
Vivanco viticulture museum at Briones nor
the medieval fortress town of Laguardia
with its surrounding bodegas and wine
shops. And you can't miss Frank Gehry's
characteristically flamboyant Hotel
Marqués de Riscal in the village of Elciego.
Start // Logrono
End // Logrono
Distance // 97 miles (140km)

ROMAN PROVENCE, FRANCE

Provence was where Rome first truly flexed
its imperial muscles. On this drive, follow
Roman roads, cross Roman bridges and
grab a seat in the stalls at Roman theatres
and arenas. Thrillingly, you'll discover that
most of Provence's Roman ruins aren't
ruins at all. Many are exceptionally well
preserved, and some are also evocatively
integrated into the modern cities. Sites at
Nîmes, Arles, Glanum, Vaison-La-Romaine
and Orange, with its massive 103m-wide,
37m-high stage wall at the Théatre Antique,
are must-sees, while the three-tiered
aqueduct of the Pont du Gard is a marvel of
1st-century engineering. You could choose
to enjoy your first glimpse of it from the river
by paddling 5 miles (8km) downstream
from Collias, 2½ (4km) west of the D981.
But even if you just stick to the road, when
you've got Provence's knockout landscape –
rocky gorges, honey-stone villages, vineyard-
lined valleys – as a backdrop to your drive,
history never looked so good.
Start // Nîmes
End // Vaison-la-Romaine
Distance // 127 miles (205km)

ON THE TRAIL OF
THE LONESOME PINE

The 574-mile route through the Blue Ridge Mountains is one of America's legendary road trips – every autumn it's the scene for a drama of change and renewal.

he two roads that run down the spine of the southern Appalachians, Skyline Drive and the Blue Ridge Parkway, were built specifically for sightseers and tourists. They are winding, sedate – the speed limit never exceeds 45mph (72km/h) – and closed to commercial vehicles. There isn't a 'Gas Food Lodging' sign anywhere in sight, nor a gleam of neon. To find fast food and even gas, you have to leave the route briefly and venture into the back roads of Virginia and North Carolina. Getting your kicks is a possibility, getting lost in the sticks is a virtual certainty.

But the rewards for forgoing roads with higher speeds and corporate amenities are immense. This is a route filled with tales of moonshine, disappearing customs, and the Appalachians' own take on jazz: old-time music and bluegrass.

It's getting close to Halloween when I join the northern end of Skyline Drive after a leisurely breakfast in the town of Front Royal. I feel like the slow speed of the roads is the whole point. There's

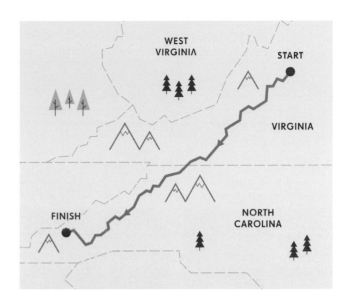

no-one behind me beeping or impatient to overtake. The route winds through mountain scenery with views that stretch for miles to distant vanishing points; the colours span a vast range: from the cheese-on-toast yellow of the tulip poplar to the vibrant red of sourwoods and maples.

Skyline Drive is the shorter of the two roads, sitting at their combined northern end. At 105 miles (169km) long, it can be covered easily in a day, though, at the higher elevations, the weather can be very fickle. Towards mid-afternoon, somewhere around milepost 78, mist swirls over the road and as I slow the car, a strange form appears on the tarmac directly ahead of me. It's a large black bear, galumphing into the trees on the other side. It's only visible for a few seconds, but the whole atmosphere of the mountain seems suddenly different: wilder and more threatening.

At milepost 105, skyline drive comes to an end; from here the route continues on the longer Blue Ridge Parkway.

Half a day's drive along the parkway, close to milepost 213, sits the storied Blue Ridge Music Center. Overnight, high winds have felled a tree and taken down the power lines. Starved of electricity, the videos and recordings in the centre don't work and, suddenly, we're a bit closer to the music's roots: two men in a shady corner, playing unamplified instruments, singing about the dark and the light of life in the mountains.

Every afternoon during the months that the centre is open, local musicians play here for free. Today, 72-year-old Bobby Patterson is plucking a resonator banjo, accompanied by Willard Gayheart,

"The slow speed of the roads is the whole point. The route winds through mountain scenery with views that stretch for miles"

82. The music – gospel and secular – is still a vital part of life in the region. Willard explains that, barely a generation ago, farmers hosted parties as a way of repaying neighbours for their help in bringing in a harvest. Hired musicians and tubs of moonshine would be the reward for a day of collective effort.

The ranger at the Blue Ridge Music Center rolls her eyes when I show her where I'm headed on the map. There's a weather warning: more heavy rain and high winds are expected towards evening. To stay off the top of the parkway, I leave the route and take the state roads, crossing the border from Virginia into North Carolina and passing small towns, Baptist churches, commercial Christmas tree plantations, and huge patches of pumpkins, grown for Halloween.

But there's no avoiding the Blue Ridge Parkway. I'm booked to stay in a cabin close to milepost 256, so in the late afternoon, I bid small-town America farewell and head off back up the mountain. The weather is worsening and the road has become astonishingly eerie: a riot of windblown leaves, heaving branches and fog gathering in the dips. By some miracle, I find the lodge just as night is falling. My cabin, overhung with waving branches and

MEN AT WORK

The construction of Skyline Drive and the Blue Ridge Parkway began after the Great Depression in the 1930s, partly under Roosevelt's New Deal. Young, unskilled, unmarried men were enrolled in the Civilian Conservation Corps (CCC) and put to work on projects to protect the country's natural resources. The construction of the roads created jobs in the region, but also displaced residents along their lengths – some voluntarily, others forcibly.

From left: scenic stops, local traffic and many bends make this a leisurely trip; the leaves and trees of Virginia ensure a vivid autumn drive. Previous page: splendid forest surrounds the Linn Core viaduct

sitting in a hollow, clearly resembles the set of a horror film, but tucked up safely in bed, I hear no bears, or serial killers, just the death throes of the storm.

By morning, the bad weather has finally passed. The rain and wind have denuded many trees, but the sun blazes through the ones that are left. At Linn Cove Viaduct I drive through some of the most uplifting scenery of the whole route. The viaduct itself is an architectural marvel. The last section of the route to be constructed, it was designed to have minimal impact on its surroundings. It seems to float above the slopes of Grandfather Mountain. From it, I look down on the huge belt of uplands that spread along the eastern seaboard of the United States all the way from New Jersey to Alabama.

I turn-off at milepost 385 to the town of Asheville, with barely half a day's drive to go until the southern end of the parkway. It's a good place to stop and celebrate the journey's conclusion – a lively, affluent place with a dynamic music and arts scene.

At the recommendation of two local musicians, I head to bluegrass night in Jack of the Wood, one of Asheville's live-music venues. The audience includes young hipsters who look like they've just finished a hard day logging or gathering ginseng. Flannel shirts, work boots, baseball caps and facial hair are the order of the day. The evening is a celebration of what's local, renewable, homemade. It seems that just as Appalachia's last mountain people are relinquishing their old ways, a new generation is looking to them for inspiration. **MT**

DIRECTIONS

Start // Skyline Drive's northern terminus lies at an intersection with US Route 340 near the town of Front Royal.
End // The Blue Ridge Parkway's southern end lies at the junction with US Route 441 on the boundary between the Great Smoky Mountains National Park and the Cherokee Indian Reservation in North Carolina.
Distance // 574 miles (924km)
Getting there // Front Royal is about 1½ hours' drive west of Washington, DC.
Further away // From the end of the drive, head to Asheville, NC – a drive of a little over an hour.
When to drive // Autumn. The broadleaved trees start their slow-motion firework display towards the end of September.
More info // www.visitskylinedrive.org; www.blueridgeparkway.org

Opposite from top: Quedlinburg in Saxony-Anhalt, Germany, is a Unesco-listed town; the sun sets on the Nashville stretch of the Natchez Trace Parkway

MORE LIKE THIS
COUNTRYSIDE CRUISING

CAVES ROAD, WESTERN AUSTRALIA

After driving a few miles of excellent surface through grazing country along Cape Naturaliste Road, turn right into Caves Road, which suffers from use by heavy trucks, so be careful. Caves Road runs inland from the rugged limestone coast but there are plenty of side roads that run down to spacious beaches and quiet campsites. Spectacular Mammoth and Lake are among the caves that gave the road its name, many of them easily accessible. Much of the road runs through Karri and Marri forests, which give the impression of being old growth. In fact, this area was clear-felled and the trees are regrowth. From the Cape Leeuwin Lighthouse you can see where the Indian and Southern oceans meet.
Start // Cape Naturaliste Lighthouse
End // Cape Leeuwin Lighthouse
Distance // 69 miles (111km)

NATCHEZ TRACE PARKWAY, USA

It began as a trail for bison and giant sloth, and still has a low speed limit at 50mph. The Parkway is exactly what its name suggests – a long, narrow park. Like most parks it has restrictions, regulating food, fuel, lodgings, advertising and even trucks. A beautifully surfaced road stretching from the banks of the Mississippi to the home of Country Music USA, the winding parkway runs through forest that changes colour with the seasons, while roadside information tablets track its history. There are services at regular intervals, as well as historic monuments, such as the eerie ruins of the antebellum Windsor mansions near Port Gibson.
Start // Natchez, Mississippi
End // Nashville, Tennessee
Distance // 444 miles (715km)

GERMAN AVENUES ROUTE

This trip is a magic anti-clockwise loop through the diverse natural beauty of the ancient German states of Saxony-Anhalt, Lower Saxony, Thuringia and Saxony. On route there are the eye-catching villages of Quedlinburg (a Unesco World Heritage town) and medieval Goslar, a steam train along the Harz Mountain Railways and a memorial to Nazi atrocities at Mittelbau Dora near Mühlhausen. The southern stretch of the circuit takes in the culture- and history-laden cities of Erfurt, Weimar (where both Goethe and Nietzsche spent their final years), Leipzig and Dresden, beautifully rebuilt after being all but wiped off the map by Allied bombing in 1945.
Start // Dessau-Rosslau
End // Dessau-Rosslau
Distance // 541 miles (868km)

ON CAPE BRETON'S CABOT TRAIL

Encounter Nova Scotia's windblown coastline, a rich blend of Gaelic, Acadian and Mi'kmaq cultures, vibrant autumnal foliage and a stunning national park on Canada's Cabot Trail.

Life on the island of Cape Breton, in the far eastern corner of Canada, goes with the flow. Lobster boats chug into the horizon; whales rise and fall beyond the shore; bears lumber through the island's boreal forests; the Atlantic wind carries the rhythmical notes of Gaelic fiddles.

Surrounded by the Gulf of St Lawrence on one side, and the Atlantic Ocean on the other, Cape Breton's northern half is home to the Cabot Trail, a beautiful 185-mile (297km) road that hugs cliffs, then winds and climbs over the Cape Breton highlands before dropping down to grass-covered sand dunes and tranquil hamlets.

Alexander Graham Bell, he of telephone-invention fame and a regular visitor to the island, declared that of all the natural places he'd seen around the world, 'Cape Breton out-rivals them all.'

But the Cabot Trail is more than a drive with stunning geography, ocean vistas, wilderness and wildlife. It's also a cultural circuit enriched by colourful inhabitants and centuries-old traditions. The Mi'kmaq people inhabited the island when the first Europeans, led by explorer John Cabot, arrived in 1497. In later centuries, many Scottish, Irish and English settled. So did Acadians, descendants of the French, all contributing to a colourful Gaelic melange.

Many fishing villages were not accessible by land until as late as the 1930s, when car travel over the Cape Breton highlands became possible. In 1936, the Cape Breton Highlands National Park was created in the northern section of the island, preserving 366 sq miles (949 sq km) of coastal wilderness, forests and mountains. The road – which encompasses much of the park – was gradually paved in sections between 1940 and 1961.

The route itself is circular so I can head in either direction (though the cliff-clinging, anti-clockwise trip offers the best views). Driving

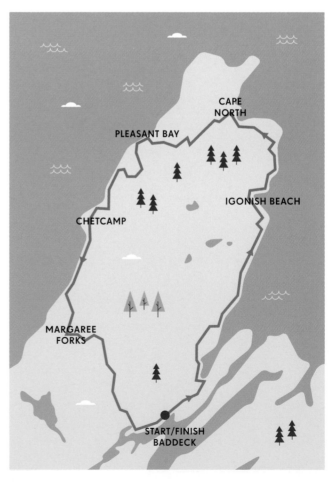

"The road winds through corridors of pine and spruce, before I emerge at a cliff edge and a view of the icy ocean"

here is a pleasant, leisurely experience. While the maximum speed on the trail is between 60km/h and 80km/h (35mph-50mph), the trail has a pace of its own; locals regularly stop their vehicles in the middle of the highway – for a pedestrian, a moose or simply a friendly chat with a neighbour heading in the oncoming direction.

Officially, the Cabot Trail starts and ends in Baddeck, a pretty harbour town on Bras d'Or Lake. I take a quick pre-drive look in the Alexander Graham Bell National Historic Site, a museum that displays Bell's fascinating inventions, including his hydrofoil.

From Baddeck, I head north to St Anns, home of the Colaisde na Gàidhlig, the only Gaelic college in North America, where you can learn to speak the language, step-dance or play the bagpipes. The road then winds through corridors of pine and spruce, before I emerge at a cliff edge and a view of the icy ocean. In its northern section the road heads around the national park, whose hiking trails and campgrounds make it the perfect stop for adventurers.

You should get used to stopping. At North River, you can jump in a kayak and paddle up an inlet while keeping an eye out for whales and otters. At Ingonish Beach, enjoy a round of golf at Highlands Links, a stunning course designed by Stanley Thompson in 1939.

I have my sights set further north. Back on the trail, at Cape North on the northernmost tip, a detour takes me to the tiny fishing port of Bay St Lawrence. Here I jump aboard a whale-watching boat and cruise alongside the bay's rugged coastline, whose numerous waterfalls and sea caves are just as beautiful as the pilot whales and dolphins that swim around the boat.

Back on land and feeling peckish, I head from Cape North to the remote settlement of Meat Cove, so named because in the 1700s, European settlers slaughtered moose, deer and bear there (for antlers and hides). It's a must-visit for the cove's only chowder hut that whips up seafood chowder, lobster rolls and crab sandwiches.

The northwestern shore of Cape Breton – between Cape North and Pleasant Bay – has magnificent 'look-offs', viewing points that frequently dot the route. These showcase the island's deciduous trees – birch and maple – that transform into an explosion of autumn colours. Bald eagles frequently soar overhead.

Heading south at Pleasant Bay, steep cliffs morph into lowlands comprising grass-covered dunes and sandy beaches. A shock of striped red, white and blue flags (and even buildings) signifies my arrival into Chéticamp, a village that proudly proclaims its French Acadian roots. A sign also states cheekily that the locals are 'Proud to be Hookers', a nod to Chéticamp's expert hooked-rug makers. The best examples of their work are exhibited in the hooked-rug museum, Les Trois Pignons (www.lestroispignons.com).

Another cultural event is the annual Celtic Colours International Festival in October, when local and international artists fiddle, pipe and dance in churches and school halls.

But whatever the time of year, it's worth the drive just to kick up your heels at a *ceilidh* (pronounced cay-lee), a Gaelic gathering where all are welcome to eat, drink and be merry to a backdrop of local folk music, and Cape Breton's exceptional hospitality. **KA**

PARKLIFE

In summer, Parks Canada (www.pc.gc.ca) offers a range of fabulous activities in the Cape Breton Highlands National Park. You can hike at sunset along the scenic Skyline Trail with a park interpreter, enjoy the gourmet contents of a Parks Canada picnic basket, or learn to cook, crack and feast on a lobster. At night, rub shoulders with the region's ghosts on a lantern walk or wander through the park with a guide to view the star-filled sky.

Clockwise from left: moose are a common sight on Cape Breton; an Acadian lighthouse in Chéticamp town; the road winds through Cape Breton. Previous page: the Cabot Trail Hwy undulates around the cliffside

DIRECTIONS

Start/End // Baddeck
Distance // 185 miles (297km)
Getting there // Sydney, the capital of Cape Breton, is a one-hour flight from Halifax Stanfield International Airport on the Nova Scotia peninsula. By car, it's a 4½-hour drive from Halifax to Sydney via the Canso Causeway.
When to drive // June to the end of October is the prime season. During autumn the deciduous trees show their true colours and hundreds of performers kick up a musical Gaelic storm at the Celtic Colours International Festival.
Where to stay // Keltic Lodge (kelticlodge.ca) is a stunning lodge above the Highlands Links Golf Course, perched on a cliff overlooking the Ingonish Beach.
Where to eat // Don't miss the fishcakes at the Rusty Anchor Restaurant (therustyanchorrestaurant.com).

*Opposite from top: Long Point Light
at the start of the Pilgrim Trail,
Provincetown, Massachusetts; the
famous ruins of Pompeii*

MORE LIKE THIS
WHERE TIME STANDS STILL

PILGRIM TRAIL, MASSACHUSETTS, USA

Your car is a time machine, transporting
you back 400 years. This region's living
museums allow you to experience what life
was like for the colonists as they settled in
the New World. Explore the churches and
trading posts, homesteads and grist mills
that are still standing from those nascent
days of the United States. Begin where
it is likely that the Pilgrims first did, even
before they landed on Plymouth Rock,
at Provincetown at the tip of Cape Cod,
before following the scenic roads around
Massachusetts Bay. As you do so, stop off
to view the restored 1640 salt box home at
Sandwich; a replica of both the Mayflower
and the settlers' village at Plymouth; the
bright lights of Boston, actually founded
by Puritans who arrived a decade after the
Pilgrims; and the interactive museum at
Salem, also the infamous location of the
1692 Witch Trials, a travesty explained here
at the town's Witch House.

Start // Provincetown
End // Salem
Distance // 136 miles (2178km)

SHADOW OF VESUVIUS, ITALY

This trip begins in Italy's most
misunderstood city, Naples, an exhilarating
mess of bombastic baroque churches,
bellowing baristas and thrilling street life.
From the labyrinthine Unesco-listed centre
packed with old churches, head up to the
Museo Archeologico Nazionale to mug up
on Pompeii and Heruclaneum. The latter
is a short journey round the bay of Naples
on the SS18 and, having been drowned in
a sea of mud in the AD 79 eruption of Mt
Vesuvius, is a remarkable fossilised relic of
a Roman town and its inhabitants. Head
inland to the summit of the great volcano
itself before resuming your coastal drive
and taking in lesser-known jewels including
ancient villas and Portici's royal getaway,
as well as the famous ruins of Pompeii,
another great city frozen in time. The final
stage of the drive towards Sorrento affords
beautiful views of the Bay of Naples and
the mountains of the Amalfi Coast.

Start // Naples
End // Sorrento
Distance // 56 miles (90km)

GERMAN CASTLE ROAD

This romantic trip will take you castle-
hopping across 370 miles (600km) of
southern Germany and through a thousand
years of the country's history. Kicking off
at Germany's biggest baroque pile in
Mannheim and finishing at Bayreuth's
Altes Schloss, it's castle-a-day time on
this route, and when palace fatigue
sets in, there's nothing easier than
escaping to a fascinating museum, or
a traditional tavern to sample the local
sausages (those at Coburg are special)
and unsurpassed beer. Particularly eye-
popping citadels and settlements include
the ruins of the Renaissance Schloss
Heidelberg towering over the old town, the
medieval walls surrounding the historical
core of Rothenburg ob der Tauber, and
Nuremberg's Kaiserburg, a huge castle
complex that poignantly reflects the city's
medieval might. And that's not forgetting
the dramatic Burg Guttenberg above the
Neckar Valley or the Unesco World Heritage
site that is Bamberg's Altstadt.

Start // Mannheim
End // Bayreuth
Distance // 316 miles (507km)

GOING TO THE SUN IN GLACIER NATIONAL PARK

Don't be surprised if you find yourself holding your breath as you ascend this thin ribbon of road at the edge of a vast glacial valley in Montana.

There are only a few locations on Earth I've been that really must be seen to be believed, and Glacier National Park, Montana, is one of them. Photographs may hint at its glory, but even the very best shots are unable to capture the sheer scale of the place, the jagged grey peaks and the steep angle of the valley walls.

In a site like this, I can almost feel the earth move – it's easy to imagine a time when ancient masses of ice carved out a path, leaving behind an utterly changed landscape. And if that's not enough, two words: grizzly bears.

Among the best ways to see and appreciate the park is by driving the aptly named Going-to-the-Sun Road. It's a high, narrow, edge-clinging ribbon of pavement, the kind of road that makes me feel as if I'm in an IMAX cinema, getting a vivid, wide-screen view of the world. It also makes me feel very small and, occasionally, a little nervous. Limited access heightens the road's appeal: it's covered in snow most of the year, and is only open end-to-end from late June or early July to mid-October, after maintenance crews have cleared the snow away and repaired any seasonal damage. Completed in 1933, Going-to-the-Sun is the only paved road that crosses the park. That means traffic is heavy, and maintenance work is more or less constant, so plan on taking it slow.

You can drive the road in either direction, or both, of course, but the scenery has the biggest impact if you go from west to east. I duly made my start in West Glacier, a small community built around the various ways of exploring the park; if you're up for more adventure, this is a good place to ask about guides, hiking trails, snowshoeing tours, river rafting, fly-fishing or whatever else you're into. I made sure I fuelled up – there are no petrol stations along the Going-to-the-Sun Road.

For many people, a brilliant drive along a beautiful route

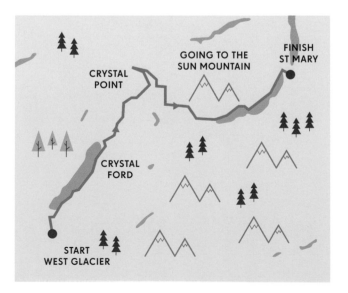

creates a certain momentum that can be difficult to resist. Swept up in the rhythm of the drive, you may find that you are reluctant to stop. But trust me: on this particular road, the stops are half the fun. Fortunately, there are numerous pullouts along the road, and I made full use of them, pausing for a photo or just to drink in the awesome views.

Heading east, I felt like I had only just got started when I was compelled to pull over. I was in tiny Apgar, a village at the edge of gorgeous Lake McDonald, the largest lake in the park. The view is sublime – a glass-like lake swept before me to the white-capped mountain peaks that clustered together at the opposite end of the lake. (For most of the winter, this is as far along the road as cars can go.) Also in the village are a permit office and visitors' centre, campgrounds, a motel, gift shop and cafe.

Back on the road, I soon reached the McDonald Creek Overlook, another worthy stop. The creek changes personalities according to the season; in summer, it's gentle and tidily contained between its wide, rocky banks, but in early spring the force of the water is strong enough to make the viewing platform I was standing on tremble.

My next stop was Avalanche Creek and by now I was ready to get out and stretch my legs. Two excellent trails start here: a 1-mile (1.6km), wheelchair-accessible boardwalk loop called the Trail of the Cedars, which takes you through the only grove of cedars in the park, and a longer, 4.2-mile (6.8km) round-trip hike to Avalanche Lake. The lake is a treat to see: a blast of bright turquoise surrounded by steep rocky walls.

AN ENGINEERING MARVEL

Early plans included 15 switchbacks along the road, snaking tightly back and forth up the valley to Logan Pass. But a team of engineers continued to study the area, eventually deciding they could use the current route instead. This meant the road would blend almost seamlessly into its surroundings. If you tire of gazing at the landscape, ponder for a moment the amount of work that went (and still goes) into building a road in a place like this.

Clockwise from above: brown bears make the park their home; humans can do likewise in Lake McDonald Lodge; the rapids at Logan Pass. Previous page: ducking through a mini-tunnel on Going-to-the-Sun

Once back in my car, I found myself on The Loop: a section of the road that's shaped a little like a hairgrip. Drifting along its gentle switchback I could not help but admire the people who dreamed up, planned and constructed this road. A trail here leads to Granite Park Chalet, a superbly situated wooden lodge built by the Great Northern Railway in 1914. It's now a National Historic Landmark.

Just beyond The Loop there's a chance to see two examples of the impressive engineering that made the Going-to-the-Sun Road a reality. First is the Weeping Wall. As a result of the construction process, several rivulets of water now stream down the hillside above the road, sometimes drenching westbound vehicles in a chilly glacial spray. A little further on are the Triple Arches, together they form an elegant solution to the problem of several gaps in the rock base supporting the road.

If every trip has an ultimate destination, for me that destination was Logan Pass. It's the highest point along the route (and a good turning-around point if you're short of time). A number of short hiking trails start from the parking lot, on both sides of the road. Venturing out on one of these will earn you some of the most spectacular views in the park, although even the views from the parking lot are good.

Drivers who continue eastward along the road will find still more hiking trails from Siyeh Bend, as well as even more ominous craggy mountaintops and a distant view of Blackfoot and Jackson Glacier. See these while you can; glaciers throughout the park have been steadily shrinking.

Towards the end of the road I made sure to stop at the St Mary Falls trailhead, a 2.4-mile (4km) round-trip hike that leads to the namesake falls and lake – it's a fitting way to end such a spectacular drive. **BO**

"Rivulets of water stream down the hillside, sometimes drenching westbound vehicles in a chilly glacial spray"

DIRECTIONS

Start // West Glacier, Montana
End // St Mary, Montana
Distance // 50 miles (80.5km). It's two hours driving, but allow twice that for stops and hikes.
Getting there // Glacier Park International Airport has car hire outlets and is located just outside Kalispell, a 30-minute drive from West Glacier.
When to drive // The road is open late June or early July to mid-October, weather permitting. Check ahead (www.nps.gov/glac).
Where to stay // Lake McDonald Lodge (www.glaciernationalparklodges.com/lodging/lake-mcdonald-lodge) is a historic Swiss chalet-style lodge with cabins, on the shore of the park's largest lake.
Park entrance fee // US$30 per car (good for seven days).

Opposite: the sun rises over Toroweap Point, Grand Canyon National Park

MORE LIKE THIS
AMERICAN LANDSCAPES

FOUR CORNERS CRUISE

This road trip is super-sized, covering the grandest views and biggest wows in the Southwest United States – from Vegas to Zion to the Grand Canyon and beyond. The timid should stay at home. Starting in Las Vegas, swing through the Valley of Fire State Park then cruise through Arizona into Utah and Zion National Park, which offers what may be the best day hike in North America, before continuing on Hwy 89 to the clifftop view of the Colorado River at Horseshoe Bend, simultaneously beautiful and terrifying. Further on, the rugged buttes of Monument Valley look, from a distance, like the remains of a prehistoric fortress, red-gold ramparts protecting ancient secrets. But their sun-reflected beauty will lure you in. There are so many stunning sights on the remainder of this loop through five states back to the awesome Red Rock Canyon that it's hard to pick standouts, but a walk along the South Rim Trail will best reveal the Grand Canyon in all its magnificence.

Start // Las Vegas
End // Red Rock Canyon National Conservation Area
Distance // 1852 miles (2980km)

THE HOGBACK, UTAH

The drive south on Route 12 from Torrey starts gently enough before climbing to a 9000ft (2750 metres) pass, frequently covered in snow. Despite that, it is a beautiful drive through the thick pine forests of the Dixie National Forest. But it really gets interesting after Boulder. There was a time when the only road that connected Boulder and Escalante in Utah was a trail called Hell's Backbone. True to its name, it was – and still is, if you care to tackle it – as nasty a piece of track as you'll find in the Old West. Eventually it became obvious that a better road was needed and work began on the stretch that would include The Hogback. A narrow, tarred road that clings precariously to the top of a razorback ridge, filled in occasionally with some soil, the Hogback is balanced between steep spills down to creeks and near-vertical canyons. There are few places to park, but stop when you can: the vistas are wonderful. And talking of wonderful, Escalante's Cowboy Blues restaurant has supreme local trout served on wooden boards.

Start // Torrey
End // Escalante
Distance // 65 miles (112km)

FANTASTIC CANYON VOYAGE, ARIZONA

This scenic route north to the Grand Canyon is a great all-rounder. It's pretty, it's wild and it embraces Arizona's rough and tumble history. Picturesque trails wind past sandstone buttes, ponderosa pines and canyon views. Wild West adventures include horseback rides, saloon crawls and standing atop a 580m mine shaft on a terrifying glass platform at Audrey Headframe Park. But the route's not stuck in the past. A burgeoning wine scene and a new ale trail add 21st-century sparkle. Tackle this drive in spring or autumn by starting in Wickenburg, which looks as you'd imagine it did in the 1890s, then heading on to further centres of the Old West in Prescott and Jerome, a copper-mining town once known as the 'wickedest in the West'. Cottonwood offers more contemporary delights via excellent food and wine, while the remainder of the drive towards the Grand Canyon offers riparian scenery, sandstone monoliths, red cliffs and expansive plateaus.

Start // Wickenburg
End // Grand Canyon Village
Distance // 285 miles (459km)

CHARGING THROUGH NAPA VALLEY

A maiden voyage in an electric vehicle – organised around available charge stations – delivers an all-new approach to Napa Valley, and to road trips in general.

For 10 miles (16km), Dan Brooks was a dot on a map. Now he was the occupant of a house my wife and I were approaching, 24 hours into a strange vacation.

As San Franciscans of the bleary parental variety, we'd been itching to ditch town. But rather than the standard road trip, we got the idea of renting an electric vehicle (EV). Like many, we'd come to occupy a funny spot regarding EVs: we sensed they were on the cusp of ubiquity, but we also had almost no idea how they worked. What's their range? What kind of chargers can you use? Which button do you push?

Operating the car turned out to be the easy part. It was the spirit of the trip that was different. Rather than following your bliss, your bliss reorients to your car's limited range, and the limited supply of charging stations. Before setting out, Amy and I pulled up a map of the country on a website called PlugShare. It was sprayed with dots, each representing available chargers. When we zoomed in, we noticed an impressively heavy concentration in Napa Valley.

Rather than charting a road trip according to spots we wanted to hit, we chose dots that we had enough range to reach – about 80 miles (130km), according to EV-owning friends. That paralysing array of options that confronts a traveller? Gone, replaced with a manageable handful. It was refreshing, frankly. My poet friend Matthew sometimes has his students stir the pot by writing poems without the letter 'e'. This would be our e-less trip: a little harder, considerably more memorable.

Thus, one spring morning, we climbed into a freakishly silent Nissan Leaf and pointed ourselves north. At times during our drive, it felt like we were from the future, darting nimbly among hulking relics of an inefficient past. At other moments, it was more like we came

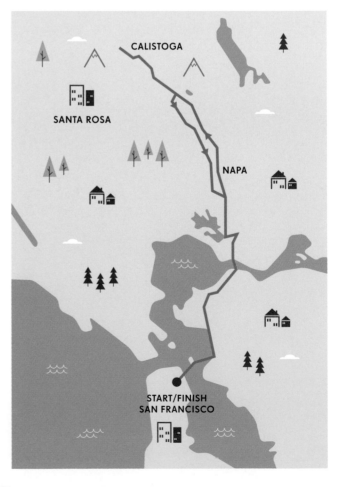

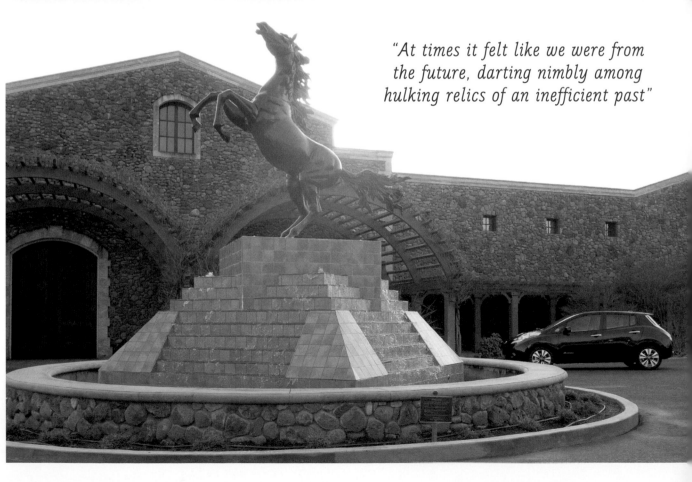

"At times it felt like we were from the future, darting nimbly among hulking relics of an inefficient past"

from the past – a Big Oil-free one. After an hour or so we rolled into Napa. After a dip in the river, we checked into the Napa River Inn, chosen not for the views or sun-dappled balcony of our room, but for the charging station in the car park. As we walked around the city that night, our Leaf quietly readied itself for the next leg.

While the PlugShare map mostly comprises businesses with charging stations (hotels, restaurants and wineries), a handful of dots stand for individuals volunteering their own private chargers. We loved this excuse for meeting a certified local on our trip – in this case, Dan Brooks, a soft-spoken guy in beach hat and sandals who offers up his home charger for e-travellers passing through.

'It's surprisingly fun to plan your trips with an EV,' he told us upon arriving. He described the video game-like thrill of trying to reach a destination on a single charge, and of driving in the most mileage-optimising way. 'Plus, you find yourself in this little community. You meet people at the charging station, or in chat rooms.'

Our community of three shot the breeze a while, and then it was time to press on. After a short drive we were on a red dirt trail on the other side of town, dry grass shushing around us. The Skyline Wilderness Park was the former grounds of a psychiatric hospital, back when this county was known not for wine but for madness. During the Napa State Hospital years, saying you were from Napa would supposedly prompt the retort, 'Who let you out?' In time, the facility took on the more collegiate 'Napa State', and roughly 900 acres of its gorgeous wildlands were declared surplus. We roamed several before pushing north to St Helena.

Raymond Vineyards is both one of Napa's greenest spots and one of its most garish; the solar powered, biodynamic vineyard features scantily clad mannequins and rooms brimming with plush velvet. While the Leaf charged, we roamed and drank and steeled ourselves for drinking again: later we'd charge at a holy site for wine historians, Calistoga's Chateau Montelena Winery. Its famed '73 Chardonnay beat the French in a blind tasting in the Paris Tasting of 1976. We were just happy to get free wattage while admiring an ivy-covered stone chateau dug into a hillside with a shimmering pond.

To point out that Calistoga Ranch has a charging station is like noting that the Taj Mahal has soap in the bathroom. Of course they charge your EV here, and if they didn't, someone on staff would rub sticks together till it was ready to go. Tucked discreetly into the hills and creeksides of an oaky canyon, the 157-acre resort is where you go after winning your third Oscar. Amy swam in the pool, I soaked in an ale bath, and in general we recharged alongside our car.

On our way back to San Francisco, we recalled the ancient and wildly unreliable Ford Falcon I once owned, and how any trip beyond our zip code risked a breakdown. It was annoying – but it also brought a level of deliberateness to our comings and goings. We really had to plan, and that gave things a whiff of adventure. When eventually we bought a dependable grown-up car, we switched to mental cruise control, and the voyage part of the trip slipped away. Now, driving the EV back to San Francisco, it felt nice to have it back, if only for a few more kilowatt-hours. **CC**

ELECTRIC LINGO

MPGE Miles per gallon 'equivalent,' an easier energy metric for our fossil-fueled brains to handle than kilowatt-hours.
Range How many miles you can travel in your EV before its battery runs out.
Range anxiety A condition that besets new EV drivers who haven't figured out how far they can go.
Hypermiling Not exceeding 55mph to 60mph (90km/h to 97km/h) on highways to conserve range, and coasting to regenerate battery power.

Clockwise from left: recharging the batteries; the vineyards of Napa Valley; the LEAF at the Black Stallion winery. Previous page: a vehicle from another era; Napa Valley view at Calistoga Ranch

DIRECTIONS

Start/End // San Francisco
Distance // 156 miles (251km)
Can I pull into any station? // No, stations are either AC Level 2, DC fast-charging, or Tesla proprietary stations. Each has a different-shaped plug. Teslas can use any station.
Do I pay to charge? // Some are free, but more than likely it'll cost around US$4. You'll need a scan card issued from the company that runs the station.
How long does it take to recharge? // About four hours at a Level 2 and 30 minutes at a fast-charging station.
How far can I go? // From Baja California to British Columbia. The West Coast Electric Highway network is installing retail-location DC chargers (and many Level 2s) every 25 to 50 miles along Interstate 5. Tesla has also built an extensive network.

MORE LIKE THIS
ELECTRIC ROADTRIPS

BOSTON TO NEW YORK, USA

California may have the highest density of charging points but if you're the owner of a Tesla you can use a growing network of Superchargers that upload 150 miles of range in 30 minutes. The east coast has enough of these Tesla-only charging points to make a roadtrip from Boston to New York City via Mark Twain's House and Museum in Hartford a worry-free possibility. Take a few days so you can stop at various places of interest along the way, zig-zagging from the classic clapboard mansions of Newport, Rhode Island, to Hartford, Connecticut, home of Samuel Langhorne Clemens, and southward to New York. Check Tesla's online map (www.tesla.com/supercharger) to plot a course between charging stations. And choose your companion wisely: as Twain noted 'I have found out that there ain't no surer way to find out whether you like people or hate them than to travel with them.'

Start // Boston
End // New York
Distance // 215 miles (345km)

WINE AND WHALES ON
AUSTRALIA'S ELECTRIC HIGHWAY

Australia's first electric highway lies along the beautiful coast south of Western Australia's state capital all the way to the southwest tip of Australia at Augusta. It passes through Margaret River, one of the country's most celebrated wine-touring regions, and if you time your trip to arrive in Augusta from June to August you'll be there for whale-watching season. The 12 charging stations have been installed by Australia's RAC (http://electrichighway.rac.com.au) and permit fast (DC) and slow (AC) charging with a ChargeStar RFID card. With no stress about reaching a charging point in this corner of Australia, take your time and hop from beach to beach before spending a couple of days in Margaret River then heading to the coastal town of Augusta.

Start // Perth
End // Augusta
Distance // 200 miles (320km)

A CIRCUIT OF MALLORCA, SPAIN

On the small Mediterranean island of Mallorca there are six charging points and a local rechargeable car club (Endesa Club de Auto-Recarga) has simplified access to them – so long as you register in advance for a charge card at their Palma headquarters. The three most commonly used connectors are available at each of the six Endesa charging stations and a free app that provides directions and also allows stations to be booked in advance. Car rental companies in Mallorca are also on-board, offering vehicles such as the Nissan LEAF. One route is to head southwest out of the island's capital Palma, top-up at Palmanova before heading into the Serra de Tramuntana mountain range. Stop halfway at Soller to explore some of the pretty mountain villages and recharge before continuing to Sa Pobla and then looping eastward through the flat grape-growing plains around Manacor and Campos (both sites of charging stations) to reach the east coast's beaches. Then head back to Palma.

Start / End // Palma
Distance // 185 miles (300km)

HIGHWAY 61
RE-REVISITED

Hwy 61 inspired Bob Dylan and countless legendary American musicians. Drive it and experience the region that shaped rock and roll.

US Rte 61 runs from Wyoming, Minnesota, to New Orleans, Louisiana. Beyond travelling from America's chilly northern plains to its steamy southern swamps, Hwy 61 is, at least for me, the world's most famous road. This is due to Bob Dylan naming his celebrated 1965 album *Highway 61 Revisited*. Both before and after Dylan gave the road iconic status, many a blues, soul and country musician travelled it in search of bright lights, big cities and maybe a record deal.

Hwy 61 spans 1407 miles (2264km) and while driving its entirety would be fascinating, I've never attempted to undertake such an epic trip. Instead, I stick with the southern end – nicknamed 'the Blues Highway' – and what a pleasure it is to drive.

Beginning in Memphis, Tennessee, I need a couple of days just to explore the city's rich music heritage – Sun Studios, where BB King, Howlin' Wolf, Elvis Presley and Roy Orbison started out; 'Soulsville USA', the neighbourhood that's home to the pioneering soul label Stax Records, which launched the careers of Otis Redding and Isaac Hayes; and then, of course, there's Graceland. There's also the National Civil Rights Museum, which puts into context the lives and struggles of black Americans throughout this era. Evening finds me eating BBQ ribs – a Memphis speciality – then hitting the bars and clubs of downtown, and soaking up the sound of the city that helped create blues, soul and rock and roll.

Leaving Memphis on the 61 is easy and, once outside the city limits, I find myself crossing the border into Mississippi. During the 1960s and the Civil Rights Movement, Mississippi gained a reputation for murderous racism, somewhere people fled from rather than travelled to. Today, the state remains one of the poorest, and racially divided, in the US, but it is peaceful. And the music that crystallised here a century ago now draws people like me, the blues tourists.

Cotton, which was once the dominant local industry, is still grown on vast plantations, but it's the sprouting casino signs that suggest the state's new growth industry. I pass Tunica, a mini Las Vegas situated right on the muddy Mississippi River. I'm looking for something more than gambling, however, and soon I start to see them, the roadside Blues Trail markers. They acknowledge

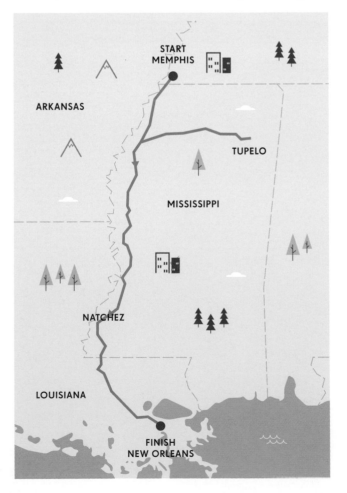

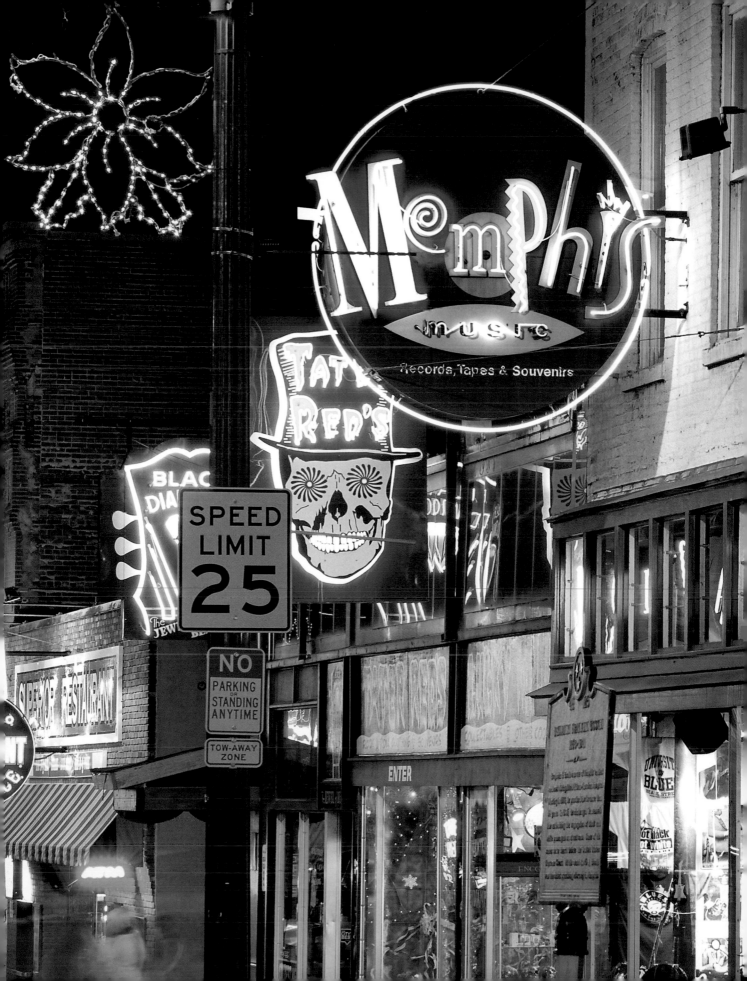

the places where so many legendary blues men and women once lived, worked, recorded and died.

Around 90 minutes south of Memphis I'm approaching Clarksdale, a run-down cotton town turned mecca for blues pilgrims. My first point of call is the excellent Delta Blues Museum, which tells the story of how the sound that was to become rock and soul took shape here. I then pay homage to the city's blues sites – here Bessie Smith died (take note: after a car crash on Hwy 61), Ike Turner and Sam Cooke were born, and you can even drive over the actual crossroads where Robert Johnson sold his soul in 'Cross Road Blues'. That certainly provides plenty of food for thought and, so inspired, I go and eat some tamales (a local favourite) in a diner.

Clarksdale's epicentre is Cat Head, a blues and folk art store, and a hive of local information. Armed with tips from its amiable proprietor, Roger Stolle, I head into town for the evening. I start out at Ground Zero Blues Club, a sumptuous live music bar owned by actor and Mississippi resident Morgan Freeman, before I wander down to Red's, a juke joint that looks as if it was due for demolition sometime during the last century. Juke joints – the African-American drinking and dancing clubs that were once prominent across much of the rural south – were the breeding grounds for blues. A few still stand and those that do often play host to local talent. At Red's, on a warm Friday night, Big-T was playing, the locals were dancing and the place was really rocking. Clarksdale also hosts the Juke Joint Festival every April: three days of beer, BBQ and blues.

MISSISSIPPI BLUES TRAIL

Since 2006, more than 200 Blues Trail markers have been placed across Mississippi. The plaques stand outside everything from cemeteries where musicians rest to juke joints, studios, record labels, homes, streets and even Parchman Farm, where many an unlucky musician did time. Maps are available and it's a fascinating drive as you explore the humble settings where one of the most atmospheric musical genres took shape.

Clockwise from top: jazz musicians in New Orleans; riding the city's streetcars; Creole architecture in the French Quarter; Clarksdale, Mississippi, draws blues fans worldwide. Previous page: Beale Street in Memphis is another bluesy essential

The next morning, in need of some fresh air, I sign on for a guided canoe trip down the Mississippi, and feel as happy as Huckleberry Finn paddling down the mighty river. Back in Clarksdale I head east to Oxford, home of the celebrated University of Mississippi – aka Ole Miss – and Rowan Oak, William Faulkner's house from 1930 until he died in 1962. A little further east is Tupelo where a certain Elvis Aaron Presley was born in a two-room shack in 1935.

Back on Hwy 61, my next stop is Indianola, now home to a museum honouring its most famous son, BB King. Close by is Greenville, a small, impoverished city that hosts the longest running blues festival in the US every year, at the very height of summer. The year I attended it was so hot I felt I was melting into the earth while the blues men casually strutted their stuff on stage. Where Clarksdale's juke joints are accommodating to visitors, Greenville's are rough: only seek out with a local guide.

Continuing south I drop into two more towns – Vicksburg, a small city that played a leading role in the American Civil War, and just east of here, Jackson, the state's sleepy capital.

For me, however, it's the swampy and near-empty, rural Mississippi landscape where the 61 really gets evocative. The cotton plantations where musical legends were born and worked still stand, often seemingly unchanged, and the small towns that have been immortalised for me in blues songs – Natchez, Yazoo City, Sunflower, Merigold, Shelby – are still working towns, even if some of them seem to be on the verge of becoming ghost towns.

In *On the Road*, Jack Kerouac and Neal Cassady drove Hwy 61 to visit William Burroughs. When this task was complete, they then carried on to New Orleans. Having soaked up Mississippi's small-town lassitude and blues bars I follow their lead and drive on to The Big Easy. **GC**

"The cotton plantations where musical legends were born and worked still stand, often seemingly unchanged"

DIRECTIONS

Start // Memphis, Tennessee
End // New Orleans, Louisiana
Distance // 428 miles (689km)
Getting there // Memphis and New Orleans are well served by flights, bus and train links, and car hire outlets.
When to drive // Spring to autumn finds the Blues Highway at its most lively, but June to August can be extremely hot and humid. Live music generally happens at weekends, except in New Orleans where the good times roll every day.
Where to stay // Mississippi is the land of cheap motels. Both Memphis and New Orleans can be expensive; book accommodation in advance.
What to take // In summer, bring lots of loose clothing – you'll sweat like never before.
Detours // When entering Louisiana drive west to Lafayette; the capital of Cajun Country is home to great Cajun and zydeco music.

Opposite: losing oneself in the music at Serbia's Guca Festival

MORE LIKE THIS
MUSIC PILGRIMAGES

GUCA FESTIVAL, SERBIA

Serbia is one of the most exciting places in the world to hear live music and its throbbing capital, Belgrade, is a great place to start, with all kinds of venues and clubs. But the event that really gets music travellers' pulses racing is the Guca brass band festival, held every year in the small town of Guca in central Serbia. This free festival – yes, that's several days of music, folk dancing and celebration at no cost – happens every August and culminates in a battle of the brass bands where a jury chooses the finest blowers from across the country. The drive from Belgrade to Guca is spectacular and, if all the brass partying becomes too much, you can head into the surrounding countryside where forests and lakes abound.
Start // Belgrade
End // Guca
Distance // 98 miles (158km)

BEATLES TOUR, ENGLAND

How Beatles obsessed are you? The world's most famous band are rightfully honoured in Liverpool and visitors can explore such sites as the band members' homes, Strawberry Field children's home, Penny Lane, the Cavern Club, the site of the NEMS record shop and other such important locations in the band's early history. Having your own car makes it an easy day outing – Liverpool is a small, lively city and the best place to start is The Beatles Museum down on the Albert Dock. Having immersed yourself in the band's story – and got a tour map – start out on your own tour of the humble suburban bungalows where pop-music genius percolated, and other locations that inspired the songs. Liverpudlians are proud of their heritage and will happily share tales of the young Beatles. If you're flying in to do this trail you will land at – of course – John Lennon Airport.
Start/End // Liverpool
Distance // From 10 to 30 miles (15km to 50km)

FLAMENCO TRAIL, SPAIN

Flamenco was born in Andalucía centuries ago, but you can still experience it in all its raw brilliance – sung, played and danced – throughout the region. Start in Seville, Andalucía's beautiful capital, where there are many bars dedicated to live performances. Next, drive northeast to Cordoba – a small city famous for its magnificent cathedral that was once a Moorish mosque. Here flamenco can often be heard echoing around the streets; Tablao Flamenco Cardenal should be noted for its exceptional performances. Finally, drive southeast to Granada, a city of intense passions where cave-dwelling *gitano* (Romani) communities have been hosting flamenco performances for centuries, and continue to enchant night after night. Add in plenty of history, architecture, the surrounding mountains, great food and drink, and you have one unforgettable musical road trip.
Start // Seville
End // Granada
Distance // 219 miles (353km)

HIGHTAILING FROM THIMPHU TO GANGTEY

A drive deep into a little-visited part of the Himalayas that unveils the wildly natural side of an almost mythical country: Bhutan.

More than one writer has described Bhutan as a 'Buddhist Disneyland', creating a cynical image of a country so obsessively happy it's almost trite – a land of painted-on smiles. But inside our car, on the highway to Gangtey, there are momentarily no smiles, and the road truly does feel like a rollercoaster.

Monsoon rains have been lashing the Himalayan slopes for weeks, and a landslip has devoured the highway. For an hour we idle as bulldozers pluck rocks from the road. I sit at the highway's precipitous edge, a rock for a stool, and watch the world plunge away below me into a gorge so deep and green I can no longer see

the river. Himalayan peaks scrape at the clouds in a hazy distance. Have I just found myself in the world's most scenic traffic jam?

At a glance, the drive from Bhutan's capital, Thimphu, to the village of Gangtey looks simple – 81 miles (130km) along the country's main highway. Google Maps will tell you it's a four-hour drive; locals say five to six. But it will be almost eight hours after leaving Thimphu that we finally turn off the highway and into Gangtey. Such are the vagaries of a 'highway' in Bhutan.

Thimphu is a good start to any journey – small, gentle and cradled by mountains, it may be the only capital city in the world without any traffic lights. As we leave, a 51m-high golden Buddha

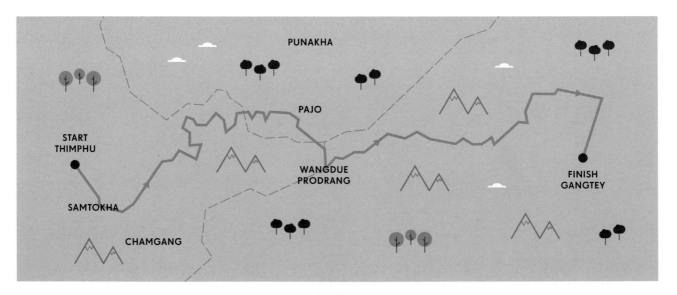

© Apsak Kanjanapusit | Getty Images

peers down at us from the slopes above. It looks like a benevolent guardian, blessing all who leave the city. Apparently we'll need it.

'The drive will be like a car massage,' my driver says with a grin as we begin the climb out of Thimphu. It's an abrupt and spectacular start to our journey, as the highway coils and contorts its way up a 900m climb to Dochula, a high pass seemingly strung this day between roiling monsoon clouds.

I've been living above 2000 metres in Thimphu for the past few days, but even so I find the air is noticeably thinner as I step from the car atop Dochula. At 3200 metres above sea level, it will be the highest point of the drive.

The pass is crowned by a temple and 108 *chortens* (shrines) built in honour of the soldiers who died in battle against insurgents from neighbouring Sikkim in 2003. Today they provide a sombre scene in keeping with the grey mist that abbreviates the view. On a clear day it's said that you can see the line of Himalayan peaks across Bhutan, including perhaps the highest unclimbed mountain in the world, 7570-metre Gangkhar Puensum. But this is not that day. We drive on, circling clockwise around the *chortens*, as is the Buddhist custom, before beginning the descent towards Punakha.

The change in landscape is even more pronounced on this side of the pass. Punakha, the former capital and the site of Bhutan's most impressive *dzong* (fort), sits almost 2000m below Dochula. The valleys are deep and green, and the climate changes from alpine to sultry subtropical in what seems like minutes.

As the forest clears, rice terraces begin to step down the slopes, each one painted green and lush by the monsoon. It's as though

THE CRANES OF GANGTEY

On a ridge between a pair of monasteries, the village of Gangtey peers down into the waterlogged Phobjikha Valley, a natural sanctuary. The wide, glacially carved valley looks almost out of place, but in winter it becomes the migratory home of several hundred black-necked cranes, which fly here from Tibet in October, returning in February or March. In November the Gangtey monastery holds a Black-Necked Crane Festival.

Clockwise from top: novice monks in Bhutan; the highway from Thimphu near Dochula; Punakha Dzong stands at the confluence of two rivers. Previous page: rice terraces in the Punakha Valley.

we've driven into an Asian highlights reel – the fields could be Vietnam or China, but with peaks worthy of Nepal rising above.

In the valley, we take a break, walking through rice fields to Chimi Lahkhang, one of Bhutan's most unusual temples. The fertility temple was built in honour of Lama Drukpa Kunley, Bhutan's so-called 'divine madman', a revered 16th-century saint with a rather unsaintly sex drive, who modestly renamed his penis the 'Thunderbolt of Flaming Wisdom'. Lama Drukpa Kunley has come to be represented in Bhutan by the phallus. In the village of Sopsokha beside the temple, stores are filled with phalluses – like sex shops for the sacred – and as we drive higher into the mountains, it seems as if every home has a spurting penis painted on its walls.

It's past Chimi Lahkhang that the highway really deteriorates, turning into one of those crazy Himalayan roads of legend. The slopes above and below are scarred with fresh landslides, marijuana grows wild at the road edge, and cars inch close to perilous drops. It's a slow but beautiful journey into the highest mountain range on Earth. The hours tick past as the road is cleared of mud and rock. At one point, a truck lies overturned across the road edge, its driver long wandered off.

By the time we reach the nondescript village of Nobding, light is fading – we will enter Gangtey at dusk – and we pull up beside a corrugated-iron shelter where half-a-dozen women sit on a concrete slab selling fruit and momos. I grab some momos and stroll off through the village to stretch my legs. Three small boys follow behind. As I stop above a gully, peering into an Afro of bush, one of the boys steps forward and points into the trees. 'Huge snake down there,' he says. 'Anaconda.' And then three hooting bursts of laughter from the boys. Before I know it I'm walking back into the village with a boy holding my hand, still spinning inflated tales of a snake more terrifying than the highway. It's hard not to smile. **AB**

"It's as if we've driven into an Asian highlights reel – the fields could be China, but with peaks worthy of Nepal"

DIRECTIONS

Start // Thimphu
End // Gangtey
Distance // 81 miles (130km)
Getting there // Bhutan's international airport is in Paro, 31 miles (50km) west of Thimphu. Bhutan's visa system assigns a guide and driver to each visitor (plus a mandatory daily fee), making it simple to get around.
Where to stay // Treat yourself at drive's end with a night or two at Gangtey Lodge (www.gangteylodge.com), commanding one of the best positions in the village, with a full view along the Phobjikha Valley. The 12 suites have floor-to-ceiling windows, the restaurant is excellent and, perhaps best of all after this drive, you'll be welcomed with a complimentary five-minute neck massage to knead away the rigours of the road.
More info // www.tourism.gov.bt

*Opposite: the road to Milford
Sound, New Zealand*

MORE LIKE THIS
MOUNTAIN DRIVES

MILFORD SOUND, NEW ZEALAND

Fiordland is New Zealand's wildest (and wettest) corner, a frayed and ragged landscape of mountains sliced with fjords. The mountains here aren't the highest in New Zealand, but they are among the most inaccessible. The drive from Te Anau into Milford Sound is the only approach by road. The first part of the drive follows the shores of Lake Te Anau, looking like an inland fjord, before entering Fiordland National Park through the Eglinton Valley. Stop here at the Mirror Lakes, which do as the name suggests, before the road climbs to the Divide, a pass that doubles as the starting point for the popular Routeburn Track. After burrowing through the mountains inside the ¾-mile (1.2km) Homer Tunnel, the road begins a steep and winding, view-filled descent into mountain-rimmed Milford Sound.

Start // Te Anau
End // Milford Sound
Distance // 74½ miles (120km)

CATALAN PYRENEES

A border anomaly heightens the intrigue of this mountainous road trip. Start in Olot, capital of Catalonia's volcanic Garrotxa region, and meander northeast to Castellfollit de la Roca, a town stacked perilously at the edge of a basalt cliff. Swing west, passing slumbering volcanoes, to Ripoll and then north to the Vall de Ribes, where roads are increasingly hemmed by rock. Hook west at Ribes de Freser and follow hair-raising route 4016, which swerves towards Puigcerdà. Road signs get interesting from here: driving north you'll leave Spain for France... only to re-enter Spain when you reach defiantly Catalan outpost Llívia. Only north of Llívia do you fully reach France; end the trip in mountain sports hub Les Angles. In winter, plan overnight stops in La Molina and Masella to turn the road trip into a ski tour. In summer, allow time to explore the gourmet enclave in medieval Llívia.

Start // Olot, Spain
End // Les Angles, France
Distance // 86 miles (138km)

ROUTE DES GRANDES ALPES, FRANCE

A true Alpine spectacular, La Route des Grandes Alpes traverses the French Alps from the shores of Lake Geneva to the French Riviera. It's a route that took almost 30 years to construct – a task you'll appreciate as you ascend and descend 16 passes, including some of the highest sealed road passes in Europe and legendary Tour de France passes, such as the Col du Galibier. There are views of Mont Blanc, the highest mountain in the Alps, early in the drive, and the road then passes through three national parks – Vanoise, Queyras and Mercantour – along its rollercoaster journey to the Mediterranean. Given that the drive climbs as high as 2800 metres, snow closes the route for much of the year – expect it to be open from June to October.

Start // Thonon-les-Bains
End // Menton
Distance // 425 miles (684km)

THE ROAD FROM
SRINAGAR TO MANALI

*Getting to Ladakh is almost as glorious as being there – two days in
and two days out, crossing some of India's highest motorable passes.*

The world is full of epic desert rides, but with the added frisson of climbing some of the world's highest motorable passes, the crossing from Kashmir to Ladakh and on to Himachal Pradesh is cinematic. The highest point – the Tanglang La – is 5328m above sea level, and the highway plunges through valleys that were old when the Silk Road was young, all in the rain shadow of the Himalaya.

My port of departure for this bone-shaking crossing was Srinagar, beautiful, troubled summer capital of Jammu and Kashmir. At times Kashmir has been one of the most dangerous places on Earth, but a lessening of tensions and the melting of snow on the high passes provided a timely window for the ride northeast.

The journey began with a gauntlet of military checkpoints, before I reached the alpine meadows around Sonamarg. With increasing altitude, the landscape seemed to morph from Switzerland, to British Columbia, until it finally turned into the barren wastelands of the Silk Road as I approached the 3528m Zoji La, the first of many perilous

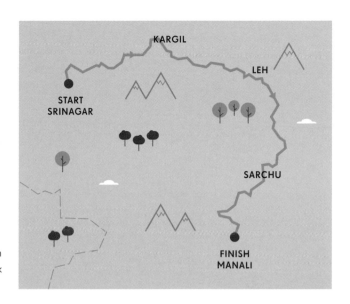

KARGIL

LEH

START
SRINAGAR

SARCHU

FINISH
MANALI

"The road from Leh is like driving on the moon. Eroded by wind, the soft sandstone is whittled into fantasy castles"

passes, and the road became a treacherous tangle of switchback loops, cut like notches into a bare rock wall. The scenery may be awe-inspiring, but drivers who let their attention wander end up as rust-coloured smears at the bottom of the valley.

Past the Zoji La, the landscape morphed into a duotone of green and grey. I was glad to find a hot meal and a bed waiting in Kargil, close to the volatile Line of Control between India and Pakistan, and the last outpost of Muslim Kashmir before entering Buddhist Ladakh.

Past the grit-grey turn off to Zanskar, the atmosphere changed profoundly. The towering bas-relief of the Mulbekh Buddha welcomed me to Ladakh, and the steely grey terrain was repainted in rich yellows and reds, punctuated by stabs of green and the gleaming white of freshly painted Buddhist *chortens*.

East of Lamayuru Gompa, there was another hair-raising test of clutch-control on the 18 breakneck turns of the Hangro Loops before the multi-coloured confluence of the Zanskar and Indus rivers burst into view at Nimmu. The final run to Leh was almost as smooth as an English motorway, if you ignore the knife-edge ridges on all sides.

Having reached Leh, my first thoughts were of hygiene. A shower, first and foremost, and a toothbrush to remove the taste of diesel and grit. For road-rattled travellers, the capital of Ladakh is the embodiment of Shangri-La – hot food, warm smiles, soft linen, and the soothing sound of Buddhist chants as a lullaby. When the time came to move on, it took most of a day to reload the bike, tighten loose bolts, and load up on fuel. Petrol stations and mechanics are rare on the road to Manali and stricken vehicles dot the highway.

The road on from Leh was like driving on the moon. Protected from rain, the badlands are eroded by wind, whittling the soft sandstone into fantasy castles. After leaving the Indus Valley, even greenery became a distant memory in the wastelands surrounding the 5328m Tanglang La. After this formidable obstacle, I zig-zagged down to the flat Moore Plains, where the road deteriorated into a sketched trace in the gravel. I was relieved to roll into Sarchu, the desolate overnight stop between Leh and Manali. Sarchu is a motley collection of canvas tents in an exposed valley, with oil fires burning in battered tin drums. If the cold and fumes don't keep you awake, the altitude will. At 4290m, I could feel the first warning signs of altitude sickness as I spent a restless night.

The second day started cold, and got even colder once I started riding. It was only when the sun cleared the mountain wall that any trace of warmth crept into my bones. Fortunately, after conquering the 4890m Baralacha La, my trajectory was sharply downhill past glacial lakes to Keylong, the only town between Leh and Manali.

Greenery filled the landscape as I rode south, but there was one more pass to cross – the 3980m Rohtang La – before the final snaking descent. After two days of grit and gasoline, arriving into the hippy hill-resort of Manali was both uplifting and anticlimactic. After the space and peace of the desert, the concrete sprawl felt pedestrian. It took several beers before I accepted the truth – that on the journey from Srinagar to Manali, it is the gruelling, mortality-testing and wonderful road that is the destination. **JB**

ACCLIMATISING

The biggest challenge on the Srinagar to Manali drive is altitude. Acute mountain sickness can be a risk above 2400m, and passes on this route tip 5000m. To minimise the risk, travellers zip from Srinagar (1585m) to Kargil (2676m) in one day, sleeping well below the highest point, the 4108m Fotu La. After rest days in Leh (3500m), you should be acclimatised enough to make the crossing over the 5328m Tanglang La to Manali (2050m).

Clockwise from left: Lake Dal, Srinagar; the Buddhist Gompa at Lamayuru; the Manali-Leh road moonscape. Previous page: a view of Leh from Leh Gompa.

TOOLKIT

Start // Srinagar, Jammu and Kashmir
End // Manali, Himachal Pradesh
Distance // Srinagar to Leh is 270 miles (434km); Leh to Manali another 298 miles (479km).
Getting there // There are international airports in Srinagar and Bhuntar, just over an hour's drive from Manali.
When to drive // The Zoji La between Srinagar and Leh usually opens from March to November; the road from Leh to Manali is usually closed by snow from October till May.
Petrol stops // Petrol is only available in Srinagar, Sonamarg, Kargil, Mulbekh, Leh, Karu, Tandi and Manali.
Where to stay // There are highway hotels in Kargil, and tented camps at Sarchu.
Where to eat // At rustic, roadside eateries; carry purified water (and purification tablets) in case of breakdowns.

*Opposite: driving Ruta 40 in the
shadow of the Andes*

MORE LIKE THIS
RUGGED ROADS

THE OLD TELEGRAPH TRACK, AUSTRALIA

Trade backpacker bars for outback survival on the mettle-testing trip from Cairns to the northernmost point in Australia. The Old Telegraph Track is only passable in the dry season from May to November, and even then, you'll have to ford a string of saltwater-crocodile-infested rivers. There are crude one-koala hamlets strung out along the route, but real bushmen prefer to camp with only crested cockatoos for company. Driving the Bloomfield Track through the Daintree rainforest to Cooktown will provide some basic training before you hit the empty country. Don't even think of attempting this without spare fuel and water and a road-worthy 4WD.
Start // Cairns
End // The Tip, Cape York
Distance // Approx 620 miles (1000km)

RUTA 40, ARGENTINA

Traversing 20 national parks, crossing 18 major rivers, climbing over 27 mountain passes and straining to 4952m above sea level, Argentina's longest highway traces the jagged line of the Andes, from the Bolivian border to the shores of the South Atlantic. This is one of the most epic drives in the Americas, a 3100-mile (5000km) slice through dramatic countryside. The northern stretch is paved and relatively civilised; on the southern stretch through mountainous Patagonia, the road surface frequently deteriorates to gravel, with barren stretches of hundreds of miles between outposts of civilisation. Watch for wandering wild guanacos – for some sections of road, they'll be your only company.
Start // Punta Loyola, Santa Cruz
End // La Quiaca, Jujuy
Distance // Approx 3100 miles (5000km)

WHITE RIM ROAD, UTAH, USA

The otherworldly terrain of Canyonlands National Park is intimidating enough from the hard-top – once you leave the tarmac for the gravel of the White Rim Road, it feels like driving on Mars. Sneaking along the edge of sheer cliff walls, and open only to 4WD vehicles and mountain bikers with special permits, this epic 100-mile (161km) loop was constructed by Cold War-era uranium miners, encircling the Island in the Sky mesa. You'll find campsites, but no potable water in this arid, desert country; if you want creature comforts and roads with safety barriers you've come to the wrong canyon. The pay-off comes in the best desert views this side of Olympus Mons.
Start // Junction of Potash Rd and Schafer Trail
End // Mineral Bottom Rd
Distance // 100 miles (161km)

ON THE TRAIL
OF HO CHI MINH

*The little-used Ho Chi Minh Rd between Ho Chi Minh City
and Hanoi is a rich mix of war and peace.*

The fighting started within minutes of us firing our bikes up and setting out from Ho Chi Minh City. Two of our group of five only trusted their satellite navigation systems, two were neutral and one, me, only trusted my 1:1,250,000 paper map.

It all came to a head a week later as we were leaving the cave town of Phong Nha. We arrived at the highway where we were presented with the option of going left or right. Satellite navigation said right but the map said left. Finally, succumbing to critical mass, I followed the others right for 25 miles (40km) before discovering modern technology was taking us across the country to Hwy One, perhaps the most direct route to Hanoi but not the one following our intended path: the splendour of the Ho Chi Minh Rd. The map resumed control.

Each member of our group was of the generation where the Vietnam War (or the 'American War' as the Vietnamese understandably call it) affected our lives and the society in which we lived. Riding the Ho Chi Minh Rd was a way of helping us understand better what had happened.

The Ho Chi Minh Trail was an icon of the American War. It was a network of tracks from the north of Vietnam to the south that carried soldiers and supplies to help the Viet Cong reunify the country. The trail's web totalled 10,563 miles (17,000km) to cover what is today a 1056 mile (1700km) drive. The trail is now primarily myth and legend, with large parts of it located in Laos and Cambodia and much of it now overgrown by jungle or reclaimed for agriculture.

The spirit of the trail lives on in the Ho Chi Minh Rd, which runs along the Truong Son range on the west of the narrow

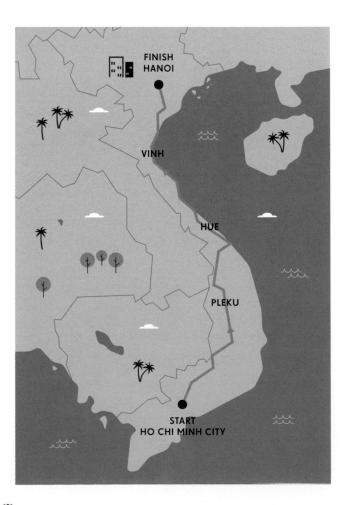

country and which uses substantial bits and pieces of the original trail, particularly in the north. Building it commenced in 2000, not as a war memorial but as a way of assisting the economic development of Vietnam's most remote regions. Regardless, reminders of the American War are everywhere. We rode it from the south to the north, as the spectacle of it builds progressively in this direction, culminating in the Western Ho Chi Minh Rd where the isolation and overwhelming presence of the jungle makes it hard to believe you're still in a country with a population of 90 million people.

The motorcycle was the obvious choice of transport: well over 80% of Vietnam's registered vehicles are two-wheelers and if you ride you join one of the world's biggest motorcycle gangs. It doesn't help much in the near-death experience of trying to get out of Ho Chi Minh City's industrial areas into clean air, and the Ho Chi Minh Rd doesn't properly start until you reach Dong Xoai. From there, the road is still busy but becomes progressively more rural as you head northwards.

In places it seems as if you could almost hit a golf ball from the road into Cambodia, and in areas like Dak Mil, the original trail and the road have frequent intersection with evidence of very heavy bombing. Parts of the original trail are available here to explore.

Climbing onto the Truong Son range gave us our first encounters with highlands ethnic minority groups variously

"Once we were recognised as travellers, we were waved at and cheered like rock stars. Tourists on the Ho Chi Minh Rd are still rare"

known as 'hill tribes' or, as the Vietnamese prefer, 'minority people'. More than 50 different groups have been identified and small concentrations of them are spread along the route. Once we were recognised as travellers (bigger hire-bikes and full-face helmets are the give-away), we were waved at and cheered like rock stars. Tourists on the Ho Chi Minh Rd are still rare. Coffee stops usually resulted in faltering conversations with students keen to practise their English and a sense that the younger generation in Vietnam is fundamentally happy. It's a bright sign for a country fast-tracking its development.

The wildness of the mountain range increases the further north you ride. The 50 miles (80km) from Prao to A Luoi, which skirts the Laotian border, is one mountain pass after another with the jungle encroaching more obviously onto the road.

Quang Tri Province was the most heavily bombed area of Vietnam during the war. Much of the agricultural land is still affected by unexploded ordinances (XMOs) and the Ho Chi Minh Rd passes Hamburger Hill where one of the most

The sheer mass of rock on the Truong Son range occasionally defeated even the resourceful builders of the Ho Chi Minh Trail. Local storytellers say when an area was judged too difficult to build through, a 'fake' camp would be set up and well lit. The roadbuilders would then retreat a safe distance and the Americans would invariably bomb the site, breaking up the rock and allowing the roadbuilding to continue.

Clockwise from left: street vendors in Hanoi's Old Quarter; on the way to Huong pagoda in Hanoi. Previous page: crossing Long Bien bridge in Hanoi

inexplicable battles of the war took place. US forces chose a ground assault on this place of no strategic importance and suffered 442 killed and injured. The US captured the hill only to quietly abandon it less than a month later. The giant US base at Khe Sanh is long unused but there's a small museum there with a modest display of war images and memorabilia. There's also a moving cemetery in Khe Sanh with a surprising number of graves with no name. Such was the ferocity of the bombing that 300,000 Vietnamese are still listed as 'missing in action'.

When you arrive at Dakrong Bridge, you have the option to turn right and take the Eastern Ho Chi Minh Rd to Hanoi or turn left for its Western branch. The Eastern road is interesting but the Western option is the highlight of the entire trip. From here to Cuc Phong National Park is really an epicentre of magic. The cement block road is too snake-like and steep for trucks and you weave in and out of jungle and over high passes, having the road almost to yourself. If you think that tigers may still roam free in Asian forests, Cuc Phong is where you'll find them. The riding experience is so intense it's almost a relief to get to the outskirts of industrialisation again for the chaotic run into Hanoi.

The Ho Chi Minh Rd won't stay the way it is forever – development will see to that. In the meantime, its great education and many pleasures await you. Oh, just be sure you take a proper, printed, paper map... **GR**

TOOLKIT

Start // Ho Chi Minh City (formerly Saigon)
End // Hanoi
Distance // 1173 miles (1887km)
Getting there // Fly to Ho Chi Minh City.
When to drive // March to September.
Where to stay // All towns and most villages on the Ho Chi Minh Rd have clean, comfy hotels (but often hard beds!).
What to take // Helmet and riding gear, wet weather gear (the Truong Son range has its own microclimates), changes of clothing (overnight laundry services available in most towns), travel map of Vietnam (www.mapvietnam.vn).
Motorcycle hire // For one-way rental from Ho Chi Minh City to Hanoi: Flamingo Travel (www.flamingotravel.com.vn). For hire bikes in Hanoi and trips north: Offroad Vietnam Adventures (www.offroadvietnam.com).

Opposite: the Confederate Cemetery at Fredericksburg, Virginia

MORE LIKE THIS
REVOLUTIONARY RIDES

CHE GUEVARA IN ARGENTINA

Although Che's famous book was titled *The Motorcycle Diaries*, motorcycles played only a small part in a much bigger adventure. Che and his mate, Alberto Granado, left Buenos Aires in January of 1952 on a 1947 Norton 500 named 'La Ponderosa 11', which meant 'the mighty one'. The bike made it across the lower part of Argentina to San Carlos de Bariloche (987 miles/1589km) and then struggled another 533 miles (857km) to the capital of Chile, Santiago, where it was abandoned through repeated mechanical failure. The bulk of the adventures in *The Motorcycle Diaries* used other means of transport. If you're retracing the motorcycle component of Che's trip, start at his place of birth, Rosario, which is close to Buenos Aires. The ride from there to San Carlos de Bariloche covers mostly grazing and farming country but there are plenty of towns along the way to break up the journey.

Start // Rosario
End // Santiago
Distance // 1520 miles (2446km)

LEE AGAINST GRANT, USA

The road that takes you through central Virginia in the US is not a particularly arduous ride or drive. Its significance is that it provides access points to the pivotal 1864 Overland Campaign that pitted two of the Civil War's chief combatants directly against each other: the South's Robert E Lee against the North's Ulysses S Grant. Virginia has a network of Civil War trails to rival the Ho Chi Minh Trail but a highlight is Grant's Overland Campaign of 1864, which pushed through the state and left Lee stranded at Petersburg before a final retreat and attempt to escape. Depending on diversions, this is a 300km drive from slightly west of Fredericksburg to the outskirts of Petersburg. To get the most from this drive/ride, some research is necessary. Just about every town you pass through on this route has its own story but there are also three national parks devoted to preserving Civil War history.

Start // Fredericksburg
End // Petersburg
Distance // 186 miles (300km)

DILI TO BALIBO, TIMOR-LESTE

Not for the faint-hearted, the road from Dili in Timor-Leste to Balibo was used extensively by Falintil, the armed wing of the Fretilin political party in the early stages of the Indonesian invasion prior to the formal invasion in December 1975. Nobel Peace Prize winner José Ramos-Horta went up and down this road with the Balibo Five and bits of it are depicted in the movie, *Balibo*. It's a trail bike or 4WD road only. When the Australian Defence Forces (ADF) were in Timor, they were banned from using it because it was considered too dangerous. If you attempt it, rely on local advice. Your reward is a rough road that winds through small, pretty villages and very green countryside up to Maliana, the capital of Bobonaro, which was a major militia stronghold. From Maliana it's a short hike up to Balibo where, from the old Portuguese fort (now a small hotel), you can see the ocean and the Indonesian border.

Start // Dili
End // Balibo
Distance // 168 miles (270km)

© Steve Heap | Shutterstock

TO THE CONFEDERATE DEAD

CROSSING THE KATHMANDU LOOP

A mountain drive with plains appeal, this dusty circuit from Kathmandu to the Terai serves up everything from medieval villages to rhinos and Himalayan views.

R oad blocks, traffic jams, irate crowds protesting this and that, and a gauntlet of sacred cows, street dogs and suicidal chickens. Leaving Kathmandu is a test of both driving skill and patience. Faced by the magnitude of the task, many drivers balk, and limp back to Thamel to settle in with a good book and a falafel wrap.

However, those willing to go the distance receive ample rewards. You don't have to go far beyond the Kathmandu Ring Road to find yourself surrounded by the pristine mountain scenery that first drew travellers to Nepal. Indeed, you're likely to find more peace and privacy on a country drive through the Himalayan foothills than at Everest Base Camp.

The Nepali capital is both blessed and cursed by its location; blessed, because of the scenery, but cursed because of the sheer impracticality of getting anywhere else by road. Most traffic still chokes its way along the hugely overcrowded Prithvi Hwy, which punches east past a forest of brick kilns towards Pokhara and the turn off to the lowlands.

Despite starting my journey at first light, it took hours to get clear of the police checkpoints and escape the relentless snarl of buses, jeeps and trucks, before I could breathe easy in the winding valley of the Trisuli River. This may be the busiest road in Nepal – and reputedly the fifth most dangerous road in the whole world – but it passes through a fantasy landscape of cascading terraced fields and isolated farmhouses clinging improbably to sheer mountainsides.

Leaving the main pack behind, I enjoyed what by Nepali standards would count as a peaceful ride, close encounters with oncoming buses notwithstanding. Savouring the clean air after the smog of Kathmandu, I paused occasionally to snap photos of particularly scenic banyan trees and suspension bridges, and sip *chiya* (tea) at dusty roadside canteens.

There's plenty to see on the way to Pokhara – the Manakamana cablecar, the palace and birthplace of Prithvi Narayan Shah at Gorkha – but my destination lay off the main highway at Bandipur, a precariously balanced Newari village that has changed only superficially since the days when yak caravans were the main form of transport into the Kathmandu Valley.

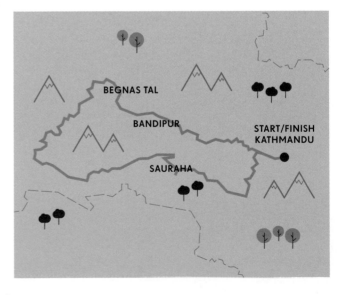

BEGNAS TAL

BANDIPUR

START/FINISH
KATHMANDU

SAURAHA

Bandipur is a place to pootle around, admiring tottering temples and tall, timber and mudbrick townhouses – several now converted into hotels – flanking the main bazaar. After a blissful night in the cool air, I freewheeled downhill to another favourite detour, the millpond-calm lake of Begnas Tal, reflecting the sawtooth ridge of the Annapurnas to the north.

For most travellers, the logical next stop would be Pokhara, starting point for treks to Annapurna and Mustang, but I had my sights on Tansen, another historic hill town to the south. Branching at Pokhara, the Siddhartha Hwy winds through a series of narrow gorges, twisting like a snake with indigestion. Even better, the rough terrain deters much of the four-wheeled traffic, making driving here a pleasure.

Once the capital of a powerful Magar kingdom, Tansen is an agreeable jumble of royal relics and traditional shophouses. I parked up and wandered aimlessly, greeting scores of inquisitive children and cheerful old men in *topis* (Nepali caps), puffing reflectively on *beedi* cigarettes. Tansen's greatest treasure though, was a hike north of town, on the banks of the Kali Gandaki River. Here, the crumbling remains of the baroque Rani

"The air was crisp and clear as I rumbled up through the foothills to find the full length of the Nepal Himalaya spread out before me"

Mahal palace recall the lonely exile of Khadga Shamsher Rana, driven from Kathmandu after plotting against the monarchy.

The Siddhartha Hwy collides with the Terai at Butwal, a hectic bazaar that feels as if it's been transplanted from India, right down to the stalls piled with glass bangles and piles of blood-red *tilaka* powder. The next step of the Kathmandu Loop is perhaps the most challenging – not because of winding mountain roads, but because of winding plains traffic.

Drivers take advantage of the flat Mahendra Hwy – the main transect through the Terai – for some of their most death-defying overtaking. By the time I limped into Sauraha, the gateway to Chitwan National Park, my face muscles were frozen into a rictus of horror from so many near-misses.

The third spike on Nepal's tourism trident, after Kathmandu and the Himalaya, Chitwan is one of the last refuges of the one-horned Indian rhino and the royal Bengal tiger. You have a reasonable chance of spotting either, or both, on guided walks through the jungle. On my last trip, I met a traveller who was jumped by a tiger and only escaped thanks to some artful stick work by his guide, so I wasn't too sorry to only see rhinos, shuffling thoughtfully through the shoulder-high elephant grass.

From Chitwan, travellers charge south to the Indian border or north to Kathmandu on the choked highway to Mugling, but wise motorists skip this in favour of the Tribhuvan Rajpath, which wriggles through the high ridge southwest of Kathmandu. Forking off the Mahendra Hwy at the nondescript Terai town of Hetauda, this is another low-traffic delight, rising in tight switchbacks through handsome stands of pine, sal and rhododendron trees to Daman at the crest of the ridge.

The air was crisp and clear as I rumbled up through the foothills, and I reached Daman to find the full length of the Nepal Himalaya spread out before me like one of those postcards on sale in Kathmandu with each of the peaks named and height-stamped. In the event, I could have used one of those postcards to work out which himal was which, though I was able to pick out Everest and the Annapurnas.

The buzz stayed with me all the way to the Kathmandu Ring Road, where it faltered, as I navigated the snarl of traffic, before reviving as I rolled into friendly, familiar Thamel. Later, sipping on a chilled mango daiquiri, I mused on the travellers' love-affair with Kathmandu: amazing to visit, but difficult to leave – both emotionally and physically. Perhaps logistics was the real reason the hippy generation came to the end of the overland trail in Kathmandu and stayed. **JB**

HIGHWAYS TO HAIL

Nepal's highways map its turbulent history. The Prithvi Hwy was named after Prithvi Narayan Shah, the king who unified Nepal in the 1700s, while the Siddhartha Hwy pays tribute to the historical Buddha, Gautama Siddhartha, born in nearby Lumbini. The Mahendra Hwy honours King Mahendra, who opened Nepal up to the world, while the Tribhuvan Rajpath is a nod to his dad, King Tribhuvan, who seized power in 1951.

Left: Bandipur village. Previous page: a wild one-horned rhinoceros in Chittwan National Park

DIRECTIONS

Start/End // Kathmandu, Nepal.
Distance // Approx 435 miles (700km) – or 4 days of driving
Getting there // Tribhuvan International Airport is just a 20-minute drive from the centre of Kathmandu.
When to drive // October to November and March to April.
Where to stay // Make overnight stops at village hotels in Bandipur and Tansen. There are safari lodges in Sauraha.
Where to eat // Dine at rustic *dhabas* (roadside eateries) in villages en route.
Logistics // You'll find puncture-repair wallahs and fuel stops all along the route.

*Opposite: the breathtaking Khardung
La pass in Ladakh*

MORE LIKE THIS
HIMALAYAN DRIVES

GUWAHATI TO TAWANG

India's northeast is a wild frontier, with remote and rarely visited tribal states pushed up against the Chinese and Burmese borders. The testing trip from Guwahati in Assam to the Tawang Valley in Arunachal Pradesh rises from the tropical floodplain of the Brahmaputra River through the foothills of the Himalaya to what is said to be the largest Buddhist monastery after Tibet's Potala Palace. Reaching Tawang involves gaining a Protected Area Permit (make arrangements with travel agencies in Guwahati) and an arduous two-day drive on what is only debatably a road – expect regular waits while road crews dynamite fallen rocks from your path. Beyond the 4170m Se La mountain pass, the route drops into the serene Tawang Valley, which feels cut off from the rest of the world, and often is from November to March.
Start // Guwahati, Assam
End // Tawang, Arunachal Pradesh
Distance // 303 miles (488km)

CROSSING THE KHARDUNG LA

Ladakh has more tricks up its sleeve than the drive in from Srinagar or Manali. From Leh, a highway seemingly built from rock and ice struggles north across the 5359m Khardung La – said to be the world's highest motorable pass – perched at a similar elevation to Everest Base Camp. On the far side is the Nubra Valley, a piece of the Silk Road preserved in a state of suspended animation. The broad, sandy basin that frames the Shyok and Nubra rivers is dotted with Buddhist monasteries, sea buckthorn berry thickets and occasional dromedaries, with a low-key traveller scene spilling over from Leh. Getting in requires a Protected Area Permit, but getting one is a formality; travel agencies in Leh can rustle up the necessary paperwork.
Start // Leh, Ladakh
End // Hunder, Ladakh
Distance // 79 miles (127km)

KARAKORAM HIGHWAY

Despite the instability along the Northwest Frontier, the epic crossing from Pakistan to China is still theoretically possible, with some strategic planning and a lot of luck. Originally part of the Silk Road, the Karakoram Hwy peaks at 4693m at the Khunjerab Pass (open May to December) before slipping down to Kashgar. This is a bone-shaking trip with few creature comforts and few amenities of any kind once you clear the idyllic Hunza Valley. Most start from Gilgit, bypassing the risky zone around the Khyber Pass, before snaking northeast into China through the high, dry valleys of the Karakoram Range. Chiselled from bare rock and ice, the terrain is humbling in scale, but with the hassles of obtaining a Chinese driving permit, more travel by bus or bicycle than by car or motorbike.
Start // Gilgit, Pakistan
End // Kashgar, China
Distance // 580 miles (933km)

SOUTH KOREA: FROM TOP TO TOE

Forget endless Seoul searching – there's more to South Korea than its neon capital. Namely an east coast blessed with beaches, a long-forgotten 'Golden City' and the buzzing port of Busan.

There's an old Korean proverb: "even if you have to crawl on your knees, get to Seoul." Today, South Korea's capital – a behemoth of 10 million people – still dominates the nation's attention. From the fast-flowing streets around Apgujeong's boutiques to the new wave bars and restaurants of Hongdae and Edae, it's a pulsing neon ocean of activity, teeming with life.

But what of those who yearn for something quieter? Visitors who'd prefer to see the *real* Korea, beyond the messy cathodic banks of the Han River? Well, for them, there's the road to Busan.

South Korea's second city is a smaller blip on the tourism radar, dwarfed by Seoul's pulsating presence 200 miles above it. But the bustling port town is a global destination in its own right – home to more than 3.5 million people and renowned for its seafood, hot springs, mountains and colourful coastal vibe.

There are plenty of ways to drive between the two cities (from top left to bottom right of the country when looking at a map), but we opt for the most picturesque: a 285-mile (459km) route in a rough figure-of-seven. Leaving Seoul we zip east to the coast, where we turn right and begin the gentle ride south towards Busan, with the Sea of Japan always on our left.

South Korean roads are smooth, modern and well maintained – but as with any major international city, it's a battle to escape the greedy tentacles of traffic unfurling from the depths of Seoul. By the time we hit the ocean at Gangneung it's mid-afternoon of day one and we're more than ready to park up, sample the extraordinary local seafood and explore pretty Gyeongpo Beach.

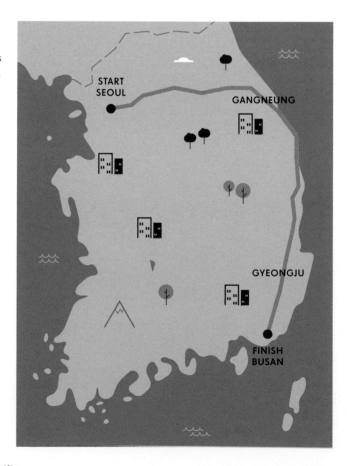

Our accommodation here is among the most extraordinary I've ever seen, let alone stayed in. The Haslla Art World Museum Hotel is designed as an enormous piece of art, exploring the harmony between humanity and nature. Each of the 24 rooms is unique, with mine containing an enormous wooden bowl – representing a mother's womb – to sleep in. Next door, a heart-shaped stone bath boasts jaw-dropping views up the coast towards the amorphous peaks of North Korea.

This close to the border, there are plenty of reminders that Korea is a nation divided. The following morning we drive past a monumental example on Gangneung's outskirts – a captured North Korean submarine, proudly displayed like a bloated hunting trophy. The 35m-long vessel, captured in 1996 while spying on military facilities near here, now sits in Unification Park – an outdoor museum dedicated to the Korean War.

Our drive south from here is both pleasant and untaxing: National Road 7 shadows the rugged coast all the way down to Busan and we take our time, snaking through rice fields, forests and mountain tunnels as golden beaches ebb and flow away to our left.

Near Samcheok we stop for lunch and a swim at Maengbang Beach, which looks and feels like a little piece of California. Everything from the lifeguards' Baywatch-style outfits to the perfect white sand, cresting waves and lookout towers screams 'SANTA MONICA'. Everything, that is, except the lifeguard with the megaphone. He screams that the beach is closing, so we

"Very much Seoul's naughty younger sibling, Busan is a hive of activity next to the East China Sea, with mountains, beaches, oceanfront bars and street food"

need to drive on.

The target for our second night is Gyeongju, the 'Golden City' from which the all-powerful Silla dynasty ruled a united Korea for more than 1,000 years. At its peak in the 9th Century, Gyeongju was home to a million people and comparable to the Rome of its day. Now it's an intriguing memory writ large: 'The Museum Without Walls.'

To get into the historical spirit, we spend the night in a traditional wooden *hanok* which, despite involving just a *yo* (padded quilt) and a heated floor for comfort, results in deep and blissful sleep.

Wandering around Gyeongju's pretty temples, palaces and gardens the following morning feels like strolling through the pages of an illustrated fairytale. Chief among the ancient capital's sights – and visible from pretty much everywhere – are the Silla royal tombs. All 56 rulers of the dynasty are buried here, beneath the Korean answer to pyramids, and you can walk freely among these rounded, grass-covered 'tumuli' mounds, which are up to 130ft tall.

Heading for a kimchi hot pot lunch, we pass another extraordinary ancient edifice: Cheomseongdae Observatory. Built in the mid 7th-Century by a Silla queen, this simple-looking tower is really a fiendish stone puzzle, designed to fracture sunlight and moonlight in arcane ways, still being analysed by experts today.

We drive off beneath the watchful eye of the stately Seokguram Buddha, a silent colossus stationed on the hillside above Gyeongju, who has been guarding the Golden City for more than 1,300 years.

From here it's just 50 miles to the south coast and the boisterous port town of Busan. Very much Seoul's naughty younger sibling, Busan is a hive of activity next to the East China Sea, where mountains, beaches, oceanfront bars and street food all mash together to create one of the most enjoyable and underrated cities in the region.

Grabbing a steaming selection of seafood from Busan's sprawling Jagalchi Fish Market (including sea worms – considerably more appetising than they sound), we picnic down on Haeundae, the city's finest beach, and toast the end of our cross-country journey.

South Korea isn't a particularly big country, but it's extraordinarily beautiful, rich and engaging once you leave the familiar international brands and bright lights of Seoul behind. Perhaps it's time to change that Korean proverb: Even if you have to crawl through traffic, get out of Seoul. **JT**

SEOUL FOOD

Some of the best food you'll taste in Seoul is from the street: from food stalls set up in market alleyways to late-night *pojenchmacha* (plastic tent bars) outside subway stations. Food is always freshly cooked and ranges from *bindaetteok* (mung bean pancakes) and *sundae* (blood sausage) to bibimbap or *twigim* (deep-fried battered seafood or vegetables). All make ideal snacks for a late night of bar-hopping, another South Korean speciality.

Clockwise from left: stopping for roadside refreshment; peaches at Maengbang Beach; the coast road; Seoul street scene. Previous page: Jeongdongjin Beach from the Haslla Art World Museum Hotel.

TOOLKIT

Start // Take the Yeongdong Expressway (Route 50) out of Seoul, heading east for Gangneung

End // Route 7 ends on the south coast in Busan's Jung District (literally 'Central District')

Distance // 285 miles (459km)

Getting there // Fly into Seoul's Incheon Airport (ICN), where there are multiple car rental options.

When to drive // Shoulder season. In May and September, South Korea's countryside is bathed in extraordinary colours, but it's still warm enough to swim at the beach. Avoid November-March, when temperatures plummet and snow regularly falls.

Where to stay // In Seoul try staying at a traditional wood *hanok* guesthouse in Bukchon or Ikseon-dong.

More info // www.visitkorea.or.kr

Opposite: the female divers of Jeju harvest shellfish without the aid of oxygen tanks.

MORE LIKE THIS
SOUTH KOREAN DRIVES

JEJU ISLAND CIRCUIT

South Korea's largest island, Jeju is also an extremely popular retreat for mainlanders. Around 2.5 times the size of Singapore, its volcanic crags, plentiful beaches and tropical vegetation have attracted favourable comparison with both Bali and Hawaii.

The best way to explore Jeju is via its coastal ring road, taking 2-3 days to fully appreciate the ancient culture and breathtaking scenery en route.

Start in the island's capital, Jeju-Si, where you'll have no trouble renting a car at the airport, then simply hug the coast either clockwise or anti-clockwise until you return. Jungmun Resort on the south coast is a great place to overnight, and keep your eyes peeled throughout for the island's infamous *Haenyeo* or 'Sea Women', who have been farming the waters off Jeju for centuries.

Start // Jeju-Si
End // Jeju-Si
Distance // 112 miles (181 km)

BUSAN TO GWANGJU

The route from Busan to Gwangju – two of South Korea's most vibrant cities – takes you neatly across the bottom of the country, via Masan, Jinju and Suncheon. A beautifully surfaced road, there are multiple options for short detours off to the left, and the beaches of Korea's southern coast.

Busan is a buzzing port town worthy of a day or two's exploration in its own right, while quirky Gwangju is Korea's art city – full of installations, sculptures and museums. It also has a high student population, making for a vibrant bar and cafe scene, particularly in the narrow alleys south of Hwanggeumgil Street.

Start // Busan
End // Gwangju
Distance // 126 miles (203km)

BAEKSU COASTAL ROAD

One of the most famous drives in Korea, the Baeksu Coastal Road (or National Highway 77 to give its official title), is one of the best ways to explore the lush rural province of Jeollanam-do. This beautiful southwestern province is one of Korea's least developed, and the road takes you through dramatically changing landscapes – from rolling green hills to precipitous coastal cliffs. There are a multitude of beach options en route – as well as hundreds of off-shore islands for those with time for a serious detour. (In particular, check out Dombaeseom Island, famed for its fishing, and Chilsando Island for its extraordinary hiking).

Start // Giryong-ri
End // Sukgumi-maeul
Distance // 10 miles (17km)

THE WINDSWEPT
WILD ATLANTIC WAY

Untamed and utterly divine, Ireland's west coast is a dramatic procession of deserted beaches and towering cliffs where traditional music and ancient castles abound.

A 'savage beauty' said Oscar Wilde and it's certainly true. Ireland's west coast is battered by Atlantic rollers, strewn with jagged cliffs and littered with wide beaches and sandy coves. It's a place where inky lakes shelter between mountains, sinewy stone walls clamber across hillsides and trees are frequently bent double by the wind. The roads here are narrow and winding, grass often grows along a hump in their middle and a herd of sheep can easily scupper all plans.

It's the part of Ireland I love most. I grew up only an hour from the coast but now that I live abroad I rarely get to spend much time here. Trips home are a whirlwind of family gatherings and, despite my best intentions, a stay on the coast never quite seems to happen. But then the contorted back roads, deserted beaches and turquoise coves of my childhood got rebranded as the Wild Atlantic Way: a 1600-mile (2600km) route that traces all the twists, turns and crenulations of Ireland's rugged west coast. I fell for it, hook, line and sinker.

Why take a day trip when I could investigate every little side road and dead end route that I never had time to take? I could wander aimlessly on a set course and just let the incredible landscape unfold along the way.

The route commences on the Inishowen Peninsula in Donegal, which is a remote and rugged place that's also Ireland's most northerly point and an area peppered with traditional thatched cottages, ancient ruins and enormous numbers of birds. Donegal is wild and mountainous and I start out on my journey by meandering down coastal roads past gloriously deserted beaches. I climb the thick walls of the Grianán of Aileách,

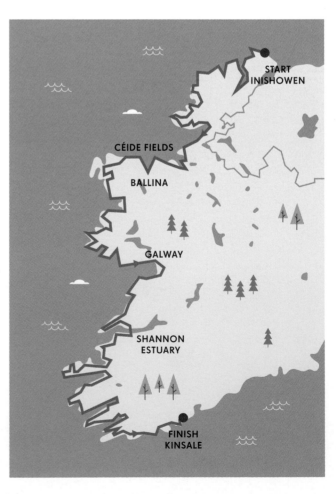

a 2000-year-old circular stone fort perched on a 244 metre-high barren hillside, sit mesmerised by the views of Mount Errigal and marvel at the Slieve League cliffs, which plunge 600 metres down into the ocean below.

Heading south, the familiar, flat-topped monolith of Benbulben soon appears, every bit as beautiful as I remember it. From Streedagh Beach the view is sublime, back to Slieve League and south to mountain tops littered with prehistoric graves. I'm tempted to climb to Queen Maeve's grave but speed off instead to Enniscrone and unwind with a hot and

slippery dip in an Edwardian seaweed bath. I forge on, aware there's a long way to go and little time to linger. I pass the Céide Fields, the world's most extensive Stone Age monument, holler in the wind on the beach at Belmullet and feel the sorrow of the past in Achill's abandoned famine villages.

Impetuous weather and tortuous roads remind me that it's a harsh place to live but it's all forgotten in a blur of colourful good cheer and rousing traditional music in Georgian Westport. I climb Croagh Patrick, Ireland's holiest mountain, and am treated to a clear view of the islands of Clew Bay. I stop for a bowl of steaming Killary Harbour mussels at the head of the moody inlet, see salmon being smoked on the pier at Ballyconneely and watch the sun set over turquoise waters from the idyllic white sands of Dog's Bay.

Vibrant, bohemian Galway soon gives way to the limestone fields of the Burren, the precipitous Cliffs of Moher and the reels and jigs that are a feature of Doolin's pubs. The driving is easy; the challenge is not getting waylaid along the way.

I make my way to places I've only ever heard of on the shipping forecast, where colourful lighthouses pilot ships to safety. In a downpour I remind myself why I set out to do this at all, to reach places just like this, that I would never have bothered to visit otherwise, where dead end roads question my commitment but reward me with incredible views.

I take a ferry across the Shannon Estuary and enter the 'kingdom' of Kerry. I drive Slea Head and round furrowed headlands to see brilliant beaches embraced by rocky cliffs. The Blasket Islands look beguiling but I struggle to see beyond the tales of unrelenting hardship recounted by author and islander Peig Sayers, which are a staple on the Irish school curriculum. I revel in Dingle's traditional pub-cum-hardware shops before blowing away the cobwebs on the sweeping expanse of Inch Beach.

Then it's on to the Ring of Kerry to wind my way around Ireland's highest peaks, Macgillycuddy's Reeks, and past the jagged Skelligs where a 6th-century monastery doubled as Luke Skywalker's secret hideaway in *The Force Awakens*. As I head south from Kenmare the traffic eases away as I make my way along the wonderfully remote Beara Peninsula. Vividly painted fishing villages and farming communities dot the mountainsides, sheep wander everywhere, some even transported to their island home by cable car.

The scenery calms as I make my way through prosperous West Cork and I can feel my journey is almost at an end. I soak up the sun in remote Barleycove before making the final push through picturesque villages with quaint names and bobbing yachts, trendy shops and organic farmers' markets to the narrow, winding streets of Kinsale, where gourmet restaurants tempt me to celebrate the end of this epic journey.

I don't really feel like celebrating, though. Instead of scratching an itch, this invigorating journey has succeeded in opening up a legion of longing. I want to go back again, to do all the things I missed this time around: to hop on ferries to outlying islands, kayak around headlands, hike up mountains, scramble over castle ruins, visit oyster beds and spend however long it takes to learn to surf.

Yes, the rain poured and the wind whipped at my skin at times, but it's only when you've given up on the downpour ever stopping that you appreciate the magic of the clouds parting and the sun lighting up the hillsides. It's only then you realise that there's nowhere quite so beautiful. **EOC**

FRUIT OF THE SEA

Great seafood is one of the consummate joys of driving the Wild Atlantic Way with everything from slick restaurants to cosy pubs and roadside trailers serving succulent lobster, oysters, mussels and salmon straight from the sea. You can forage for seafood with a local guide, visit smoke houses and mussel farms, tour oyster beds or join in a food festival to see how the landscape and customs influence the fine foods the region produces today.

Left: the still waters of Derryclare Lough in Connemara. Previous page: Fanad Head lighthouse, close to Inishowen Peninsula

DIRECTIONS

Start // Inishowen
End // Kinsale
Distance // 1600 miles (2600km)
Getting there // Just across the river from Inishowen, Derry has a small airport but Belfast, 95 miles (150km) away, has more choice. Kinsale is 12 miles (20km) from Cork Airport.
When to drive // April to October when its marginally less inclined to rain.
What to take // Raincoats, wellies, hiking boots, umbrellas, wet suits, an ark; whatever it takes to withstand the changeable weather.
Car hire // At Derry and Belfast airports in Northern Ireland but returning to Cork Airport will incur a hefty fee. It's better to hire and return to the same spot in the Republic.
More info // www.thewildatlanticway.com

Opposite from the top: a pelican colony on the Islas Ballestas, Peru; the Pan-American Hwy near the Nazca Lines

MORE LIKE THIS
COASTAL DRIVES

PAN-AMERICAN HIGHWAY, PERU

With deserted beaches on one side and towering mountains on the other, the southern section of Peru's Pan-American Highway is a dramatic route that takes in everything from pre-Inca history to world-renowned wineries. The road winds its way through coastal desert, tiny fishing villages and colonial-era towns revealing a side of the country few visitors ever get to see. En route you can go river rafting and wine tasting, visit the mysterious Nazca Lines, chill in charming Chala or take a boat trip to the magnificent Islas Ballestas with their sea lions, penguins and boobies. As you head south the landscape becomes harsher until finally, in attractive Moquegua, you edge into the Atacama, the world's driest desert. For safety only drive during the day and fuel up wherever you can.

Start // Lima
End // Tacna
Distance // 767 miles (1234km)

CHAPMAN'S PEAK DRIVE, SOUTH AFRICA

It's less than 10km long and it's a toll road, but it has 114 curves and offers breathtaking views of Hout Bay (the bay, not just the fishing village) and the mountains across the water. Affectionately known as 'Chappies', the Drive was originally built during World War I, but has seen significant upgrading since then. Chappies was a dangerous road at one time; between 1998 and 2000, rock falls caused four deaths and numerous serious injuries. Remediation included a 155-metre half tunnel and various canopies. It reopened in 2003, but the road is still closed in particularly bad weather. Riding or driving Chappies is quite exhilarating: apart from the view and equally spectacular canopies and other protection from rock falls, the road also offers a steep cliffside climb to Chapman's Point below the 593-metre Peak. From there it follows the cliffs until it drops back to near sea level just short of Noordhoek, where it turns inland. On a sunny day this is an unbeatable drive.

Start // Hout Bay
End // Noordhoek
Distance // 5½ miles (9km)

D-DAY BEACHES, FRANCE

The beaches and bluffs are quiet today, but on 6 June 1944 the Normandy shoreline was the destination for more than 6000 Allied ships, the largest armada ever assembled. This part of the French coast will forever be synonymous with D-Day (Jour-J to the French), and is strewn with memorials, museums and cemeteries – although victory was won on the Longest Day, it came at a terrible price. There is no better place to start than the town of Caen and its award-winning Un Musée pour la Paix (Museum for Peace), for an overview of the events of D-Day and its context in World War II, before you head north to the coast itself, to take in German artillery guns, shell craters and the landing points at infamous beaches such as Omaha, Juno and Utah. Standing by the many thousands of graves at locations including Bayeux and Omaha is a stark, somber way to remember those who gave their lives to defeat fascism in Europe.

Start // Caen
End // Utah Beach
Distance // 88 miles (142km)

THE MAGIC CIRCLE

Discover haunting lava fields, wild coastline, powerful waterfalls and majestic ice caps on an elemental journey around Iceland's Ring Road.

t's mid-morning on Iceland's east coast, but it might as well be midnight. Fog cloaks the road, blending land, sea and sky into a spectral grey. Now and then, black peaks materialise from the gloom, and slashes in the cloud reveal sudden glimpses of coastline: rocky cliffs, grassy dunes, wild beaches of black sand. Gulls bank and wheel in the wind.

Wild weather is par for the course on Iceland's Ring Road – or Route 1, as it's designated on highway maps. Circling around the island's coastline for 830 miles (1336km), the Ring Road is an engineering marvel as well as a national emblem, and this year celebrates four decades of service.

Naturally enough, all distances along Route 1 are measured from Iceland's capital, Reykjavík. Even here, among the art galleries and pubs, hints of Iceland's wilder side are easy to find. Looking north across the bay of Faxaflói, a craggy finger of land extends along the horizon, terminating in the snow-capped summit of Snæfellsjökull, used as the setting for Jules Verne's classic adventure tale, *Journey*

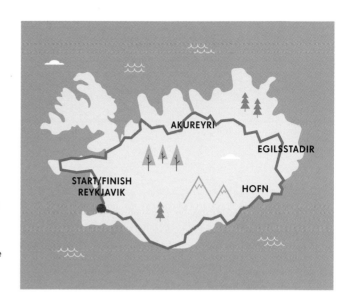

AKUREYRI

EGILSSTADIR

START/FINISH
REYKJAVIK

HOFN

to the Centre of the Earth. The volcano remains a brooding presence as the Ring Road heads north from Reykjavík's suburbs – a reminder that the forces of nature are never far away.

Verne wasn't the first writer to find inspiration among the fjords and valleys of Iceland's west. To Icelanders, this area is synonymous with the Sagas, the tales that are a cornerstone of Icelandic culture. First written down by historians in the 12th and 13th centuries, but rooted in an older tradition of oral storytelling, these tales of family feuds, doomed heroes, warrior kings and tragic romances are part genealogy, part history, part drama.

As the Ring Road swerves inland across the humpbacked hills northwest of Borgarnes, it passes many locations from the Sagas: a farmstead that features in Egil's Saga, a hot spring where the hero of Grettir's Saga soothed his battle-weary bones. While most of the stories are rooted in fact, many have a fantastical streak that stems from Iceland's pantheon of myths and legends: strange tales of trolls, giants and dragons, as well as the island's *huldufólk* (hidden folk) of gnomes, dwarves, fairies and elves.

It's easy to see how Iceland's otherworldly landscape inspired such tales. Sculpted and scarred by thousands of years of geological activity, it often appears not altogether of this world.

Nowhere is this more true than around Lake Mývatn and Krafla, Iceland's most volcanically active area. Here, as the Ring Road drops from the uplands, it loops past Goðafoss (Waterfall of the Gods), a deafening mass of foaming white water that seems to emanate from a ragged crack in the Earth's crust.

"To Icelanders, this area is synonymous with The Sagas: tales of doomed heroes, warrior kings and tragic romances"

The cascade is the prelude to an even stranger landscape. As the Ring Road nears Lake Mývatn's shoreline, shattered boulders and volcanic pillars litter the sides of the highway, the geological remnants of ancient eruptions. Geysers gush and mud pools bubble. Fissures in the earth spew out columns of steam, a reminder that this part of Iceland sits on top of the Mid-Atlantic Ridge, the unstable meeting point of the Eurasian and North American tectonic plates.

As the Ring Road circles around the eastern coast, the landscape becomes wilder and emptier. Isolated villages hunker at the bottom of glacial fjords. Abandoned shepherds' cabins line the roads. Waterfalls cascade down hills, carving canyons through the rock, including the maelstrom of Dettifoss, Europe's most powerful fall.

The east coast has always been isolated, cut off by distance and geography. Prior to the arrival of the Ring Road, many villages were only accessible via mountain passes, which were often snowbound, forcing the delivery of supplies by air or sea. Reaching these villages was a big challenge for the Ring Road's engineers, and required tunnels, embankments and bridges to overcome the topography.

Iceland's most epic playground, the Vatnajökull ice cap, covers 3000 sq miles (7770 sq km) of the country's southeast, making it the

TOLKIEN'S ICELAND

Iceland's legends were an important inspiration for JRR Tolkien, a scholar of Old Norse and the Sagas. Many Tolkien enthusiasts believe Iceland's turf houses, built from peat bricks topped by grass roofs, may have given him the idea for Bilbo Baggins' underground home, Bag End, in *The Hobbit*. They certainly resemble hobbit houses, but they were actually a pragmatic solution to one of Iceland's enduring problems – a shortage of timber.

Left to right: pure-bred Icelandic horses; a characteristic red-roofed church; working the annual sheep round up; Seljalandsfoss waterfall; statue of explorer Leif Eriksson outside Hallgrímskirkja in Reykjavík. Previous page: Þingvellir National Park

largest volume of ice anywhere in Europe. Driving west from Höfn, a small port in one of Iceland's southeastern fjords, the glacier looms along the skyline, a frozen white sea slicing through a jawbone of dog's-tooth peaks.

As the Ring Road leaves Vatnajökull and cuts west, it enters the flat pastureland of Þingvallavatn, and passes two spectacular waterfalls – Skógafoss, one of Iceland's highest, with a sheer drop of 60m, and Seljalandsfoss, where the spray refracts the sunlight like a prism, conjuring rainbows from thin air. Bit by bit, countryside gives way to civilisation. Towns and villages become more frequent, and greenhouses appear along the roadside. This is also equine country, home to numerous farms that raise Iceland's pure-bred horses.

Further west, and a short detour north from the Ring Road, lies Þingvellir National Park. A place of wild beauty, it was here that the Vikings established the Alþing, an open-air assembly and Iceland's first parliament. Established in 930 AD, the Alþing has a legitimate claim as the world's oldest form of democratic government, and holds a deep historical and symbolic significance for Icelanders.

Appropriately enough, the beginning of Iceland's recorded history also marks journey's end for the Ring Road. As it snakes across the magma fields of the Reykjanesfólkvangur nature reserve, it drops down into Reykjavík's suburbs, bathed under streetlights that seem strange after a week of clear skies and starlight. Far ahead across the bay of Faxaflói, the Snæfellsnes ice cap flashes in the evening light, and the Ring Road begins its circular journey north again – a never-ending thread unspooling beneath a silver sky. **OB**

DIRECTIONS

Start/End // Reykjavík
Distance // 830 miles (1336km)
Getting there // Iceland has become far more accessible in recent years, with more flights arriving from more destinations. Ferry transport (from northern Denmark) is a good alternative for Europeans wishing to take their own car.

When to drive // June to August is peak season, with higher prices and bookings required way ahead. This is also endless-daylight season, with plenty of activities and festivals to draw you ever onward. May and September are optimal if you prefer fewer crowds and lower prices over cloudless days.

Hot tip // Don't rush – allocate 10 to 14 days to driving the Ring Road, at a minimum. With just a week to spend in Iceland, concentrate on one or two regions in detail.

Opposite from the top: Montauk
Lighthouse, Long Island; New York
City beach life

MORE LIKE THIS
ISLAND CIRCUITS

LONG ISLAND, NEW YORK, USA

Beginning and ending in New York City, this Long Island loop takes in wide ocean and bay beaches, renowned vineyards, mega mansions and important historic sites. Heading out of Manhattan on the 59th Street Bridge, go east on the Long Island Expressway and Rte 25A right up till you hit the hip and handsome town of Montauk, then return down Long Island's southeasterly coast. Allow around four days to do the circuit, which should mean you can take in highlights such as the near-30 vineyards and unspoilt farmland of North Fork, and the prime examples of beautiful Hamptons real estate at Shelter Island. Consider a detour (on foot) to the car-free slither of land that is Fire Island.
Start // Central Park
End // Coney Island
Distance // 267 miles (429km)

WAIHEKE ISLAND, NEW ZEALAND

Just an hour out of Auckland, Waiheke Island is blessed with its own warm, dry microclimate and has long been a favourite escape for both city dwellers and travellers. The island drive takes in wonderful beaches at Man O' War Bay, and Onetangi, which you'll share with the homes of millionaires, plus an excellent sculpture park at Connells Bay. The bold may also wish to soar above vineyards and native forest at EcoZip Adventures. More sybaritic diversions include the many vineyards – several have restaurants – that evoke a South Pacific spin on Tuscany or the south of France, and irresistible seasonal ice cream at Island Gelato in Oneroa.
Start // Auckland
End // Te Whau Point
Distance // 38 miles (62km)

THE LONG WAY ROUND, IRELAND

Ideally undertaken as a two-week break, this trip explores Ireland's jagged, scenic and spectacular edges, and there's a case to be made that its dramatic coastlines are the very best that the Emerald Isle has to offer. Travelling out of Dublin towards the North, and then circuiting the island's northern, western and southern fringes, here is a journey of splendid scenery, mountain ranges, traditional villages and vibrant urban centres, among them Belfast, Galway, Sligo and Cork. For an island-within-an-island circuit, explore the Arans beyond the desolate beauty of Connemara, and make the seaside village of Ardmore your final destination, as it's one of the southeast's loveliest.
Start // Dublin
End // Ardmore
Distance // 807 miles (1300km)

THROUGH THE GRAPEVINE: ROUTE DES VINS D'ALSACE

On one of France's finest drives, every turn reveals hamlets with storybook appeal, vine-swathed views and open-doored cellars with glasses for tastings at the ready.

I have the peculiar sensation that I've somehow been drafted as an extra on a Disney film set. The village I'm exploring is too ludicrously cute to be true – there are half-timbered, wonky-gabled houses in colours as bright as liquorice allsorts, their window boxes overflowing with geraniums. Storks are balancing protectively on the huge nests they've built atop chimney pots. Cobbled lanes polished smooth with centuries of boot leather weave past patisseries scented with gingerbread and displaying *macarons* in every shade. Beyond the medieval town walls, row after neatly tended row of vines march up hillsides watched over by the hazy Vosges Mountains in the distance.

This is northeastern France, but not as many people know it. Alsace does things a little differently. Sidling up to Germany, it has ping-ponged between the two countries over hundreds of years, finally being returned to the French post WWII. Listen carefully and you'll hear the Germanic cadence of Alsatian, the local dialect. Look carefully and you'll notice the mix of French and German cuisine on menus – *choucroute garnie* (a gutsy dish of sauerkraut garnished with sausage and smoked meats), *wädele* (pork knuckle in pinot noir) and *lewerknepfle* (liver, shallot and parsley dumplings).

Even the oft-blasé French go misty-eyed at the mention of Alsace, considered something of a national treasure for its cross-cultural idiosyncrasies. And the 105-mile (170km) Route des Vins wine route, which corkscrews largely along scenic backroads between Marlenheim – 13 miles (21km) west of Strasbourg – and Thann, is the region's pièce de résistance. It's easy driving; the landscapes are soothingly green and you are never more than a few miles from a village with fairy-tale looks, an excellent restaurant, or a *cave* (cellar) where you are welcome to stop and sample the local wines. Unlike

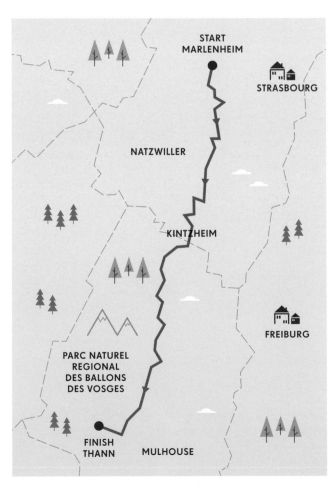

in more prestigious regions like Champagne, say, or Bordeaux, no appointments are usually necessary for a *petite dégustation* (tasting), and the wines on offer are often surprisingly good. At the white end of the spectrum are light, citrusy sylvaners, tangy rieslings, spicy gewürztraminers and aromatic, honeyed muscats. Light-bodied pinot noirs, full of ripe fruit notes, dominate the reds.

Like a fine meal, the Route des Vins is best broken down into several courses and savoured slowly. Stopping overnight not only allows you to see the towns and villages at their lantern-lit best, it also means you can sensibly factor in the wine tastings post-drive.

After a spin of Strasbourg's historic centre and Gothic giant of a cathedral, I'm ready to drive south. It's early autumn and already the vine-draped hills are beginning to turn gold and the scent of new wine is drifting from roadside *caves*. The road wends past sleepy villages that recline at the foot of rolling, low-browed hills. This is gentle countryside that grows on you with its quiet beauty. There are no grand chateaux. The delightfully old-world villages I pass have an air of model railway perfection and they smell like Christmas.

In Obernai, I wander aimlessly in the backstreets of a town where life still revolves around the market square – this one sports a Renaissance-style six-bucket well and a bell-topped corn exchange. I follow a trail that takes me beyond the town walls and up into the vines, and am later rewarded for my efforts with a slab of *zwiebelkuchen* (onion tart) and glass of effervescent new wine at a cosy *winstub* (wine tavern).

Grand cru wines can be found in the nearby village of Mittelbergheim, none of which are finer than those sold at Domaine

COLMAR CHARM

Strasbourg is better known, but Colmar is a delightful base to explore the Route des Vins. Its old town is crammed with half-timbered houses in chalk-box colours, but its canal-woven Petite Venise (Little Venice) quarter steals the show – rent a rowboat in summer. Colmar's other claim to fame is as the birthplace of Frédéric Auguste Bartholdi, the Statue of Liberty sculptor. The Musée Bartholdi (www. musee-bartholdi.fr) is where the legend was born in 1834.

Clockwise from above: grapes ripen on the vine; the canal in nearby Strasbourg; Riquewihr, one of the route's prettiest villages. Previous page: the vast vineyards of Alsace

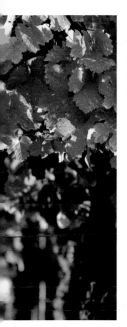

Gilg, hailing from the slopes of Zotzenberg and Moenchberg. The 16th-century stone cellars are their pride and joy, as are their rieslings and sylvaners, which have won many accolades.

Heading on further south brings me to Dambach-la-Ville, another chocolate-box village, this one lined with late-medieval houses painted in shades of pistachio, caramel and raspberry – they look almost edible. Lifted high on a wooded crag above a sea of vines is Dambach-la-Ville's most evocative sight: the nearby 12th-century Château du Haut-Koenigsbourg. A riot of red towers and turrets, it was elaborately rebuilt by Kaiser Wilhelm II in 1908. On cloudless days, the views reach west as far as the bluish-green Vosges and east to the rolling mountains of Germany's Black Forest. Occasionally, if visibility is really good, the faint outline of the Alps is distinguishable to the south.

Competition is stiff for the prettiest town title on the Route des Vins, but the twin settlements of Ribeauvillé and Riquewihr are both as lovely as they come. They brim with history, too – the former with its Pfifferhüs which once housed the town's fife-playing minstrels, and the Tour des Bouchers (Butchers' Bell Tower); the latter with its ramparts enclosing a maze of twisting lanes and half-timbered houses that twist up to the Tour des Voleurs (Thieves' Tower). For an insight into Alsatian wines, I opt to visit the museum and cellars of the Cave de Ribeauvillé, leaving an hour later more the wiser and several glasses of wine merrier.

But it is in the tiny hamlet of Kaysersberg that time really stands still and I get a sense of what makes this region tick. After trying organic wines at Vignoble Klur, I strike out on foot on trails that taper off into the hills, now burnished by the last light of day. Up here I find myself alone, surrounded by row after row of ripening grapes. There is much harvesting still to be done. And though the open road and Colmar await, I'm in no hurry to leave. **KC**

"Stopping overnight allows you to experience the villages at their best and factor in the wine tastings post-drive."

DIRECTIONS

Start // Marlenheim
End // Thann
Distance // 106 miles (170km)
Getting there // Strasbourg (www.strasbourg.aeroport.fr) is the closest airport, served by a raft of airlines. All major car hire companies are represented at the airport.
When to drive // The road is accessible year-round and each season has a different appeal – from summer wine festivals to golden autumn days to the festive sparkle of some of France's best Christmas markets.
Where to stay // The villages on the route all have plenty of hotels and restaurants. Tourist offices can provide details of local *chambres d'hôtes* (B&Bs).
More info // For the lowdown on sights, attractions, hotels and restaurants on the drive, visit www.alsace-wine-route. com. Local tourist offices can supply you with the excellent English-language map/brochure *The Alsace Wine Route*.

*Opposite from the top: terraces of vines
along the Douro River; wine barrels at
Quinta do Pacheca*

MORE LIKE THIS
GRAPE TRAILS

DOURO VALLEY, PORTUGAL

Portugal kept this one up its sleeve
for a long time, but oenophiles have
finally clocked on to the romance – and
increasingly outstanding wines – of
the Douro Valley. The world's oldest
demarcated wine region (in 1756, for the
record) is a real beauty, with mile after mile
of twisting, terraced vineyards that rise
sharply from the Douro River. Its true heart
is the Alto Douro (Upper Douro), a Unesco
World Heritage site. The drive kicks off in
the grand port lodges of Porto, gradually
inching east to the Spanish border. En
route expect to find an abundance of
historic wine estates – Quinta Nova and
Quinta do Crasto are names to remember.
And you'll want to linger at the Casal de
Loivos lookout, where the gasp-eliciting
view over the vines is the Douro reduced
to postcard format. Allow five days to a
week to do the drive justice.
Start // Porto
End // Miranda do Douro
Distance // 222 miles (358km)

CHIANTI ROAD, ITALY

Toscana simply doesn't get more *bella* than
this classic drive on the SR222 through
Chianti country. Linking two great medieval
cities, the road meanders languorously
through gently rolling countryside striped
with cypress trees, olive groves and vines.
After an art and architectural feast in
Florence, it's time to head south to Siena,
crowned by its magnificent cathedral
and 12th-century Piazza del Campo. In
between are honey-coloured hill towns,
where life revolves around the town square,
and is punctuated by the chiming of the
campanile. Stop by *enotecas* (wine shops),
open for tastings of the region's revered
red wines, including Chianti Classico, a
sangiovese-dominated drop. The road
is technically drivable year-round, but is
perhaps at its most photogenic during the
late springtime eruption of poppies and
other wildflowers.
Start // Florence
End // Siena
Distance // 44 miles (71km)

LAVAUX VINEYARDS, SWITZERLAND

Easily doable in a day trip from Geneva, this
short but sublime drive takes in the Unesco
World Heritage-protected Lavaux vineyards,
which stagger up from the northern shores of
Lake Geneva in a series of sheer, stone-
walled terraces that beggar belief. The road
trip along Rte 9 begins in the higgledy-
piggledy French-speaking city of Lausanne
and takes in pretty lakeside towns like Vevey
before swinging southeast to Montreux (of
summer jazz festival fame) and Château
de Chillon, an extraordinary 13th-century
fortress, brought to world attention in 1816 in
Lord Byron's poem 'The Prisoner of Chillon'.
Painters William Turner and Gustave
Courbet subsequently immortalised the
castle on canvas. In the vineyards, pause
at a cave to taste beautiful chasselas white
wines that are crisp, minerally and usually
only produced on a small, artisanal scale.
Lavaux Vinorama in lakeside Rivaz whisks
you through the region's 300 wines and
offers insightful tastings.
Start // Lausanne
End // Château de Chillon
Distance // 25 miles (40km)

THE CÔTE D'AZUR'S THREE CORNICHES

Roll down the roof, slip on the shades and enjoy France's most cinematic drive, from belle époque Nice all the way to the Italian border – and back again.

I t's early morning on the clifftops of the Côte d'Azur, and today, the coast is living up to its name. I'm standing at a roadside viewpoint on the Grande Corniche, and my gaze is fixed out to sea, trying to work out where the sea ends and the sky begins.

The horizon is a rainbow of blues. From pale duck-egg to bright turquoise through to deep aquamarine, it's a blue symphony; a meditation on blue. I find myself thinking of the many artists who've been inspired by this coastline – from Henri Matisse and Pablo Picasso to Yves Klein, who even patented his own colour, International Klein Blue, in 1960.

I stand for a while, breathing in the scents so characteristic of Provence: sweet lavender, pine sap, salty sea air. Then I hop back in my car and set off again along the clifftop road, heading higher into the crimson hills as sea birds hover and the blue Mediterranean shimmers below.

I've come to Provence to tackle France's most famous trio of roads: the Three Corniches, which zig-zag along the Côte d'Azur between Nice and Menton. Named Basse, Moyenne and Grande (Lower, Middle and Upper) after their respective elevations, each road has its own character. The Basse Corniche is the one for hedonists and high-rollers, winding through a

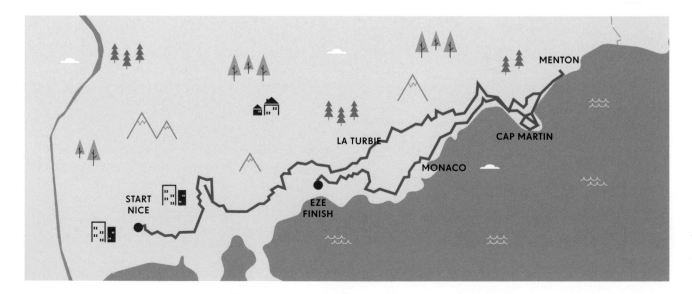

glitzy string of Riviera towns and beach resorts, where the traffic stretches bumper-to-bumper in the height of summer, and life revolves around the cafes, clubs and casinos.

The Moyenne Corniche is something of a quieter affair, meandering between sleepy, sun-drenched *villages perchés* (hilltop villages) where old men sip shots of pastis in streetside cafes, and every evening there's a game of *pétanque* on the village square. Highest and wildest of the three is the Grande Corniche, which climbs to a vertiginous 500m above sea level. It was built by Napoleon I in the 19th century, and memorably provided the backdrop for Alfred Hitchcock's 1955 Riviera caper, *To Catch A Thief*, starring Cary Grant and Grace Kelly. The drops are dizzying, the hairpins are hair-raising and the bends are bottom-clenching, but for driving thrills, no French road can compare to the Grande Corniche.

I set out early from Nice, rolling along the quiet boulevards, past pavement cafes and boulangerie windows stocked with freshly baked croissants and baguettes. I head out into the suburbs of Nice, and pick up the Grande Corniche as it criss-crosses up into the parched Provençal hills. Shrubs and pines dot the hillsides. The white dome of Nice's observatory zips past. Civilisation thins, and the Grande Corniche hits its stride.

It's more rollercoaster than road. It twists and switchbacks along the cliffs, winding through wild forests, surrounded by swathes of tangled maquis, fragrant with wild rosemary and thyme. The hairpins mean that it's essential to keep a close eye

"The Grande Corniche isn't only awe-inspiring, it's ancient, having been in service for at least 2000 years"

on the road ahead, but occasionally I can't resist stealing a glance out to sea, where the Mediterranean sparkles like a mirror in the morning sunshine.

At the little hilltop village of La Turbie, I take a break and wander beneath the great Roman arch known as La Trophée des Alpes. Built by the Emperor Augustus to commemorate his conquest of Gaul in 6 BC, it's a reminder that the Grande Corniche isn't only awe-inspiring, it's also ancient; it's been in service for at least 2000 years. The road largely follows the course of the Via Julia Augusta, which was begun around 13 BC, although the present route was the work of Napoleon I, who ordered its construction to facilitate the movement of troops and supplies during his Italian campaign of 1796.

From La Turbie, I continue east, following the Grande Corniche as it winds down the hillside and joins the Basse Corniche, zig-zagging out along the coast. Wildness gives way to civilisation. Elegant villas and belle époque mansions appear, lined up like dominoes along the shore. Near the Italian border, I feast on seafood in the seaside port of Menton, then make a volte-face west to the pretty headland of Cap Martin, a haunt of ex-pat

THE MONACO CONUNDRUM

At just 0.78 sq miles (2.02 sq km), Monaco is small, but it punches way above its weight. With a population of about 38,000, it's the world's second smallest and most densely populated country. It's a sovereign state, ruled by the Grimaldi family since 1297, with its own flag, anthem and stamps – not to mention lax tax laws. The casino – a favourite of James Bond – is in the harbour district of Monte Carlo.

Left to right: Eze, a sleepy village perché overlooks the Côte d'Azur; lavender from a roadside store; a stone arch bridge on the Moyenne Corniche; roof rolled in Beaulieu-sur-Mer. Previous page: high above the beach at Villefranche-sur-Mer

writers like F Scott Fitzgerald and Ernest Hemingway. Next comes the maze of Monaco, famous for its hedonistic lifestyle and historic casino – not to mention more millionaires per square mile than anywhere else on Earth. Once a year, Formula One drivers descend on Monaco's corkscrew streets for its glitzy Grand Prix, but the rest of the year, it's a tangle of traffic. It's a blessed relief to leave the high-rises behind and climb back into the quiet, rocky hills.

I pick up the Moyenne Corniche as it twists back into wild, barren countryside. I climb steadily, swerving and veering round the road's rollercoaster curves. The evening sun sinks towards the horizon, and dusk begins to fall. Around me, the landscape begins to turn technicolour, blazing with a painter's palette of oranges, ochres, russets and browns. Mist drifts over the coast below, and suddenly it feels more like I'm flying than driving, floating on a sea of silver cloud.

By the time I reach journey's end at the hilltop village of Èze, the sun has almost disappeared. I head for the bar of the Château Eza hotel for a cocktail, and a smartly dressed waiter brings me a martini as I watch the sun snuff itself out in a blaze of terracottas, scarlets, mauves and pinks.

'When I realised that every morning I would see this light again,' wrote the painter Henri Matisse in 1917, 'I couldn't believe how lucky I was.'

As I sip my martini and listen to the breeze stirring through the pines, I know precisely how he felt. **OB**

DIRECTIONS

Start // Nice
End // Eze
Distance // 45 to 50 miles (72km to 80km), depending on the exact route taken.
Getting there // Nice airport has regular international flights to destinations across Europe and further afield.
When to drive // Summer traffic can be a headache; May, June and September are quieter.
What to take // Sunscreen, swimming gear and a stylish pair of sunglasses.
Where to stay // Hôtel Windsor (www.hotelwindsornice. com), Hostellerie Jerôme (www.hostelleriejerome.com), Château Eza (www.chateaueza.com), Napoléon Menton (www.napoleon-menton.com).
More info // Visit www.frenchriviera-tourism.com

Opposite: a view along the
Gorges du Verdon

MORE LIKE THIS
FRENCH DRIVES

TUNNEL DU MONT-BLANC

OK, this one's France with extras! Hop two borders and drive through a mountain on this riveting route between Switzerland and Italy. Drive from Geneva across the French border (direction Annemasse), and you'll see the Alps dead ahead. For a bird's-eye view, stop in Chamonix for a cable car ride up to the Aiguille du Midi (3842 metres). Steep, rocky hills flank both sides of the highway as you cruise towards the Tunnel du Mont-Blanc (tolls are charged). Views of the ice-streaked mountain – towering 4809 metres high – increase in drama as you approach. The tunnel burrows for 7.2 miles (11.6km) from Chamonix directly beneath Mont Blanc. You'll emerge in Courmayeur, gateway to Italy's Aosta Valley. Some 22 miles (35km) beyond Courmayeur, rest your weary car engine in Aosta: a town of Roman ruins and aqueducts, and a welcoming base for skiers. The high-adrenaline roads are maintained throughout winter.
Start // Geneva, Switzerland
End // Aosta, Italy
Distance // 84 miles (135km)

THE CÉVENNES

In 1879, Robert Louis Stevenson (of *Treasure Island* fame) documented an epic, and hilarious, hike through the hills of the Cévennes in the company of a recalcitrant donkey known as Modestine. These days you can trace part of his route by car, starting in the village of St-Jean-du-Gard (Stevenson's end point), and climbing up through the forested hills to Florac. From here take a cliffside spin along the craggy Gorges du Tarn to Millau, which is set among the strange, stark plateaus known locally as *causses*. The scenery is wild, wooded and gloriously empty – except in July and August, when half of France seems determined to take a holiday here, and the traffic jams can be horrendous. Come in spring or autumn, and you'll have it all to yourself. End the drive with a cruise over the Viaduc du Millau, the highest bridge in the world (no donkeys allowed).
Start // St-Jean-du-Gard
End // Viaduc du Millau
Distance // 88 miles (142km)

GORGES DU VERDON

Cutting a 15-mile (25km) swath through the limestone hills of Provence, France's answer to the Grand Canyon makes for a truly unforgettable day's drive. The usual route begins in the hillside town of Moustiers-Ste-Marie, and creeps around the edge of the gorges, at times teetering above sheer cliffs that are nearly a kilometre high. There are roadside viewpoints galore, and several optional detours along the way, such as the Rte des Crêtes, a 14-mile (23km) loop with 14 lookouts. Keep your eyes peeled for eagles and vultures – and if you haven't got a head for heights, don't look down.
Start // Moustiers-Ste-Marie
End // Castellane
Distance // 54 miles (87km), including the Rte des Crêtes

ROVING THE BALTIC: ESTONIA TO LITHUANIA

Take a drive through the crossroads of several mighty European powers: the Baltic countries twist their own brand of Northern culture with a history steeped in millennia.

At a dinner in Riga over a decade ago, as I pushed around a slab of grey pork and side of boiled potatoes, I learned that the Latvian language – one of the oldest tongues still spoken on the planet – had no word for 'mountain'. The term *kalns*, or hill, serves as the best substitute, as there are no true mountains in the entire region – no borrowed term has been added to the local lexicon. And there's really no need for one: from cobbled alleys of coastal Tallinn to the desolate recesses of the Curonian Spit, the entirety of the Baltic shield is blanketed by an undulating current of towering pine.

The green carpet – unbothered by the brutal winter weather – seems uniform from the car window year after year, no matter how many times I return to visit. But a turn onto a lonely side road reveals thousands of years of fascinating geopolitical history.

Sure, Tallinn, Riga and Vilnius, the triad of Baltic capitals, each stir their own brew of old-meets-new, but it's the countryside – the veritable battlefields of both ancient and modern empires – that narrates a more nuanced history of subjugation and glory.

Latvia's largest national park, the Gauja, follows its namesake river as it snakes between tribal war mounds and medieval castle ruins; I do the same. Subtle bumps in the terrain mark the strongholds of the tribes that waged war in the region over 2000 years ago – archaeologists have uncovered old stones from other parts of the planet lending credence to the notion that the area was an epicentre of global trade.

A rich medieval history comes to life at the rosy-red tower of Turaida Castle and at the ashen stone spires of Cesis castle. In Sigulda, I spot my first Soviet relic – a cluster of tenements and a strange ribbon of concrete. In the cities, the austerity of the

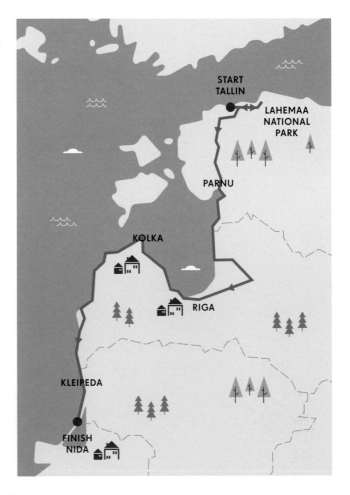

architecture seems like an unassuming patch of the urban quilt, but in the forest, surrounded by swatches of deep greens, the structures are shockingly dour.

It was in Sigulda that the Soviet bobsled team trained for international championships, like the Olympics. The facility was abandoned after the fall of the USSR, and today local business owners offer introductory spins on the track with various sleighs.

Following a stomach-churning ride down the concrete corkscrew, I meet up with a friend-of-a-friend who has invited me to his *pirts* (sauna). Like the Finnish, Estonians and Latvians have an elaborate and enthusiastic sauna culture, but without any of the modesty assigned to the ritual by other Western nations.

After a hardy shake of hands, my friend-of-a-friend strips to his birthday suit and lies upwards on the thin birch planks of his pond-side sauna. I follow and an older woman, the sauna master, immediately enters the chamber holding bushels of dried twigs and flowers. What follows is a choreographed dance – almost in nature – as she swishes her branches through the air to raise the humidity then beats us with garlands to open our pores. The branch-beating session lasts some 15 minutes, after which I'm grabbed by the arm and tossed in the chilly lakelet out the door. Lather, rinse, repeat with a splash of vodka and some cured meats, and by the end of the afternoon I feel fully indoctrinated into the Baltic way of life and ready to continue my journey.

The trees continue to march on like noble warriors, save the odd clearing marking a cool, dark lake in the near distance, until suddenly the crash of the frigid Baltic Sea breaks their stride. The

LITGATNE BUNKER

In Latvia's pine forests lies one of the most compelling artifacts from the Soviet Era, lending the land's dystopian history some context. Discovered early this century in the basement of a convalescence home, the nuclear shelter was to protect the highest officials of the Union. And no item has been changed since the 1980s: propaganda scrawled on the walls, levers in the control room, and one single bed – for the senior commandant.

Clockwise from top: Tallinn's colourful facades; blue skies over a Baltic beach; the skyline of Tallinn from Toompea Hill. Previous page: Turaida Castle above the Gauja River

seaside enclave of Jurmala softens the transition between worlds with its cottage architecture and art nouveau flourishes. In the summer months the beach teems with day-tripping Rigans, but out of season the veneer fades on the holiday town, and the so-called sanitariums lie bare along the coast like beached cruise liners.

Latvia's coastline swerves up to a point at Kolka where the Baltic Sea meets the Bay of Riga. A line, where the purple seas lap over the clearer waters of the bay, can be seen from the haunting sea stacks formed by faraway timber. The area was strictly off limits to civilians during the Soviet occupation, and therefore feels lost in time, save the odd concrete wartime watchtower along the shore.

The Cape of Kolka is the indigenous territory of the Livs, or Livonians, one of the ancient regional tribes that guarded their land claims with the legendary ferocity of the Vikings. Today, only a handful of ethnic Livs remain – fewer than a dozen are native speakers – their sea-blue eyes catch your attention as they tend to the small cottages and fish-smoking shacks along the shore.

The solitude of the cape crescendos with activity as I pass through seaside towns. In laid-back Pavilosta locals are zipped to the neck in neoprene, battling the Baltic waves on their kiteboards. Further on, grungy Liepaja provides interesting contrast, with its roaring nightclubs built in old port-side warehouses.

Then the road quite literally comes to an end on the Lithuanian side of the border, and suddenly the Baltic's trademark pines are gone – replaced with a landscape so severe that it feels almost Soviet in nature: a desert. Small vacation villages with adorable chalet-style architecture have popped up where the sand meets the sea, but the vast expanse of dunes, seemingly ripped from the depths of the Sahara, always make me wonder what's more surprising: the lack of Baltic vocabulary for 'mountain' or the fact that locals have seven words for 'desert'? **BP**

"The area near Kolka was strictly off limits to civilians during the Soviet occupation and feels lost in time"

DIRECTIONS

Start // Tallinn, Estonia
End // Nida, Lithuania
Distance // 948km (589 miles)
When to drive // June is the optimal month for travel, when the three Baltic nations embrace their pagan roots with celebrations held around the summer solstice; July, August and September remain delightfully busy along the coast as well.
Where to eat // Tallinn offers plenty of hipster hangouts: start with Must Puudel (the Black Poodle); in Riga try upmarket Vincents, which pioneered the down-to-earth food movement that supplanted pork and potatoes and put Latvia on the culinary map.
What to take // Much of the terrain between towns is undeveloped tracts of land, which lends itself well to some blissful camping experiences – pack all the accoutrements for a summertime tenting adventure.

Estonia to Lithuania

Opposite from the top: dawn at Mont
St-Michel; the skyline of Charleston,
South Carolina

MORE LIKE THIS
WAR HISTORY DRIVES

NORMANDY & BRITTANY, FRANCE

In much the same way that castle ruins and crumbling tenements cut the pristine pine forest of the Baltic, spartan watchtowers and solemn cemeteries haunt the idyllic coastline of Normandy and Brittany. A drive around France's northwest reveals some of its most iconic destinations, like the demi-island Mont St-Michel, and the quintessential Breton township of St-Malo. The area embraces roots that predate the nation's union. But the rocky coastline famed for its dramatic tides and purple-pink twilight also reveals some of the biggest scars from WWII.
Start // Caen
End // St-Malo
Distance // 182 miles (293km)

THE AMERICAN SOUTH

Warm hospitality and soul food brighten any road trip in the southern United States – the 'other America' best explored by Eisenhower's interstate highways connecting hubs below the Mason-Dixon Line. Sites such as the Fort Sumter National Monument near Charleston, South Carolina, or the Antietam National Battlefield near Sharpsburg, Maryland are reminders that the country isn't blanketed in a single definition of America, but a patchwork of values, customs and cultures. The Civil War occurred in the early 1860s; its series of bloody battles moved steadily from the Deep South up towards the Union states, costing more than 600,000 soldiers their lives in four years. Richmond, Virginia, was the capital of the Confederacy and is filled with relics to retell the story of the war. Finish in Gettysburg, Pennsylvania, famed as the site of Abraham Lincoln's 1863 address, but also the place that marked the turning point in the war when General Lee could first see that the South's campaign would end in surrender.
Start // Charleston, South Carolina
End // Gettysburg, Pennsylvania
Distance // 660 miles (1062km)

SCOTLAND

A separatist sentiment and an assertion of independence has long been the hallmark of the Scottish vis-à-vis their British neighbours, and dozens of ruins mark the fights for freedom over the centuries. A drive through the highlands is one of the most breathtaking road trips in its own right, but marrying the ethereal landscape to its storied past enhances the experience. Fittingly, the Wallace Monument marks the area where the Scots earned their first decisive victory against the English – Stirling Bridge, a narrow pass that split the English forces in two just before the start of the 14th century. Locations of several important battlegrounds inscribed in the history books remain a mystery, but Glencoe has become mainstream due to James Bond *Skyfall* fame, and Culloden, near Inverness, is a handsome reward for intrepid road trippers travelling to the Isle of Skye and beyond.
Start // Stirling
End // Inverness
Distance // 234 miles (377km)

CROATIA'S ADRIATIC HIGHWAY

The Adriatic Hwy stretches nearly 400 miles (643km) along Croatia's coast and provides a front-row seat for 1185 islands, an embarrassment of cultural riches and slow-food prowess.

My first brush with Croatia came 20 years ago on the Jadranska Magistrala, or Adriatic Hwy, which hugs the country's shoreline from Rijeka, in the north, to the border with Montenegro. It passes nearly 1200 islands, endless vineyards, Unesco sites, national parks and olive groves. But I knew none of this at the time. I was just cruising the sea. On that initial drive, the two-lane ribbon of tarmac – part of the E65 roadway funnelling into the smaller D8 – unfurled beneath my rented, yellow Fiat as I drove between the Dinaric Alps, a string of jagged limestone cliffs teetering above me on one side, and the sea below on the other. Zen-filled open roads, extending to the horizon, would suddenly give way to white-knuckle hairpins and crawling along in first gear as a rainbow of sailboats appeared on the rocky beach below.

In those nascent days as a travel journalist, my sophomoric goal was to choose one of the many secluded villages and hole up in a writer's bungalow. There I would craft something special to stagger my non-existent editors. Salty fishermen sitting in the sun mending nets while puffing cigarettes would be a bonus. Perhaps skiffs would be scattered along a pebble beach, the deep-blue Adriatic slapping at their weathered sterns. I knew I was in the right place when I had to slow to a snail's pace behind a man, rope in hand, coaxing along his donkey loaded with baskets of grapes.

There were fishermen, by the way. And twice each day I joined the procession of villagers filling jugs with fresh spring water that flowed from a pipe sticking out of a rock wall. During those communal moments, I learned of secret beaches, caves,

and where to go for activities I had, until then, not associated with the recently independent country.

Not much has changed, for me, over the past two decades. Every year I use the Adriatic Hwy for both business, as a journalist, and for pleasure. However, Croatia is no longer such a secret. But, in many ways, the popularity makes this road of slow discovery even more special.

These days, as time-pressed tourists rush to reach their must-see spots, those with a slower pace in mind, travellers in search of authentic adventure, know better.

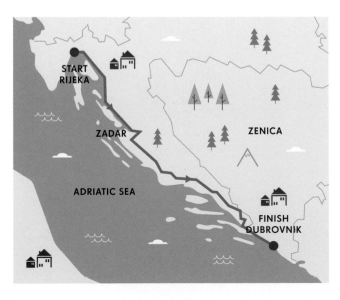

"Five Unesco World Heritage sites crowd the highway, not including the Roman and Hellenic ruins along the route"

'Driving along this highway – or even better, riding on a motorbike – is a great way to experience the diversity of Croatia,' says Veselka Huljic, the general manager of AndAdventure (www.andadventure.com). The Split-based adventure tourism operator offers trips and excursions that include activities such as sea kayaking, hiking and cycling, but specialises in customer-driven, tailor-made tours. 'You can't really get to know the depth of this country until you travel without a schedule,' says Huljic. 'Stop as you please along the coast, take in amazing views of the sea, and hop onto islands to experience culture, the parks, the incredible food and wine. At this speed the country starts to feel like yours.'

Over the years, the Adriatic Hwy has become the ultimate insider reference tool for me as I learned about the country's angles and traditions. It would also be a surefire suggestion for the continuous stream of visiting friends and family.

For instance, the highway provides access to five national parks, which each open a window into the character of the coast. Northern Velebit National Park, with sweeping sea views, is a jumping-off spot for long-distance hikers heading into the Velebit mountains, part of the trans-Balkan Via Dinarica trail running from Slovenia to Macedonia. Paklenica National Park, a confluence of sheer canyons, is a famous climbing destination. Krka takes visitors to some of the continent's most beautiful waterfalls. And the island-based Kornati and Mljet National Parks give travellers a sense of the coast's hallmark remoteness.

Four Unesco World Heritage sites crowd the highway: the Cathedral of St James in Šibenik, the historic town of Trogir, the Diocletian's Palace in Split, and Dubrovnik's walled Old Town. Each offers an insight into the timeline of the Adriatic. And this doesn't even include the Roman and Hellenic ruins strewn along the route with such nonchalance that it's common to pass by people milling about atop ancient blocks. The city of Zadar, for example, acts as an open-air museum with the original Roman forum and streets still in daily use.

For those who have heard that Croatia is a gastronomic wonderland, the Jadranska Magistrala is as much a progressive dinner as it is a road trip. The island of Pag, in northern Dalmatia is the country's sheep's-cheese capital and specialises in a sort – paški sir – that is flavoured by the salty grasses and herbs the animals graze upon. The road then passes through the village of Posedarje, known for its pršut (dry-cured ham). Further south, travellers wheel past the Pelješac Peninsula, where drivers-turned-diners pair oysters, pulled directly from the bay moments earlier, with some of the region's best red wine, from a local variety called plavac mali.

Two decades ago, the tastes and the images and the notebooks filled with illegible chicken scratch stayed with me long after I pulled off the Adriatic Hwy and returned the yellow Fiat rental. I can't remember if I sold a single magazine story from the trip. I know, for certain, that it was the beginning of my life as a writer. More importantly, the drive changed me forever as a traveller. **AC**

REFUELLING

Forget petrol, it is the ingestible liquids on the Adriatic Hwy that will rev your engine and rewire your taste buds. All along the drive you'll see roadside stands selling homemade wine, *rakia* (fruit brandy), olive oil and honey. Sure, you can purchase excellent versions of each in a spiffy, labelled, glass vessel. But don't hesitate to sample the rustic versions sold in plastic bottles. They are as fresh and good as any you'll taste on the planet.

Clockwise from left: sheep on Pag island; Croatia's coast road; Prozura locals; looking over Dubrovnik. Previous page: the beautiful Majarska Riviera, north of Dubrovnik

DIRECTIONS

Start // Rijeka
End // Dubrovnik
Distance // 368 miles (593km)
Getting there // Fly in and out of Zagreb, the inland capital, and then drive or take the bus to Rijeka.
When to drive // Avoid the crowds and visit in the shoulder seasons of May to June and September to October.
How to drive // Head north to south, with the setting sun and all of Croatia's 1185 islands to your right.
Where to stay // There is a bevy of hotels and private homestays. The latter are marked with signs and the word 'sobe' (rooms).
Rules of the road // Learn about Croatia's specific laws and where to look for roadside assistance via the Croatian Auto Club (www.hak.hr).

Opposite clockwise from top: La Rambla, Barcelona; a Spanish bull billboard; the Cabo de Gata park

MORE LIKE THIS
BESIDE THE SEASIDE

ALENTEJO & ALGARVE BEACHES, PORTUGAL

Portugal's southern coasts offer a Mediterranean ideal, with fragrances of pine, rosemary, wine and grilling fish drifting over some breathtaking beaches. Only this isn't the Med, it's the Atlantic, so add surfable waves, maritime history and great wildlife-watching to the mix. Your drive should take in the finest beaches in the region, including the Praia da Amoreira near Aljezur, backed by wild dunes; the remote stretch of whitish sand that is Praia de Vale Figueira; and, towards Faro, the 4-mile (over 6km) Praia da Falésia. Also explore the intriguing towns, particularly old Aljezur, remote Sagres, touristy Lagos and the capital of the Algarve, Faro.

Start // Vila Nova de Milfontes
End // Cacela Velha
Distance // 225 miles (360km)

MEDITERRANEAN MEANDER, SPAIN

From the Costa Daurada to the Costa del Sol, from Catalan pride in Sitges to Andalucian passion in Almería, from the Roman ruins of Tarragona to the Modernisme buildings of Barcelona: this drive proves that not all of southern Spain is a beach bucket of cheesy tourist clichés. Follow the A7 northeast out of cultural highlight Málaga for a 680-mile (1095km) trajectory through four regions, two languages, the buzzing urban centres of Barcelona, Valencia and Malaga, and too many beaches to count. Roman ruins, heavyweight art and great festivals also pepper this cultural coastline. Explore the wild Cabo de Gata for a feel of the Costa del Sol before the bulldozers arrived.

Start // Málaga
End // Barcelona
Distance // 680 miles (1095km)

HIGHWAY 1, FLORIDA, USA

Glittering Miami provides a spectacular finale to an epic coastal trip featuring miles of beaches interspersed with historical sights. Starting from the port of Amelia Island, drive the length of the Florida coast and you'll get a sampling of everything we love about the Sunshine State. You'll find the oldest permanent settlement in the United States in St Augustine – founded by the Spanish in 1565; family friendly attractions such as the visitor complex at Kennedy Space Center; historical curiosities like the Kingsley Plantation at Fort George Island, which offers a fairly unflinching look at slavery; and the Latin flavour of Miami. Plus all those beaches, inviting you to stop as often as you want.

Start // Amelia Island
End // Miami Beach
Distance // 475 miles (764km)

BLACK FOREST HIGHS

Layered with mountains and rippled with mysterious woods, the Black Forest High Road is a drive with altitude, serious curves and scenery straight from a Grimm's fairy tale.

It's like a Christmas card come to life: overnight a fresh layer of snow has blanketed the highest peaks of the Schwarzwald (Black Forest), some topping out at around the 1400m mark. Frosted fir trees glitter in the morning sun, some bent under the weight of ice-laden branches. Down in the valleys, toy-town villages huddle below slender-spired churches and smoke curls from the chimneys of farmhouses, their steep-pitched roofs shingled with wooden tiles. The Schwarzwaldhochstrasse (Black Forest High Road) is quiet at this early hour but, this being Germany, still drivable, *natürlich* – it has been groomed by a snowplough while the world was still fast asleep.

Of all the roads that carve up the Black Forest, the Schwarzwaldhochstrasse, otherwise known as the B500, is regularly touted as being the most beautiful – and with good reason. This is a road with spirit-soaring views and more twists and turns than a pretzel. One of Germany's oldest panoramic drives, the road climbs steeply from the swish little spa town of Baden-Baden to Freudenstadt, 37 miles (60km) distant, running right through the densely forested heart of the Black Forest National Park. At elevations of between 600m and 1000m, the road opens up the landscapes of the Schwarzwald like a pop-up book. Every gear-crunching bend reveals glorious spruce forest on repeat and landscapes plucked from a bedtime story: a gingerbread village, a castle-crowned hillside or a cuckoo clock that's the size of a house. On clear days, the views stretch to the Upper Rhine Plain and the Vosges Mountains over in neighbouring France. And thankfully, this is one of them.

I've chosen a crisp winter day for the road trip and the contrast to the traffic-clogged autobahn is striking. Up here the cars are

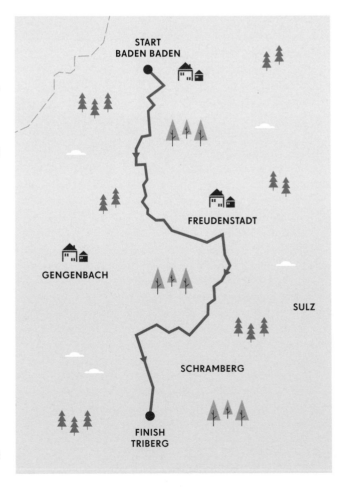

few and far between and the silence is near total. Viewpoints on the road abound as do trails; within just a couple of minutes' walk of the car, I can find myself alone in a forest of tall firs and pines, which sprinkle me with blizzards of snow at the slightest touch. Listening carefully, the only sound I can decipher is the tentative hammering of woodpeckers.

The Black Forest might be easily accessible and family-friendly, but it is also a pocket of true wilderness that can feel properly remote. Some liken the region to Canada in miniature – minus the bears – and they've got a point. The Schwarzwald is lovely at any time of year: in spring when in bud, in summer when the heather flowers up on the high moors and in autumn when the forest goldens and mushrooms pop up in mossy glades. But it is never lovelier than in the monochrome midwinter, when the first snow cloaks the hills that roll west to France and south almost to the border with Switzerland. For it is only really in winter that you can see how the forest earned its name, its dark hills plumed with trees standing out in bold relief, looking black and impenetrable.

Stretching 100 miles (160km) from top to toe and 37 miles (6okm) east to west, the Schwarzwald is not only the Germany of your wildest childhood dreams, it's also blessed with some darn fine road trips, many of which are short enough to squeeze into a weekend of leisurely cruising.

The major attractions on the Black Forest High Road are of the natural kind, such as my first stop: the Geroldsauer Wasserfall, now encrusted with icicles. Beyond the falls, a trail picks its way

"Minutes from the car I am alone in a forest of firs and pines, the only sound the tentative hammering of woodpeckers"

through the woods to the Waldgaststätte Bütthof, which is a tavern full of woody warmth and local characters sipping spiced *Glühwein* (mulled wine) and devouring thick-cut bread topped with smoky *Schwarzwälder Schinken* (Black Forest ham). It's a great stop for a snack before easing back into the drive, which weaves through a delicate fretwork of forest, high moors and gently rounded hills.

I crank up the *Volksmusik* on the radio and drive on to Mummelsee, a forest-rimmed glacial cirque lake full of local legend; the myth goes that an underwater king and nymphs dwell in its inky depths. From the lake, it's just a short hike up to Hornisgrinde, the highest peak in the Northern Black Forest at 1164m. The plateau is quiet but for the occasional swish of a passing cross-country skier disappearing into the twinkling white woods. Daylight is fading swiftly as I crest the summit and gaze across overlapping hills, silhouetted in a sunset that's like the embers of a dying fire.

After a night at the rustic-chic Berghotel Mummelsee on the lakeshore, dawn lifts a curtain on another bright day.

BLACK FOREST FOOD STARS

Four miles (6km) north of Freudenstadt is Baiersbronn. The village may have fewer than 16,000 residents, but it shines with an incredible eight Michelin stars, including two restaurants with three-star status. At Schwarzwaldstube, Harald Wohlfahrt performs culinary magic while staying true to French cooking traditions, while at Restaurant Bareiss, Claus-Peter Lumpp has won plaudits for his brilliant seasonal menus.

Left to right: half-timbered houses in Schiltach; the region is known for its clockmaking; pausing in a forest glade near Wolfach; lush valley near Gutach. Previous page: the hills of the Black Forest beckon

The morning's itinerary is an easygoing one: a visit to the Allerheiligen falls, which stagger over cliffs in a series of cascades. Here a short trail leads through a wooded gorge to a ruined Gothic abbey, its nave exposed to the sky. The onward road takes me past an area that was reforested in the wake of Hurricane Lothar in 1999, a fierce windstorm that whipped through the Schwarzwald at speeds of up to 100mph (160km/h) felling vast tracts of woodland.

The drive officially ends in Freudenstadt which, despite having Germany's largest town square (219m by 216m, for the record), is something of an anticlimax. Heavily bombed in WWII, it lacks the charm of other Black Forest towns. So I push on further south, tagging on an extra couple of days to linger in the horseshoe-shaped Kinzig Valley, lined with half-timbered, candy-coloured villages such as Schiltach, Hausach and Gengenbach – each one prettier than the last.

From the Kinzig Valley, the B33 dips south to castle-topped Hornberg en route to Triberg, where one of Germany's highest waterfalls thunders and the world's biggest cuckoo clock calls on the hour. The town is quite literally the icing on the cake to my road trip. For here is Café Schäfer, home to the original 1915 recipe for *Schwarzwälder Kirschtorte*, or Black Forest gateau. 'Baking a good gateau isn't rocket science, but it takes time, patience and fresh ingredients,' Claus Schäfer tells me, as I try a forkful of the real deal. It is every bit as deep, dark and delicious as the region it hails from. **KC**

DIRECTIONS

Start // Baden-Baden
End // Triberg
Distance // 37 miles (60km) on the Black Forest High Road; 75 miles (121km) including the Kinzig Valley and Triberg.
Getting there // The closest airport is Karlsruhe/Baden-Baden (www.airport-baden-baden.com).
When to drive // The road is accessible year-round, though check weather conditions before setting out. Be prepared for flurries of snow in winter; fit snow chains and winter tyres.
More info // For details of sights, attractions, hotels and restaurants, visit www.schwarzwaldhochstrasse.de. General information is available at www.blackforest-tourism.com.
Visitor centre // The Black Forest National Park (www.schwarzwald-nationalpark.de) visitor centre is in Seebach on the B500. Stop by for maps and information.

Opposite: navigating Norway's Unesco-listed Geirangerfjord

MORE LIKE THIS
DRIVES AT ALTITUDE

GROSSGLOCKNER ROAD, AUSTRIA

There's a reason the Grossglockner Road is often cited as the finest drive in the Alps. The scenery is nothing short of epic on this 30-mile (48km) rollercoaster of a road, with views of glacier-encrusted mountains, waterfalls, forested slopes, jewel-coloured lakes and 4000m peaks on almost every distractingly lovely bend. And what bends! You can't help but marvel at the nerves (and thighs) of steel that cyclists must have to tackle these hairpins. As you climb ever higher to the Edelweiss Spitze (2571m), classic Alpine scenery unravels like the credits of a biker movie. The crowning glory is, of course, the 'Big Bell' of Grossglockner itself, Austria's highest peak at 3798m and its rapidly retreating Pasterze Glacier. Listen out for whistling marmots on the approach to Kaiser-Franz-Josefs-Höhe lookout point. The road is open from early May to early November – weather permitting. Check conditions before heading out.
Start/End // Bruck, Salzburgerland
Distance // 60 miles (96km)

FURKA PASS, SWITZERLAND

Something of a rite of passage for hardcore Alpine cyclists, Switzerland's Furka Pass is also enshrined in motoring legend thanks to its starring role in the Aston Martin/Ford Mustang car chase scene in the James Bond film *Goldfinger*. It's an Alpine pass and a half, with some hairy switchbacks to negotiate and big views of snow-streaked Alpine summits en route to the austere beauty of an otherworldly plateau at 2431m. Park at the Hotel Bélvèdere to glimpse the Rhône Glacier, a swirl of deeply fissured ice that is melting fast, and its shimmering blue ice grotto. Trust us, you don't want to get caught in a snow blizzard on this road, which is off-limits in winter, so it's one to save for a fine midsummer day. Add on a few extra days to explore the Goms Valley – it's picture-book stuff.
Start // Gletsch, Valais
End // Realp, Uri
Distance // 19 miles (31km)

GEIRANGER-TROLLSTIGEN, NORWAY

Not for the faint of heart or nervous of heights, this Norwegian National Tourist Route (Rd 63) is one hell of a drive. Its steep inclines – the average gradient is 9% – helter-skelter hairpin bends and slam-on-the-brakes-and-grab-the-camera views make for terrific slow touring. The Trollstigen, or 'Troll's Path', bombards you with the full shebang of Norwegian loveliness: mountains of myth with names like Kongen (the King) and Dronnigen (the Queen), waterfalls spilling down sheer cliff faces and deep-gouged fjords of bluest blue. The road's pride and joy is the Unesco-listed Geirangerfjord, which scythes its way through lush green slopes that rise to snow-dusted peaks. Drive this one if you dare, but be sure to pick a clear day – the road is usually open mid-May through October, but can close due to snowfall or wet conditions.
Start // Langevatn
End // Sogge Bru
Distance // 64 miles (104km)

IN PURSUIT OF THE TARGA FLORIO, SICILY

Motor racing started on public roads before moving to specialised racing tracks and none of those early road circuits conjures up the magic better than Italy's ultimate test.

The photograph was taken in 1970 and I had no trouble tracking down its location in Campofelice. The coastal town is an easy drive east of Palermo, on the north coast of Sicily. Campofelice di Roccella has a long beach, an important church, a 14th-century castle, and nearby there are the Greek ruins of Himera, but it's what's happening in the street on that Sunday in May that has clearly entranced a large contingent of the local population. Under the building balconies, which I found so easy to identify, the citizens of Campofelice are lining the pavements, leaning out into the street, waving ecstatically, clearly cheering loudly for a local Palermo schoolteacher.

The schoolteacher is Nino Vaccarella and he is hurtling towards them, obviously travelling at something approach warp speed, in a bright-red 600 horsepower Ferrari 512S – and he is in the lead of the Targa Florio. He didn't go on to win the Targa Florio that year, but he did the following year and again in 1975, when he clinched his third Targa victory. That 1970 photograph summed up what made the Sicilian sports car race so utterly irresistible: the setting, the enthusiasm and the sheer absurdity of it. You simply do not let people stand in the street, totally unprotected, when racing cars are hurtling past.

From 1906 to 1977, however, the world's oldest sport cars race did exactly that. At first the race was a complete circuit of Sicily, and over the years assorted other routes were tried, but from 1951

the race used the Circuito Piccolo delle Madonie. The Madonie is one of Sicily's principal mountain ranges, and since *piccolo* is Italian for 'little' this was the small racing track in the mountains. The short one, the little track with more than 700 corners. You went around it 11 times if you were going to win the Targa Florio. And although the long straight that stretches along the

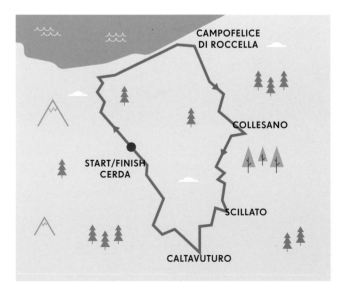

coast towards Palermo might have given Signor Vaccarella the opportunity to push his Ferrari to its maximum speed, all those twisting corners as the circuit climbed up into the hills meant that the fastest anyone ever got around the circuit was an average of just under 80mph (129km/h).

Nino Vaccarella, now in his 80s, still turns up at historic motoring events to demonstrate the fire-breathing racing monsters of his heyday. Although he did drive in a handful of Formula 1 Grand Prix races, sports cars were his speciality, when he could get away from his day job: teaching accounting. He won all sorts of races, including the Le Mans 24-Hour-Race, but it was the Targa Florio where he was always the popular favourite. When he crashed his Ferrari into a wall and out of the race in 1966, 'Viva Nino' was graffitied on the wall he hit.

From Campofelice, where I tracked down that evocative motor racing photograph, it's about 6 miles (10km) along the coast to where the track turns sharp left and starts to climb – and twist and turn – from sea level towards the town of Cerda at 272 metres. Cerda was the start and finish point of the Targa Florio; on such a narrow winding track it was impossible to start the cars together so, like the Mountain Circuit Tourist Trophy (TT) motorcycle track on the Isle of Man, the cars started one by one, 15 seconds apart. The starting order was often a confusing jumble, but even if they didn't all start together there would soon be plenty of racing on the road. The pit counter still stands beside the old starting line, and manufacturers still like to bring their latest creations down to the track to try them out. The

SICILIAN PIT STOPS

Casale Drinzi, which is just a short stroll out of Collesano, features an acclaimed Slow Food restaurant that serves hearty Madonie mountain specialities on the menu and pizzas at night. If you've imbibed too much Sicilian wine there are also B&B rooms available. With Casale Drinzi's food, wine, architecture, old churches, history and beautiful Sicilian mountain scenery, motor racing almost comes as something of a surprise bonus.

Clockwise from top: the town of Collesano; central Palermo; Mondello beach, Sicily. Previous page: Luigi Tarramazzo's Ferrari 250GTO takes a bend in the 1964 Targa Florio

impossibly beautiful countryside with its photogenically perfect driving roads certainly helps.

If the road wasn't already torturous enough, from Cerda it really beings to corkscrew as it hairpins its way up to Caltavuturo, the 'Fortress of Vultures,' at 635 metres altitude. From the coast the track has been running south, but now the route turns north and starts the descent back towards the coast, dropping down through Scillato and Collesano at 468 metres before the final breakneck plunge down towards the sea. Collesano has Greek and Arab historic connections, the remains of a Norman castle and an assortment of interesting churches. It also boasts the official Targa Florio Museum, which features a model of every race winner.

Targa simply means 'plate' and the plate in question was presented as a prize by Vincenzo Florio, a wealthy Sicilian businessperson, wine merchant and fast car enthusiast. The name lives on in the Targa Tasmania, an annual race around the Australian island state, and in every Porsche 911 Targa to cruise Rodeo Drive in Los Angeles or the King's Rd in London's Chelsea. Porsche was a Targa Florio specialist; it won the race 11 times, although that's only once more than Alfa Romeo.

In the Targa Florio's racing days, drivers would often practise when the road was open to everyday traffic, and dodging wayward donkeys was part of the fun. But with so many corners to memorise, regular racing practice time was clearly inadequate. The Circuito Piccolo delle Madonie is still a wonderful road to drive, although you're obviously not going to do it in anything like the sub-34 minute lap record. Two hours and seven minutes is the suggestion from Google Maps, an average speed of just over 20mph (35km/h). Given the 700 corners, the twists, the turns, the climbs, the descents... that's probably quite fast enough. **TW**

"In the Targa Florio's racing days, drivers would practise when the road was open to traffic – donkeys included"

DIRECTIONS

Start/End // Cerda, Sicily
Distance // 45 miles (72km) and – apart from 5 miles (8km) along the coast, good for 200mph (322km/h) when the roads were closed – it's all either corkscrewing uphill or twisting and turning down.
Getting there // Palermo, the capital of Sicily, which welcomes frequent flights from all over Europe and plenty of ferry services from other Italian ports, is just 31 miles (50km) to the west.
When to drive // Avoid summer crowds or go very early: venturing out at dawn for a pre-breakfast Targa lap is recommended.
What to drive // A Porsche or an Alfa Romeo are totally appropriate, but in Italy, for anything requiring some speed, a Ferrari can't be beaten.
Where to stay // Lots of excellent little hotels along the coast or in the mountain villages.

*Opposite: a 1922 Fiat 501 S in
the 2015 Mille Miglia rally*

MORE LIKE THIS
RACING CIRCUITS

CANNONBALL RUN, USA

The 1973 oil crisis took maximum speed limits away from the US and introduced the 'double nickel': no one could travel at more than 55mph. Clearly Brock Yates saw that coming and dreamt up the Cannonball Run, the 'Sea-To-Shining-Sea Memorial Trophy Dash'. The rules were simple: you started from the Red Ball Garage on Manhattan anytime on the starting date and drove to the Portofino Inn on Redondo Beach, not far south of LAX Airport. In 1971 Mr Yates, assisted by Formula One driver and Le Mans 24-Hour-Race winner Dan Gurney, completed the trip in 36 hours at an average speed of 80mph (129km/h), slightly slowed by snow in the Rockies and sorting out his only speeding ticket – for doing 135mph (217km/h). The record is currently just under 29 hours.
Start // Manhattan
End // Pacific Ocean
Distance // 2863 miles (4608km)

SNAEFELL MOUNTAIN COURSE, ISLE OF MAN, UK

Since 1911, the world's oldest motorcycle race has taken place on the Snaefell Mountain Course. The circuit has been raced by cars and bicycles, but it's famous for the Tourist Trophy (TT) motorcycle races. The roads are closed for the TT from late May to early June, but any other time you can cruise out of Douglas, the capital of the small Irish Sea island, and follow the course through assorted pretty little villages up to the top of the Snaefell mountain road at 1385ft (422 metres) before plunging back downhill to Douglas. Hopefully at far less than the 134mph (216km/h) average speed of the current lap record. Apart from being very very fast, the mountain course is also very very dangerous. Country stone walls mean that falling off is never a good idea; more than 250 riders have been killed.
Start/End // Douglas, Isle of Man
Distance // 38 miles (61km)

MILLE MIGLIA, ITALY

Starting in Brescia in northern Italy and heading south to Rome and then back to Brescia, the Mille Miglia covered 1000 miles. Miles, real miles, not those newfangled kilometres. It ran between 1927 and 1957, attracted up to 5 million spectators and was finally halted because far too many people – spectators more than drivers – had been killed. The classic Mille Miglia win was by British driver Stirling Moss in a Mercedes-Benz 300 SLR in 1955. His co-driver Denis Jenkinson – later famous as motor racing journalist 'Jenks' – read out instructions like a human version of a modern satnav from an 18ft roll of paper. Their average speed of just under 100 mph (161km/h) was never beaten. Today the Mille Miglia survives as an annual rally for cars from 1957 or earlier that have a connection with the original race.
Start/End // Brescia
Distance // 1000 miles (1609km)

A DAY ON THE BELFAST LOOP

Often overlooked for the classic cliffs and loughs of the Irish Republic, the lonely shores of Northern Ireland might just be the perfect day-tripping antidote to Belfast's urban core.

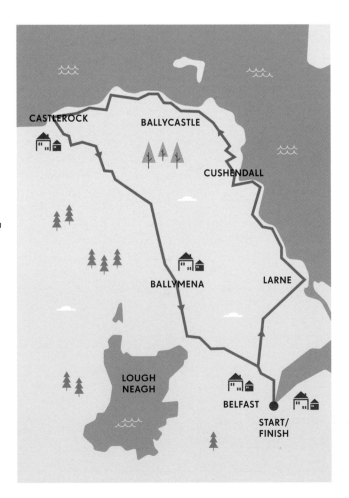

ere's our best of the day,' the waiter says, pushing a porcelain dish across the table. 'We usually send the megrim to Portugal or Spain, but every so often we keep some of the finest catches for our customers.' I gently tuck into the white fish and glide my forkful through some tapenade. Moments later, barefoot in the sand, I toe the clear, curling tide as it rolls towards me, in the same gingerly manner with which I approached my lunch.

I need to rub my eyes. The beach is broad and filled with bathers, and the sea Caribbean-clear – but I'm not on a tropical island, I'm staring down the public beach in Portstewart along the upper crest of Northern Ireland. The cloudless weather seems more unlikely than it does unseasonable, forever turning my prejudiced imagination of a realm of beiges and grey into a vibrant scene of lapis and green like the one that lays before me.

For many, I would think, the small seaside town of Tudor-style row homes feels like a daytripper's coda along the coastal road due north of Belfast. But as I furiously inhale my honeycomb ice cream before it succumbs to the summer's heat I find myself strangely enraptured by my mini road trip's 'in-between' experiences.

From Belfast, the so-called Causeway Coastal Route is a world-in-one circuit easily completed in a day's journey. It is, by design, a path to its namesake attraction, Giant's Causeway – a Unesco World Heritage Site of mythic hexagonal stone located about two hours away when following the seaside roads.

But as I begin the drive, it becomes immediately apparent – despite my urgency fuelled by years of ogling moody snaps of Giant's Causeway on Instagram – that it will take me far longer than a couple of hours to reach the intended destination. Each

© Greg Sinclair | 500px

"Road signs advertise the Dark Hedges ahead — one of the many recesses of Ulster made famous by Game of Thrones"

swerve on the coastal route begs me to turn off the road and explore its tangential attractions. And several times the road succeeds.

After Larne, stony cliffs – like fortress walls – flank seas for nearly 100 miles, breaking only nine times where deep glens burrow a verdant path to the countryside. Each valley, collectively known as the Glens of Antrim, promises a distinct and unique vibe, further exaggerated by the fickle North Atlantic weather casting a cloak of fog over one village while bathing the next in sun.

In Glenarm I pause to wander through the preserved village. In Carnlough, I have lunch along the scenic harbour, and in Glenariff I follow the boardwalk path through the lush, boggy forest to an inland constellation of secret waterfalls.

While the valleys are steeped in story (as locals will endearingly remind you in an unsolicited fashion) the ruins further north at Dunluce best bring the legends of sword-brandishing heroes to life. Built circa 1500 by the MacQuillian clan, the stronghold passed through several ruling parties until it became the County Antrim earls' seat in the 1600s. Perched on the cliff's edge, the gables of old stone are said to have inspired C.S. Lewis' *Chronicles of Narnia*.

Of the many other stops on the way to Giant's Causeway, Carrick-a-Rede is worth the longest detour, as it's only from here that one can fully appreciate the awesomeness of the Irish bluffs from below. A thin rope bridge connects the mainland to a rocky islet offshore that's home to soaring razorbills and kittiwakes. On a clear day, every crack and crevice of the cliffs are easily discerned, as are the Scottish islands skulking above the horizon in the distance.

I can feel the anticipation in my throat as I follow the final signs for Giant's Causeway, and seeing the rocky outcrop for the first time feels like one of those strange moments in travel when you can't help but weigh a big-ticket destination's worth against its hype. The counterculture of modern travel, too, further eschews classic attractions for local, un-touristy points of interest.

I clamber down Shepherd's Steps with the basalt stone rising like organ pipes around me – even more impressive than I'd imagined. From far away, the latticework of strange smooth stones resembles the scales of a beast sleeping along the water's edge. According to legend, the collection of rocks was created by giant hero Finn McCool to fight Benandonner, another giant from Scotland across the straight – a colourful reimagining of the scorching volcanic activity that carved up the area 50 million years ago.

After an hour of hopping from stone to stone like an frog leaping between obsidian lily pads, I find my way back to my car ready to turn inland back to Belfast. Road signs advertise the Dark Hedges up ahead – one of the many recesses of Ulster County now famous as a backdrop for the TV phenomenon *Game of Thrones*.

The infinite summer sky, however, encourages me to push on, just a little bit more down the shoreline to Portrush and perhaps all the way to Portstewart. Although no longer coasting through the 'in between' Belfast and Giant's Causeway, I continue on in search of more serendipity, rumours of fresh fish, soft sand, and perhaps even some honeycomb ice cream. **BP**

HIDDEN GEMS

It's not apparent when you zip through the coastal village of Glenarm that one its local businesses, Steensons, is responsible for some of the jewellery featured on *Game of Thrones*, such as Daenerys' dragon brooches and Lannister's lion pendants. Fans of the show can grab their own pieces, made from the same moulds as the originals; the perfect souvenir after touring the sites where many pivotal scenes of the series were shot.

Clockwise from left: local langoustines; the beech trees of the Dark Hedges road at Ballymoney; the Causeway coast road. Previous page: the Giant's basalt columns

DIRECTIONS

Start // Belfast
End // Belfast
Distance // 143 miles (230km)
Getting there // Fly into Belfast International Airport.
Where to stay // Splurge on Belfast's Merchant Hotel (www.themerchanthotel.com) set in a refurbished bank.
When to drive // Summer months offer the best chance for cloudless weather and Caribbean-clear waters offshore.
Where to eat // Try fresh fish at Harry's Shack in Portstewart, then top it off with some honeycomb ice cream at Morelli's down the street; or enjoy steaks and tunes at Berts Jazz Bar in Belfast.
What to take // Even in just one day the weather can be fickle – pack layers. And don't forget your zoom lens for cross-glen photo opps.

239

A Belfast Loop

*Opposite: equipped for adventure
in Acadia National Park*

MORE LIKE THIS
ESCAPES FROM THE CITY

PORTLAND, MAINE

Portland is quaint by any American standard, but in Maine – tucked in the United States' northeast corner – it's a metropolitan centre and a veritable base camp from which to explore the so-called Downeaster shoreline of rocky outcrops and lonely lighthouses. The vistas become more dramatic and amplified as the road slides north towards the Canadian Maritimes, and tiny fishing towns perfectly punctuate the ride, providing room for pause (and plenty of lobster rolls). Pull over in Brunswick, Bath, Rockport and Camden – and finish the day in Bar Harbor, famed for its storybook charm and backyard trailheads that wind through Acadia National Park. The drive is best undertaken during the summer months when the constellation of villages bursts to life with festivals, boat tours and seasonal eateries run by a coterie of noted chefs who are escaping the big smoke.

Start // Portland
End // Bar Harbor
Distance // 156 miles (251km)

DUBLIN, IRELAND

The Emerald Isle is synonymous with its misty cliffs, but the rugged mountains of the interior are just as prone to those perfect #nofilter snaps on Instagram. Leave the gothic streetblocks of Dublin for Wicklow Mountains National Park, where stony peaks hide quiet loughs and windless forests of beech and pine. Thread the mountain pass at Sally Gap and wend your way through the Glenealo Valley – another realm of sacred stones, crumbling relics and flowing rivers. Follow the mirror-like lakes to find the way west towards workaday Portlaoise, or double back to the coast for a leisurely ride back to the capital. Coastal riders on the return leg shouldn't miss a stop in Bray at the very end of the day to visit the Harbour Bar for tea or tipples, and a some of the best local music around.

Start // Dublin
End // Portlaoise
Distance // 85 miles (137km)

SYDNEY, AUSTRALIA

There are few cities in the world that are more dramatically sited than Sydney, with its picturesque communities spilling over a dramatic series of bays shaped like a row of crocodile teeth. But a drive north out of Australia's largest city leads to an inlet – Port Stephens Bay – of even greater splendour. Pass dramatic dunes and quiet palm-flanked waters, then pause in the tiny coastal towns of Shoal Bay and Anna Bay for the genuine smiles of small-town Oz; you'll reach Nelson Bay at the end of the day for whale watching and dinner along the waterfront promenade.

Start // Sydney
End // Nelson Bay
Distance // 134 miles (215km)

WINDING UP ON NORWAY'S WEST COAST

Norway may not be the cheapest country for a drive, but the upside is you will mostly have its majestic beauty and prize-winning roads to yourself.

Norway means 'narrow way through the straits', rather apt, given the mighty glacial fjords that lacerate its western coast. Admittedly there's not much that's spellbinding as I roll north out of Bergen. The majesty comes later; for now I'm passing the engineering workshops and other small factories serving the oil and gas industry that has made the city rich – again. The charming buildings that surround the harbour are a reminder that Bergen was a successful business centre for many centuries, going back to its days as a Hanseatic port.

I'm riding out in the wonderful, slightly watery, sunshine typical of Norway. As I follow the fjord first east and then north before turning inland again to Voss, the rugged, often vertical countryside begins to work on me, raising thoughts of Vikings and moody gods.

Norway's roads, bridges and tunnels are sparkling examples of their builders' skill and tenacity, but they shrink to scratches on the mile-high cliffs if you look up a little. Whoops! Not enough attention on the road and a long frost break is trying to turn my front wheel

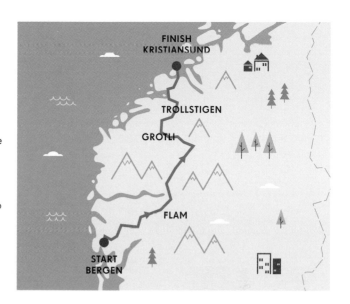

into oncoming traffic. Norway's main roads are excellent, but not all back roads survive the brutal winters unscathed.

I turn north at Voss and then take Stalheimskleiva, the loop of road which runs between two waterfalls and offers 13 hairpins on its mile-long 20-degree climb to the eponymous hotel. It took seven years to build the whole 6 miles (10km) of road, finishing in 1849. The view towards Gudvangen from the hotel is spectacular, with near-vertical cliffs boxing in the narrow green valley bottom.

Not far past Flam, I face a decision. Carry on straight ahead through the world's longest road tunnel, a 16 mile (28km) marvel, or take the old road across the top? I've ridden through the tunnel before, so the choice is easy. I don't regret it. There are deep snow banks alongside the 30 mile (48km) stretch of narrow, steep and twisting road but its surface is clear and tempts my inner boy racer.

Back at sea level I am speeding along one of the tentacles of Sognefjord. I cross it on a ferry and turn west along its shore before another ferry takes me across to Dragsvik and on to the E39 main road. It's an intoxicating run north and east from here, always either alongside a fjord or crossing a rocky range by hairpins, smooth, long curves and regular blinks of tunnels.

At Grotli I turn west again, and after following the waterside for a while, climb back up to the high, icy country that interrupts the fjords. The drop back down to sea level at Geiranger is a superb stretch of road, which deservedly won a prize at the 1924 World Expo in Paris. Climbing back up from Geiranger is just as impressive. This is Ørnesvingen, the Eagle's Road, and it has a wonderful lookout like a long tongue of concrete at the top.

The high valley before Trollstigen is renowned for its strawberries, and the fields stretch as far as I can see. A quick visit to Jordbaestova, a cafe advertising the best strawberry cakes in Norway, and then I reach the top of the Troll's Ladder. I pull in at the car park and walk to the viewing platform. Piles of stones, balanced on one another, dot the rocks. 'The tourists think the trolls like them,' says a local. 'They don't. Anyway, there are no such things as trolls.' I'm not sure about that. There's one outside the futuristic information centre, with its odd looks combining humour and veiled threat.

The brochure about Trollstigen claims only 11 hairpins for the descent. That may be true in the strictest sense, but it feels like a lot more, as my bike takes me over bridges spanning the white water tumbling the 762 metres to the valley floor, and along short straits with steep drops on one side and more sheer rock on the other. Then it's a short run along Romsdalsfjord and up the peninsula that has Ålesund at its tip. This is a lovely town, best seen from the hill behind its sprawl around the waterways that define it.

There is one more marvel to tackle – the Atlantic Rd to the north, on the way to Kristiansund. It's only 5 miles (8km) long, but it squeezes eight bridges into that distance, including the twisting Storseisundet Bridge, which you've probably seen in a car commercial on TV. It's an exhilarating ride, especially when the sea is up, and when I finally reach the long tunnel that will take me to Kristiansund, I'm ready for a beer. **PT**

KNOW YOUR LIMITS

Alcoholic drinks are expensive in Norway, so it pays to stock up on duty-free en route. You won't be the only traveller on the ferry with a shopping cart of beer, spirits, wine or magnums of champagne. There is a limit to what you can bring in, so don't be as confident as many locals who believe that no-one checks. Check alcohol and tobacco limits at Norwegian Toll Customs (www.toll.no/en/goods/alcohol-and-tobacco/quotas/).

Clockwise from left: Ørnevegen viewpoint over Geirangerfjord; Ålesund; Bergen's shopfronts. Previous page: the Trollstigen mountain road; Geirangerfjord and the Seven Sisters waterfall

DIRECTIONS

Start // Bergen
End // Kristiansund
Distance // 650km (404 miles), depending on which side roads you take.
Getting there // Take a ferry to Oslo or Kristiansand and ride or drive. Alternatively, take a Hurtigruten ship. These run up the coast frequently and carry both bikes and cars.
When to drive // Between June and August, when Trollstigen is open.
Where to stay // Pre-book hotels or cabins at the many camping grounds.
Visas // Norway is part of the Schengen area. Many Europeans won't need a visa, other nations should check.
Vehicle hire // It's best to bring your own. It's possible to rent both motorcycles and cars, but expensive.

Opposite: the forested Zagorohoria region of Greece

MORE LIKE THIS
LESSER-DRIVEN EUROPE

MOLDOVA'S MONASTERY ROUTE

A largely untouristed country, squeezed between Romania and Ukraine, Moldova transports you to its pastoral past beyond the multi-lane mayhem of capital city Chisinau. Headscarved heather vendors stand by the northbound M2, and traffic slows for horses and carts. Take the Ivancea turn-off towards Trebujeni and the scenery transforms from hay bales to ridges of limestone. Encircled by cliffs is Orheiul Vechi, an archaeological complex of cave monasteries. Rejoin the M2 to Orhei for more sacred sites. Turnoff to Tipova, a 10th-century cave sanctuary, before continuing to Saharna Monastery, where you can see a treasured relic of the Virgin Mary's footprint. You can hire a car in Chisinau.
Start // Chisinau
End // Saharna
Distance // 100 miles (160km)

CURONIAN SPIT, LITHUANIA

This soothing route rolls from open meadows to the Curonian Spit, a slip of land connecting Lithuania with Russian exclave Kaliningrad. Begin in Šiauliai, site of the Hill of Crosses, where 100,000 crucifixes are amassed as a symbol of Lithuanian identity. Drive west on the E272 until you reach Palanga, the country's merriest seaside town. Then dip south along the Baltic coast to Klaipeda, a port town with a German feel and crammed with waterside taverns. Drive on to a ferry to Smiltyne, then south to Juodkrante, along roads shaded by mighty sand dunes. Pause at Juodkrante's outdoor gallery of pagan sculptures, known as Witches' Hill, then continue to Nida for smoked fish and Baltic beers.
Start // Šiauliai
End // Nida
Distance // 137 miles (220km)

ZAGOROHORIA, GREECE

Mountainous Epirus is largely untouched by the sunshine seekers flocking to Greece. Take the scenic route from Ioannina across Pindos National Park to the Zagorohoria villages of slate and stone, while marvelling at views of the Pindos Mountains. North out of Ioannina, veer east towards the national park. Stop in Dilofo, one of the prettiest of the region's villages. Continue east to Vovousa, and pose by its stone bridge over the Aoös River. At the eastern edge of the national park, roads get smoother (if not straighter). Finish in Grevena, known for weathered churches, forests and tasty mushrooms. Roads are steep and narrow, herds of goats are a distraction and you'll stop for photos by every stone bridge.
Start // Ioannina
End // Grevena
Distance // 100 miles (160km)

SLOVAKIA'S STORIED ROUTE 59

Rte 59 weaves together Slovakia's most legendary landscapes. Along this scenic road, you'll delve into folklore and revolutionary heroics, and meet monsters from history and myth.

Rte 59 (the E77) begins with a UFO and culminates at a vampire's lair. It's not your typical itinerary, but this is Slovakia. Villages in this Central European country look plucked from a fairytale, and dark history slumbers beneath the meadows.

Infused with tales of fallen heroes, central Slovakia is a rewarding region to explore by car. Rte 59 winds among some of its most intriguing sights, starting with the town of Banská Bystrica, home to the space-age SNP Museum.

Plotting my route while in the leafy grounds of the museum, it feels as if I am sitting in the shade of the Starship Enterprise. This large dome of concrete and glass is one of the country's most unforgettable brutalist buildings. The SNP Museum within honours the Slovak National Uprising, an anti-fascist rebellion that took place during WWII, and the bloody reprisals that followed. Cradled between the two halves of the dome is a haunting statue that represents the lost, and is illuminated by a coppery shaft of sunlight.

The Slovak National Uprising gathered force right here in Banská Bystrica, but central Slovakia has harboured a spirit of revolution for much longer. Wartime revolutionaries took inspiration from Juraj Jánošík, a 17th-century highwayman who went down in legend for robbing wealthy merchants and sharing his loot with the poor. One partisan group even named themselves after Jánošík. Rte 59 leads me right into the heart of Jánošík's old stomping ground.

The road out of Banská Bystrica heads straight to the mountains, darting between two national parks. Veľká Fatra, to the west of the road, gargles with mineral springs, with spa

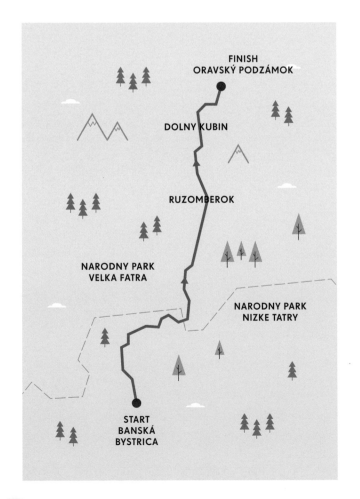

towns huddled around its western fringe. Spreading east of the road is Slovakia's largest national park, Nízke Tatry (Low Tatras), a 281-sq-mile (728-sq-km) swath of limestone canyons and wind-buffed plains, its valleys furred with maple and beech tree groves. Both parks are thickly forested and dotted with caves: perfect hiding places for a renegade highwayman.

Driving north, my car passes a blur of boxy guesthouses and buttercream-coloured chapels. After an easterly bend, the road is suddenly lined with spruce trees, towering high on both sides of the road. At every bend, mountains whip teasingly into view, only to disappear as I zoom into another corridor of fuzzy greenery. Only the occasional ray of light penetrates, dappling the smooth tarmac in sunshine.

The trees begin to thin out and rockfall litters the road. My car engine whines as the road climbs to reach Vlkolínec (718m), one of Slovakia's most enchanting villages. Here, a congregation of wooden statues startles me into parking my car...

Vlkolínec – which has a population of 19 – is a village of wood-cutters, where wooden statues far outnumber their craftsmen. Hand-carved figures stand guard around the village, most of them illustrating characters from Slovakia's rural past: bread-makers, shepherds, women cradling infants, and the occasional glowering grandmother.

Barely changed since it was founded back in the 14th century, Vlkolínec's 45 houses are painted with jaunty bands of mauve and yellow. Apple trees sway above their dark wooden roofs.

"Clinging to a rocky outctrop, the Gothic towers of Orava Castle rise high above the road – almost like a warning"

Crowning the village is the bell tower of the 1875 Roman Catholic Church of the Annunciation of the Virgin Mary, who gazes out sadly from a stone alcove.

The setting is equally beguiling. Vlkolínec is perched on a hill against a backdrop of the Veľká Fatra mountains. Its meadows are flecked with a late bloom of purple marsh orchids and bird's-eye primrose. The valley below is choked by fog. Even the village's name carries mystique: 'vlk' is the Slovak word for wolf, and I can almost imagine Little Red Riding Hood tottering out of one of the log-lined houses.

Back on Rte 59, I steer past towns that snooze in the shade of mountains. First I pass Ružomberok, once a major trading crossroads, snuggled between three mountain ranges: the Low Tatras, Veľká Fatra, and the Choc Mountains. Pressing further north, along roads hemmed by oak trees, I reach another former powerhouse. Dolný Kubín, a medieval quarrying centre, is now resolutely ignored by visitors speeding towards Orava Castle.

Inevitably, this spectacular 14th-century castle is my final destination. For the concluding few kilometres of the road trip, I can see its Gothic towers rising high above the road – almost

SLOVAK SHEEP'S CHEESE

A smoky aroma will tickle your nostrils long before you see a Slovak cheese stall. *Ovci syr* (sheep's cheese) is sold at roadside kiosks. Pungent *bryndza* is a key ingredient in the dumpling dish *bryndzové halušky*. The prettiest cheeses are palm-sized, usually patterned *oštiepky*. *Korbáčiky*, cheesy plaits, and *parenica*, shaped like a snail shell, are moreish snacks. Just beware the lingering cheese odour in your rental car...

Left to right: beehives in Vlkolínec village; Korbáčiky braided cheese; Low Tatras national park; colourful houses of Vlkolínec. Previous page: the Museum of Slovak National Uprising in Banská Bystrica

like a warning. The castle clings to a rocky outcrop above the village of Oravský Podzámok. Tick forest is wrapped around the base of the hill like a cloak.

For a horror movie fan like me, its silhouette is thrillingly familiar. Orava Castle was a filming location for FW Murnau's vampire film *Nosferatu* (1922), a masterpiece of expressionist cinema that is regarded as one of the greatest horror films of all time. The silent movie belongs to an era before vampires became teen heartthrobs that sparkled handsomely under the sun.

Climbing weathered stone staircases, I wander between Orava Castle's grand hallways and chambers. Their walls are decorated with bear skins and coats of arms, and it's all too easy to picture *Nosferatu*'s villain, Count Orlok, scuttling around the fortress. But the castle's horrors aren't confined to the silver screen. Among the successions of aristocrats who moved through these stone walls was Nicolaus Draskovics, a man rumoured to have skinned his servants alive. Also residing here was George Thurzó, the judge who decided the fate of 'blood countess' serial killer Elizabeth Báthory. The infamous Hungarian noblewoman went down in history for murdering hundreds of young women and reportedly bathing in their blood.

These dark legends seem at odds with the glorious serenity of the castle's setting. Peering through embrasures in the castle walls, I can see a tapestry of green meadows rolling towards the High Tatras. But if I've learned anything from this drive, it's that Slovakia's idyllic landscapes conceal its greatest mysteries. **AI**

DIRECTIONS

Start // Banská Bystrica
End // Orava Castle
Distance // 56 miles (90km)
Getting there // Slovak capital Bratislava has a convenient airport, 130 miles (210km) west of Banská Bystrica.
When to drive // May to September has the best weather.
Timing // The drive can be done in a day, but it's better to stop halfway. This will allow time for cheese stalls, walks in Vlkolínec, and reaching Orava Castle before closing time.
Where to stay // Ružomberok is a pleasant place to stay the night. Cosy and marvellously friendly Penzión Andrej (www.penzionandrej.sk) is very convenient for drivers.
Hot tip // The road is cleared of snow in winter and you can ski at Park Snow Donovaly, 17 miles (27km) north of Banská Bystrica, en route.

Opposite: Bran Castle in the
Transylvanian mountains of Romania

MORE LIKE THIS
FOLK CULTURE DRIVES

BRAN PASS, ROMANIA

Careening between fortresses and frozen-in-time villages, Bran Pass is a hair-raising route through Romania's medieval history. Start in the old town of Brasov, where according to legend the Pied Piper of Hamelin emerged in the main square. Drive southwest along Rte 73 to Râsnov, where a maze-like citadel teeters on a high hill, then venture onwards to Bran Castle, whose sharp Gothic towers and forested location have forever linked it with legends of Dracula. Bran, roughly half-way, is packed with romantic places to stay the night; The GuestHouse (www.guesthouse. ro) is a snug but sophisticated choice. The onward drive from Bran to Rucar is as spine-chilling as the folk tales: the road ducks and dives between forlorn country villages, and its hairpin bends overlook the Bucegi Mountains. Drive it between May and October (the Bran–Rucar stretch can be perilous in winter).
Start // Brasov
End // Rucar
Distance // 40 miles (65km)

WOODEN CHURCHES
ROUTE, POLAND

Southern Małopolska's churches are Unesco-listed for their unique style and religious art. Locals credit divine intervention with the survival of these all-wooden medieval churches through countless wars. Shaped like dainty wizard's hats, the churches are waystations along an enchanting road trip east of Kraków. Your first stop is Lipnica Murowana, where Gothic St Leonard's Church has stood since the 15th century. Continue east to Binarowa, whose centrepiece is a richly decorated 16th-century church. Dip south to Sekowa's steep-eaved church, which narrowly escaped destruction by fire in WWI, then return north to the main road. A pleasant drive through farming country leads you east to the treasured church of Haczów. It's the largest Gothic-style wooden church in Europe, and a miraculous survivor of Tatar attacks. Finally, trundle into Blizne to see its uniquely decorated log church. For the best weather, set out between May and September.
Start // Kraków
End // Blizne
Distance // (140 miles) 225km

LIVRADOIS-FOREZ, FRANCE

Plunge deep into Livradois-Forez Regional Park via time-honoured folk crafts and cheesemaking. Begin in Vichy, famed for healing thermal waters, and drive south into the verdant hills of Livradois-Forez. Pause in time-trapped Thiers; powered by a thrashing river, artisans have fashioned knives here for over 600 years. Local wisdom insists that when giving a Thiers knife as a gift, the receiver must reciprocate with a coin, to ensure the knife doesn't sever the friendship. Further south, brake in Ambert for creamy blue cheese Fourme d'Ambert, one of France's oldest unchanged cheese recipes. Pull over at La Chaise-Dieu's enigmatic abbey church and finish in Le Puy-en-Velay, where chapels perch on towers of volcanic rock. Stop-offs are part of the fun of this scenic north-south drive: linger in Vichy for spa treatments and allow an overnight stay to fully appreciate Le Puy-en-Velay's green Verveine du Velay liqueur.
Start // Vichy
End // Le Puy-en-Velay
Distance // 100 miles (161km)

THROUGH THE PICOS DE EUROPA

*The food is the big attraction on this exhilarating drive through northern Spain.
No, the scenery; or maybe the people. Ah, the drink! No, it's the food. I think...*

There can be few better beginnings to a road trip, or any other trip, than Frank Gehry's convoluted titanium Guggenheim Museum in Bilbao. Let its otherworldliness work on you, have a snack and a glass of the local cider in its outdoor cafe and you'll be ready for new experiences. There are many of them on this tour. Head north and east from Bilbao and enjoy the adventurous coast road which takes you to San Sebastián, the real beginning of this drive.

San Sebastián, on its sweeping bay, is a twin city. The new is all rectangular and formal as it hugs the beach, and the old a warren of back streets and lanes tucked away under Monte Urgull.

I spent an evening – a long evening, which actually didn't seem long at all – enjoying the super-sized tapas called *pintxos*, paired with local white wine and increasingly amusing company as I endeavoured to improve my basic Spanish.

I spent much of the next day riding through the pretty and fertile country south of San Sebastián, crossing Usateguieta Pass and finally reaching Vitoria-Gasteiz. The capital of the Basque country is an open, green and relaxed city with a strong cider heritage of its own. Beware the pouring ceremony – it's best done by a local! I wasn't smart enough to do that and ended up soaked in cider from the knees down. Another great night.

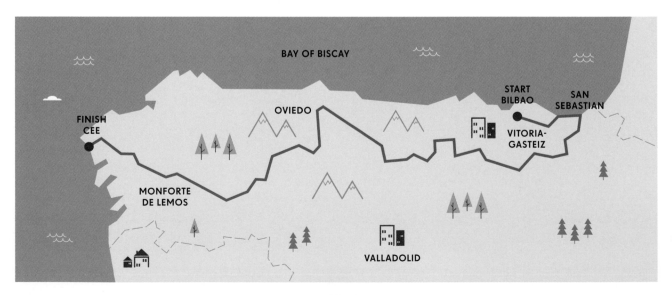

From here I stayed in the back country, heading for the Picos de Europa mountains over snaking back country roads – some in better condition than others. I passed the Sobrón Reservoir on a narrow road through small tunnels. Rivers frequently flow in deep canyons here, their slightly sloping walls covered in vines or other crops, and, on the roads, the 180 degree 'paella turns' as they're known locally made for a particularly enthusiastic ride. Traffic is almost unknown here, although you may see the occasional pilgrim making their way to Santiago de Compostela.

The vast stone pillars of the Picos point to the sky, deriving their name from the fact that their height made them the first land visible to ships returning from the New World. They offer wonderful photo ops in different light, and I was tempted to stay to see in the evening, but the road was calling and I went on. One local told me the motorways were paid for by the EU, but the back roads – some good, some, well... not so good – 'are all our own'. They certainly take you to outstanding places such as Tarna Pass, the border with Asturias at 1492 metres, and Redes National Park.

Oviedo, its 'real' name Uvieo in the local but nationally unrecognised Bable language, is a surprise. It's not just the statue of Woody Allen but the many others dotting the city's streets.

Heading west and then south took me through the mountains and Somiedo National Park, a wonderful drive along winding roads, with good surfaces, into the mountains and up to a high pass by the same name which is one of the first to be covered in snow every winter. Eventually the road drops to the Babia Valley, a favoured holiday destination for León royalty, where they could forget their

REGIONAL TASTES

Crossing northern Spain, you pass through four provinces with distinct food and drink. Many of Spain's best chefs are from the Basque country, and San Sebastian is famed for the micro-cuisine of 'pintxos'. Cantabria's *cocido montañés* is no ordinary stew due to its range of ingredients, and in Asturias you'll find *Fabada Asturiana*, another hearty bean stew, black pudding. *Pulpo a la Gallega*, octopus with potatoes, is Galicia's signature dish.

Clockwise from top: delicious Spanish specialities; a relaxed resident; Santiago de Compostela's cathedral; culinary capital San Sebastian. Previous page: the Picos de Europa

troubles. The phrase *'estar en Babia'*, meaning to be distracted or dream, derives from here. So did El Cid's famous horse, Babieca.

The Pozo de las Mujeres Muertas is a relatively unknown pass road which is one of the treasures of northern Spain. I'm usually keen to see new things when I'm travelling, but I rode a stretch of this pass three times – up, down and up again. I was booked into the Parador at Monforte de Lemos, and I could see the old, refurbished Benedictine monastery on its steep hill from miles away, across one of the few flat bits of country I encountered.

My targets for this ride were Compostela and the Cabo de Finisterre, both to the north-west. But I had been told about the challenging ride along the Sil River, to the south, so I turned that way and enjoyed a drive through a country that might have been made by giants – enormous slopes, 500 metres down to the river, covered in vineyards – and a road that followed every twist and turn of the huge hillsides. No paella bends here; the corners were gentler, but also longer and even more exhilarating.

I eventually turned north to Santiago de Compostela. The target of thousands of pilgrims every year following the Way of Saint James, Compostela somehow remains an impressive example of classical architecture and devotional gravity. It also has one of the grandest hotels in Spain, on the cathedral square, the Parador Nacional de Santiago de Compostela. But my journey wasn't over.

The Camino de Santiago doesn't end in Compostela. There is another stretch of road to cover, to Finisterre – the end of the world. I rode out past the wind turbines through the Montes de Buxantes to Cee, a fishing village just short of Cabo de Finisterre. This isn't really the most westerly part of Europe, but it was thought to be since prehistoric times when pilgrims came here and burned their clothes as a sign of a new life. No need to burn your clothes now, but it's always a good idea to reconsider your life's path... **PT**

"I'm usually keen to see new things when I'm travelling, but I rode part of this pass three times – up, down and up again"

DIRECTIONS

Start // Bilbao/San Sebastián

End // Finisterre

Distance // 620 miles (1000km)

Getting there // Fly to Bilbao. Or, if you're in England, take your own vehicle on the ferry from Portsmouth.

When to drive // Summer. The sea breezes stop it from becoming too hot.

Where to stay // The Paradores: castles, palaces and monasteries that are now beautiful hotels. Printed and internet guides (www.parador.es/en) are available.

What to take // An appetite and a Spanish phrase book.

Car hire // Rent a car or motorcycle, most easily in Bilbao. Or take your own on the ferry.

Formalities // Spain is a Schengen country, so be guided by those visa regulations. Take an International Driving Permit, or your vehicle may be impounded in case of an accident.

Detours // All over the place. Really. You can't go wrong.

*Opposite clockwise from top:
central Bologna; market stalls
on Bologna's Via Pescherie
Vecchie; a bolognese correctly
served with tagliatelle*

MORE LIKE THIS
FOODIE DRIVES

EMILIA-ROMAGNA, ITALY

Sandwiched between Tuscany and the Veneto, Emilia-Romagna is a foodie's dream destination. Many of Italy's signature dishes originated here, and its regional specialities are revered across the country. This tasty trip takes in the culinary centres of Parma, Modena and Bologna, as well as the charming Renaissance town of Ferrara and art-rich Ravenna, celebrated for its glorious Byzantine mosaics. In Parma, stock up on the country's finest ham and most revered cheese, sample the famed balsamic vinegar, pig's trotters and pork sausages of Modena, and, in Bologna, tuck into a plate of the eponymous bolognese sauce (*ragu*) in the vibrant city of its inception, also the birthplace of lasagne and tortellini. For the first half of this trip, from Palma to Bologna, you'll be following the region's most famous road, the ruler-straight Via Emilia, built by the Romans in the 2nd century BC.

Start // **Parma**
End // **Ravenna**
Distance // **152 miles (245km)**

CAPE ANN, MASSACHUSETTS, USA

Somebody (a New Englander, no doubt) once said that 'the humble clam... reaches its quintessence when coated and fried'. The big-bellied bivalve – battered and fried – supposedly originated in Essex, Massachusetts, so Cape Ann is an ideal place to sample it. This North Shore route takes you from clam shack to clam shack, with breaks for beachcombing, bird-watching, gallery-hopping and picture taking. Before you head south down the 1A from Newburyport, take a detour to Plum Island to visit the Parker River Wildlife Refuge and its 800-plus species of birds, plants and animals. Further down the coast, break at Crane Beach, one of the longest and sandiest in the region, and, of course, Essex, for its maritime history, antique shops and succulent clams. With plenty of picnic tables overlooking the estuary, there's no better lunch stop.

Start // **Newburyport**
End // **Gloucester**
Distance // **54 miles (86km)**

TYROL & VORALBERG, AUSTRIA

As you drive east from opera-festival-famed Bregenz on the shores of Lake Constance, you'll discover a different side of the Alps to the dizzying drives of the Grossglockner Road. A food- and culture-filled trip through mountain valleys offers up more than 50 schnapps distilleries in the village of Stanz, the medieval-castle-housed brewery Starkenberger Biermythos and several Alpine dairies. After discovering the cheese-making secrets of show dairy Bergkäserai Schoppernau you may be tempted to set off from Schoppernau itself on a detour of the Bregenz Forest Cheese Road, to explore dairy farms, peek inside huge cheese cellars, take factory tours and dine alfresco on *Kässpätzle* (hand-rolled noodles with cheese, topped with crispy fried onion). Back on the road northeast towards your destination, Salzburg, explore the monumental ochre-and-white abbey Stift Stams and the treasures of Innsbruck.

Start // **Bregenz**
End // **Salzburg**
Distance // **238 miles (383km)**

REACHING THE ISLE OF SKYE

From Portree on the Isle of Skye to the coastal township of Applecross on the mainland, here is a breathtaking journey around and up the Scottish Highlands.

Portree and Applecross are only 74 miles (119km) apart by road, but the route between them is epic in the most elemental sense. Driving in an arc from one to the other, the panorama from the passenger's side window is a near-constant of bruised-blue open seas or gaping loch, these waters often churning and frothing. The landscape is otherwise one of verdant pine forest, even greater expanses of rugged, rock-strewn moorland and towering mountain ranges. Separating these two townships, one located just off the West Coast of Scotland, the other just on, is the highest and the most otherworldly pass traversable by car in the British Isles.

The first time I took this extraordinary drive was in the summer of 2011, going in the reverse direction. Today, I depart from Portree on a frigid midwinter's morning with a bank of gun-grey cloud brooding over the humpbacked peak of Ben Tianavaig, one of the two prominences that flank the town's natural harbour. Within a mile I'm in the midst of Skye's open country, panoplies of rolling, craggy dun-coloured moor dotted with battalions of pine. A bubbling stream runs parallel to the road. Tendrils of mist snake over the water, a common sight here. In the 9th century, Viking invaders from Scandinavia gave the island the name Skuy, Norse for 'misty isle'.

Even those marauding Norseman must surely have been struck by the Cuillins, the twin mountain ranges that bisect the island at its midpoint. The A87 winds right through them: the Red Cuillin – triangular-shaped peaks as if a child's drawing or a Martian landscape – looming on one side of Glen Sligachan; on the other the more ominous Black Cuillin, jagged like a row of broken teeth. I drive up and around the Cuillin, which provide company until the

road drops onto the flatter land of Broadford Bay, where I can look out at Skye's little sister isle, Raasay, high and rocky.

I follow the bend of the bay to the southern tip of the island and the Skye road bridge. Opened in 1995 and spanning the picture-postcard Lochalsh Sound, this replaced a ferry service that had been sailing in one form or other since the 1600s. From the outset, the bridge was controversial. The private operating company appointed by the government to run the bridge imposed a prohibitive toll which locals refused to pay. More than 100 arrests were made, but Skye folk did what they have been doing for

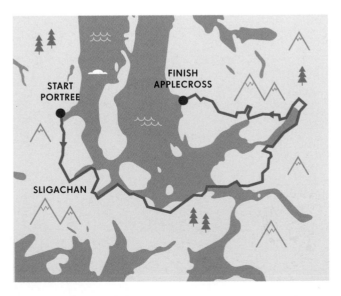

"At the plateau, an alien netherworld unfolds: a wilderness of black rock, a blacker sky, snow and ice on the ground"

centuries, which is to say dug in, and in 2004 the toll was scrapped. This region as a whole demands hardiness. That much is apparent as I head out of the town of Kyle of Lochalsh towards the buttresses of Glen Shiel, menacing black slabs stretched across the horizon, with a cold wind howling in off the Sound.

Turning left off the A87, roughly three miles (5km) further down the road and just after the tiny village of Auchtertyre, I join the Wester Ross coastal route. I might as well be passing into Middle Earth. As the meandering road rises, falls and climbs again it does so through curtains of pine and silver birch. Ahead of me are the sheer peaks of the Torridon range, snow-capped and foreboding. To the right, banks of steep hillside are flecked with deep purple heather; below, glistening, is the enormous spread of Loch Carron. Raven stalk the higher ground; a buzzard perches on a roadside sign, motionless and watchful.

Unspoilt, untamed beauty surrounds me for 20 miles (32km), yet it is a mere prelude to the wild heart of the drive. The turn off for Bealach na Bà – the Pass of the Cattle – is two miles (3km) on from the township of Kishorn. Ahead of it, a large red sign spits out warnings: 'Not suitable for caravans, large vehicles or learner drivers! High risk of snow!' Like Frodo Baggins, I am off to Mordor.

In total, Bealach na Bà stretches out and up for 11 miles (18km), rising at a one-in-five gradient to 2053ft (626 metres) and then plunging back down to Applecross Bay. Initially, it is deceptive, almost benign. As I guide the car up a gently climbing bend, I am afforded a view out to sea with the sun breaking through the cloud. On the hillside, I spot a pair of red deer, stags, standing sentry and watching me. Soon enough, though, the road tapers to a single track and the true drama begins. Here, the road bucks and with it the car engine whines in protest. At the same time, the bends become more acute until the route is but a series of head-spinning hairpins – a rusty barrier all that stands on one side between narrow track and a straight drop of hundreds of feet. More than enough to make one's stomach churn.

At the plateau, a kind of alien netherworld unfolds. This is a wilderness of black rock, a blacker sky, snow and ice on the ground, all else indistinct in the gloom. And then, magically, at the apex of the descent and under the charcoal cloud line, there is clear sky and the sun once more kisses the land and sea, lighting them up in a chorus of greens and blues. Down, down I go towards Applecross. Its Gaelic name is A'Chomraich, 'The Sanctuary', and entirely apt. Such as it is, the town is but a ribbon line of white-walled houses, a shop and an inn set along the seafront, looking out to a deep, wide bay. It is hushed, peaceful and welcoming.

I drive another three miles (5km) west of Applecross and pull off the road at a small, rough-hewn car park. A track leads off it and down on to a bowl-shaped beach of golden sand, a bank of it rising 70ft (21 metres) back up to the roadside. There is no one here but me. The tide is out, and I walk across wet sand to the sea's edge. From there, I am able to regard, across the water, Raasay and Skye beyond. So close, but also seeming so very far away. **PR**

WEE BEASTIES

The West Coast of Scotland is home to rich wildlife. Both white-tailed and golden eagle have become a familiar sight in the skies over the Cuillins and Raasay, while it is not unusual to spot common and bottlenose dolphin, harbour porpoise and even minke whale from sites on the Skye shore, as well as common and grey seal and otter. Take one of the boat trips from Portree, Elgol or Shieldaig, and you might also glimpse rarer visiting whales.

Clockwise from left: a white-tailed sea eagle; the Bealach na Bà road; sunset at Portree. Previous page: stunning scenery on the Isle of Skye

DIRECTIONS

Start // Portree
End // Applecross Inn car park
Distance // 74 miles (119km)
Getting there // The nearest major airport is Inverness, 129 miles (217km) away, where car hire is available. The Skye Bridge means that the island is accessible by road from anywhere in the UK.
Where to eat // Lunch or dinner at the Applecross Inn (www.applecross.uk.com/inn) is a must, especially the divine fish and chips, and fresh seafood platters. You can stay the night, too (from £65 p/p), but will need to book in advance.
Hot tip // Before setting off, check on travelscotland.org that the Bealach na Bà route is open. It often closes in winter.
More info // There are helpful tourist information offices in Portree and Applecross.

MORE LIKE THIS
GREAT BRITISH DRIVES

ALNWICK TO
LINDISFARNE, ENGLAND

This picturesque route drinks in
Northumberland's panoramic coastline,
one of Britain's best-kept secrets. Drive
from the pretty market town of Alnwick,
north up the A1 and across to the Holy
Island. Before setting out from Alnwick,
visit Barter Books. Sited in an old Victorian
railway station, Barter is one of the largest
second-hand book stores in Europe and a
veritable wonderland. Its cafe also serves
the best fruit cake in England, bar none.
On route to Lindisfarne, the views to the
passenger's side are a bucolic delight
of rolling hills and moorland and on the
driver's side serve up the dramatic spread
of the North Sea. There are also three of
the UK's best-preserved castles to visit:
Alnwick, made famous by the *Harry Potter*
films; Bamburgh; and Lindisfarne, which
is hauntingly evocative. Lindisfarne is only
accessible by car at low tide, so check the
tide times before departing *and* making the
return journey. It's worth noting also that
Lindisfarne Priory is closed from November
through January.
Start // Alnwick Castle
End // Lindisfarne Priory
Distance // 35 miles (56km)

THE ABERGWESYN
MOUNTAIN PASS, WALES

Not a long journey, but one to truly excite
the senses and the pick of the many
fine drives that Wales can offer. The
Abergwesyn Pass, like Bealach na Bà, is a
challenge of steep sections, and includes a
series of daunting hairpin bends known as
the Devil's Staircase. Yet the rewards make
it irresistible: within just a couple of miles of
setting off from the market town of Tregaron
– 35 minutes' drive inland from Aberystwyth
– you are bedazzled by staggering views
out over the Cambrian Mountains and the
route as a whole serves up a scenic feast
of forest, valley and lake-land. For a lovely
diversion, take the detour road to Llyn
Brianne reservoir, which is man-made but
enchanting. Pick a clear spring or summer's
day to get the best of the views, but
whatever the season take care as the going
is rough and dotted with potholes.
Start // Tregaron
End // Abergwesyn
Distance // 18 miles (29km)

GLASGOW TO FORT
WILLIAM, SCOTLAND

Scotland spoils drivers for choice, but this
route is the perfect introduction into its
Highlands. Not long out of Glasgow, the
landscape changes to the rolling greens
of the Loch Lomond and the Trossachs
National Park, as the road passes through
the villages of Tarbet and Crianlarich and
is flanked for miles by the great loch itself.
Then there is another, still more dramatic
shift into huge, imposing Glen Coe,
the gateway to the Highlands. It's well
worth stopping off here at the Glencoe
Mountain Resort, open all year round.
Take the ski-lift to the top and walk the
high plateau. The views are spectacular
and there is the chance of spotting a
golden eagle and red deer. Back on
the road, head onwards to Fort William,
nestled in the shadow of the mighty Ben
Nevis range. You could always finish your
drive at the Nevis Range Resort, seven
miles (11km) north of Fort William, just off
the A82. On a clear day, the Snowgoose
Restaurant affords an uninterrupted view
of Britain's highest peak and serves fine
coconut cake year round.
Start // Glasgow
End // Fort William
Distance // 108 miles (174km)

THE WILDS OF ABRUZZO

With its thrilling mountain scenery, rural back-country charm and snaking roads, the little-known Italian region of Abruzzo makes for exhilarating driving and wild encounters.

There was so much snow, the wolves came into town looking for food. You couldn't go out at night.'

We're sitting on the shores of Lago di Scanno, an idyllic lake surrounded by tree-clad slopes in Abruzzo, the Apennine region about two hours' drive east of Rome. The water is twinkling in the midday sun and a local kiosk owner is telling us about the realities of life in the mountains. Heavy winter snowfall had forced the animals to come down from the woods, he explained, and one day 'I came out to check my kiosk hadn't caved in under the snow, and saw a bear, right there, with a cub.'

As the crow flies we're only about 68 miles (110km) from Rome, but Abruzzo is a world away from the bright lights of the Italian capital. Where Rome has art, history and more than a little urban chaos, Abruzzo has brooding mountains and ancient forests, wide vistas and remote hill towns, where little appears to have changed in centuries and age-old traditions still hold sway. It's one of my favourite parts of Italy.

It's also epic driving country, as I discovered on a summer road trip I undertook with my wife and two young kids. Our route took us deep into the Parco Nazionale d'Abruzzo, Lazio e Molise and up to the mighty Gran Sasso massif. Our starting point was Sulmona, a handsome provincial town famous for its 'confetti' (a sugar-coated almond sweet), where we got our first taste of local hospitality. Dining at the family-run Hostaria dell'Arco, the owner insisted on lighting the charcoal grill just for us. The lamb chops, he insisted, just wouldn't taste the same otherwise.

We left Sulmona's cobbled lanes the next morning and headed into the big country of the Parco Nazionale della Majella. Climbing steadily, we weaved smoothly through wooded hills

while foreboding peaks loomed on the blue horizon. A few kilometres beyond the Bosco di Sant'Antonio beech forest we came to Pescocostanzo. Set amid lush, almost alpine, plains, this surprisingly grand hilltop town harbours a pristine historic core that dates back to its time as one of the most important staging posts on the Via degli Abruzzi, the traditional trans-Apennine route that linked Florence to Naples.

We pushed on towards Pescasseroli, the primary centre in the Parco Nazionale d'Abruzzo, Lazio e Molise. The going had become fairly easy by now and it was wonderfully relaxing to meander past the Lago di Barrea on the SS83 and enjoy the unspoiled verdant scenery. Pescasseroli is reasonably quiet even at the busiest of times, and it was positively sleepy when we arrived. But we were keen to stretch our legs, and the children, who had uncomplainingly braved the twisty roads – thank you, Travel Gum – were itching to ditch the car, so we decided to stop over for the night.

The plan for day two was to double back to Sulmona via Scanno, a route that would take us through a gorgeous rocky gorge known as the Gole di Sagittario, and then head further up to the Gran Sasso. This promised some tough climbing and so it proved as we motored up to the Passo Godi mountain pass at 1630 metres. From there we inched our way down a slow, tortuous descent to Scanno.

Scanno is a decidedly picturesque town with steep alleyways and a cluster of slate-grey stone houses grafted on to the mountainside. We paused for a quick look around before heading

SNAKES ALIVE

Some 12½ miles (20km) west of Sulmona, Cocullo is home to one of Italy's weirdest festivals. The Festa dei Serpari (Festival of the Snake Catchers) is the highlight of celebrations to honour St Dominic, the village's patron saint, held on the first Thursday of May. The main focus of attention is a statue of the saint that's festooned with writhing serpents – all caught for the event in the surrounding hills – and paraded through the village.

Clockwise from top: the town of Scanno; the medieval village of Pacentro in Abruzzo; Lago di Scanno. Previous page: Monti Marsicani in the Parco Nazionale d'Abruzzo, Lazio e Molise

down to the lake, a couple of clicks beyond the main centre. There wasn't a lot going on there but the boys were soon playing with a local lad, and his grandfather was cheerfully regaling us with tales of bears and hungry wolves.

So far, we'd been on roads I'd covered at least once before. But the next leg took us into virgin territory. And on to one of the highlight stretches. The road up to Santo Stefano di Sessanio was a true white-knuckle drive with a series of sharp second-gear switchbacks and sweeping views at every turn. I was concentrating too hard to take in the scenery, including the remote Rocca Calascio castle when it came into view, but there was no denying the drama of the landscape. If ever they decide to make a horror film in Italy, this would be the ideal place.

Three and three-quarter miles (6km) further on, Santo Stefano di Sessanio is similarly haunting. Formerly a 16th-century Medici stronghold, it suffered damage in a 2009 earthquake and many of its stone buildings are still under scaffolding. As we strolled through its semi-deserted lanes, we began to notice a boy shadowing us. We eventually worked out that he wanted us to go to his cheese shop. We obliged and picked up a hefty wedge of fresh pecorino that made for a tasty addition to our picnic lunch.

We were now at an altitude of about 1200 metres and the rest of the world felt a very long way away. This sense of isolation grew as we pushed on to Campo Imperatore, a rolling highland plateau known as Italy's 'Little Tibet'. Mussolini was briefly imprisoned here in 1943, and it's a stark and majestic place.

Overlooking everything was the great grey fin of Corno Grande, the summit of the Gran Sasso massif and, at 2912 metres, the highest point in the Apennines. I'd long wanted to climb it – it's a tough but do-able summer hike – but now wasn't the time. It would have to wait for another day. **DG**

"The sense of isolation grew as we pushed on to Campo Imperatore, a highland plateau known as Italy's 'Little Tibet'"

DIRECTIONS

Start // Sulmona
End // Fonte Cerreto
Distance // 161½ miles (260km)
Getting there // Nearest airports are Rome's Fiumicino and Ciampino. Car hire is available at both.
When to drive // May through September. The weather's warm, colours are brilliant and it's great for hiking.
Where to stay // Albergo Ristorante Stella (www.albergostella.info) offers modern three-star rooms in Sulmona's historic centre. Sextantio (www.sextantio.it) has smart, tasteful rooms in Santo Stefano di Sessanio.
Where to eat // Hostaria dell'Arco is a family-run trattoria serving hearty, local fare in Sulmona.
Local information // Tourist offices at Sulmona and Pescasseroli.
Hot tip // If travelling with kids, car sickness pills are a trip saver. There's great hiking, so bring walking boots.

*Opposite: the town of Ragusa in
southern Sicily*

MORE LIKE THIS
RUGGED ITALY

THE DOLOMITES

Ranging across the northern regions
of Veneto and Trentino Alto Adige, the
Dolomites boast some of Italy's most
spectacular mountain landscapes. Huge
cathedrals of rock soar skywards like
great craggy fangs, forming a cinematic
backdrop to the Grande Strada della
Dolomiti (Great Dolomites Rd). This
exhilarating road takes in inspiring
views, vertiginous switchbacks and lofty
mountain passes as it weaves its way from
Bolzano up to the chic ski resort of Cortina
d'Ampezzo. Route highlights include the Val
di Fassa, a magnificent valley framed by
forested slopes and gigantic rock summits,
and the Alta Badia, a stunning area on the
Sella Ronda massif embraced by the peaks
of Pelmo (3168m) and Civetta (3218m).
There's magnificent skiing in winter, hiking
and rock climbing in winter, and fabulous
food all year round.
Start // Bolzano
End // Cortina d'Ampezzo
Distance // 73 miles (118km)

SICILY'S SOUTHEAST

Taking in remote gorges, rocky hills and
some of Italy's most beautiful baroque
towns, Sicily's southeastern corner makes
for an eye-opening road trip. Towns such as
Noto, Modica and Ragusa host stunning
examples of baroque architecture, much
of which was built in the aftermath of
a devastating earthquake in 1693. The
surrounding landscape is harshly beautiful.
A huge canyon, the Cava d'Ispica, extends
near the town of Ispica, its grey rock
honeycombed with prehistoric tombs, while
grey drystone walls line tracts of citrus
groves. All around, vivid Mediterranean
colours bloom in the sharp light. The route
starts in Noto and heads to Modica by
way of the hilltop town of Ispica. From
Modica, continue inland to Ragusa and on
to Chiaramonte Gulfi, famous both for its
olive oil and its delicious pork.
Start // Noto
End // Chiaramonte Gulfi
Distance // 44 miles (71km)

SALENTO

Italy's coastal splendours are legion,
including such greats as the plunging cliffs
of the Amalfi Coast, Cinque Terre's pastel
villages and Sardinia's silky beaches. Lesser
known but equally as inspiring in its own
way is the wild coastline of the Salento in
the southern region of Puglia. Backed by
a harsh, sun-baked interior, it's a magical
stretch of jagged rocks, hidden coves and
shimmering waters in a hundred shades
of blue. Huge prickly pears line the road
as it follows the contours of the coast from
Otranto down to Santa Maria di Leuca, the
point the Romans called the *finibus terrae*
(end of the world) at the tip of the Italian
heel. From here, push on to the kicking
summer resort of Gallipoli and the limpid,
sky-blue waters of the Ionian Sea.
Start // Otranto
End // Gallipoli
Distance // 73 miles (117km)

SOUTHERN ALPS EXPLORER

Combine the absolute best of New Zealand's renowned alpine and lake scenery with myriad opportunities to test your mettle in the great outdoors.

I am kicking off one of New Zealand's most spectacular road trips with one of New Zealand's most spectacular snacks. A steak-and-mushroom pie from the Famous Sheffield Pie Shop is the perfect sustenance for a drive towards the craggy spine of the Southern Alps.

Sheffield is located on the expansive Canterbury Plains, but I'm soon traversing long bridges across braided rivers, and winding through sub-alpine rainforest to be surrounded by glacial valleys and mountain peaks. Kea, those cheeky – and bold – alpine parrots, jump on my car's roof in Arthur's Pass village but before they pull their usual trick of gnawing on the car's aerial, I depart across the sweeping curves of the Otira Viaduct and downhill through farmland to meet the South Island's West Coast.

Approximately 12 miles (20km) further south, Hokitika's history is derived from gold, and though the 19th-century's prospecting frenzy has passed, the town's wide streets are still framed by grand buildings. *Pounamu* (jade or greenstone) is the region's modern

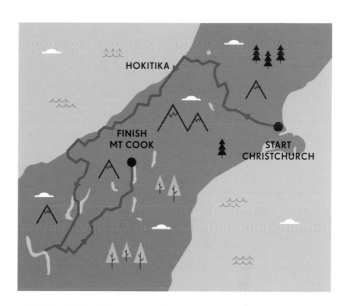

"The diversity in landscapes on my three-hour drive from Queenstown to Aoraki/Mt Cook is astounding."

bounty, and local galleries feature work crafted from rocks that were retrieved from remote valleys.

From Hokitika, SH6 diverts inland, winding through a rugged collage of farmland and forest to the former mining town of Ross. After stretching my legs on the Water Race Walk taking in old gold diggings, caves and tunnels, I make the day's final drive to Franz Josef Glacier past stony river valleys merging with the Tasman Sea.

I get lucky the following morning: the West Coast's weather can be capricious, but a blue-sky day dawns to banish the rain or mist. On an earlier visit I splashed out on a helicopter flight and a guided hike high on the glacier, but this morning I'm happy to negotiate the Ka Roimata o Hine Hukatere Track alone for excellent views of Franz Josef's imposing terminal face.

I push on further south to Fox Glacier, and the serpentine 23km journey cradled by the bush-clad mountains of the Westland Tai Poutini National Park is quite possibly New Zealand's most spectacular half-hour drive.

At Fox Glacier, I make an essential detour to Lake Matheson. The weather gods continue to behave, and the soaring, snowy profile of Aoraki/Mt Cook is reflected perfectly in the lake's tranquil waters. As the crow (or kea) flies, it's only a distance of 15 miles (22km), but my ongoing road journey to New Zealand's highest peak includes another 280 miles (460km) of spectacular South Island scenery.

From Fox Glacier to Wanaka is around a three-hour drive as I continue down the west coast to the remote settlement of Haast. Just beyond the easily accessible waterfalls and careful switchbacks

of the Haast Pass, the middle-of-nowhere village of Makarora – a base for adventure trips combining jetboating and hiking in the forbiddingly named 'Siberia' region – is the last fling for Westland's forested mountains before entering the more open and sparsely covered peaks and valleys of Central Otago. Following a snaking route along Lake Hawea and Lake Wanaka, I arrive at my destination around mid-afternoon.

Wanaka is often overshadowed by Queenstown to the south, but Central Otago's other (less busy) lakeside town is arguably even more enjoyable. A late afternoon kayak on Lake Wanaka segues to watching a movie seated on a comfy old sofa – unfortunately the airplane seats and the old Morris Minor car are already taken – at the quirky Cinema Paradiso. Add pizza and freshly baked chocolate chip cookies at intermission and you can see why I'm sold.

Arriving in Queenstown the next morning, I trade in four wheels for two knobbly wheels and ride the Skyline Gondola up Bob's Peak to the Queenstown Bike Park. Multiple downhill runs taking in arcing views of Lake Wakatipu and the indigo peaks of the Remarkables mountain range set me up well for a pint of Queenstown's very own Altitude craft brew at the wharf-side Atlas Beer Cafe.

© Pakawat Thongcharoen | Getty Images, © Paul Viant | Getty Images, © Philip Lee Harvey | Lonely Planet

© Matt Munro | Lonely Planet

STAR ATTRACTION

The skies around Lake Tekapo in the Mackenzie Country are among the planet's clearest, and the region is an International Dark Sky Reserve. The cafe atop Mt John has great food, coffee and 360-degree vistas of the lakes and mountains of the Mackenzie Basin, while at night Earth & Sky (www.earthandsky.co.nz) runs stargazing tours to the University of Canterbury's observatory. Lake Tekapo is an hour from Aoraki/Mt Cook.

Left to right: lakeside Queenstown; the ideal wheels for the trip; a curious kea parrot; the road to Mt Cook. Previous page: across Canterbury Plains to the Southern Alps

Bungee jumping, ziplines and paragliding reinforce Queenstown's reputation as an adventure sports hub, but I'm headed for outdoor thrills in the shadow of the country's highest mountain instead.

The diversity in landscapes on my three-hour drive from Queenstown to Aoraki/Mt Cook is astounding. Craggy schist peaks rise above the riverside road threading past the vineyards of the Gibbston Valley and through the Kawarau Valley. From Cromwell, the steep cliffs above Lake Dunstan give way to the Lindis Pass crossing to the massive basin of the Mackenzie Country. The Lindis can sometimes be closed to snow during winter, but my own journey across the peaks and valleys of grey ribbon is illuminated by sunshine and cloudless cobalt skies.

Cobalt gives way to intense turquoise as I drive along spidery Lake Pukaki to Mt Cook Village. The lake's electric blue colour is due to a phenomenon known as glacial flour, and it's a similarly surreal hue infusing the water on the terminal lake of the Tasman Glacier. Boarding an inflatable Zodiac, I join an international crew of travellers negotiating the otherworldly vista of icebergs that have sheared off from the vast Tasman Glacier. So close to the country's highest peak, the last thing I expect to see is a maze of giant shards of ice resembling a polar seascape, and in delicate winds some of the icebergs are drifting slowly across the lake's surface. Come back in a few weeks and the view could be quite different.

As the sun sets an alpine chill seeps quickly into mountain breezes, and I'm happy to finish the day beside a warming open fire in the cosy bar of Mt Cook's heritage Hermitage Hotel. **AB**

DIRECTIONS

Start // Christchurch
End // Aoraki/Mt Cook
Distance // 851 miles (997 km)
Getting there // Fly in and out of Christchurch.
When to drive // February to April is warmest, but winter's snowcapped mountains make this stunning year round.
Where to stay // This drive includes some of the country's most spectacular Department of Conservation campsites.
Where to eat // The Central Otago vineyard restaurants around Queenstown and Cromwell.
Getting active // There are excellent day walks around Aoraki/Mt Cook and Wanaka. In Queenstown, you're bound to be enticed to go bungee jumping or jetboating.
More info // www.centralotagonz.com; www.mackenzienz.com; www.westcoast.co.nz.

*Opposite: verdant vineyards in
Marlborough's Wairau Valley*

MORE LIKE THIS
THE SOUTH ISLAND

SOUTHERN SCENIC ROUTE

Embark on this long U-shaped journey
around New Zealand's deep south for
wild surf beaches, spectacular coastal
cliffs and the atmospheric forest-clad
sounds of Fiordland. From the Scottish
history and creative university town vibe
of Dunedin, negotiate rural highways and
coastal backroads through the sleepy
Catlins. Essential stops include the Lost
Gypsy Gallery at Papatowai and the
wave-battered islets of Nugget Point.
Continue via Invercargill, New Zealand's
southernmost city, past isolated beaches,
before travelling deep into Fiordland and
the chance to go sea kayaking or cruising
on remote Doubtful Sound, or hiking the
Kepler Track or Milford Track from Te Anau.
Start // Dunedin
End // Te Anau
Distance // 376 miles (606km)

KAIKOURA COAST

This stretch of State Highway 1 is a
relatively quick route between Picton and
Christchurch, but it also boasts several
highlights. The beautiful Marlborough
Sounds and Blenheim's world-class
wineries can hardly be missed, but hidden
attractions also abound. The main draw
for wildlife watchers will be the Kaikoura
peninsula, which offers the chance to
see shearwaters, petrels, albatross and
other seabirds, plus seals lazing around
at Point Kean. Several species of whale
and dolphin either live in the Kaikoura
area or swing by. Your other key chance to
spot beasts comes at Willowbank Wildlife
Reserve in Christchurch, which provides a
rare opportunity to view kiwi.
Start // Picton
End // Christchurch
Distance // 219 miles (352km)

NELSON & MARLBOROUGH EXPLORER

Explore the top of the island on a diverse
journey of outdoor activities, wineries,
craft beer and gourmet food. Highlights
in Nelson include the World of Wearable
Art Museum and Saturday morning Nelson
Market. Continuing north through the
Moutere Valley, pinot noir at Neudorf
Vineyards and brews at the Moutere Inn
are tasty diversions. Incorporate a detour
for a boat trip in the Abel Tasman National
Park, before looping south via St Arnaud
and the Nelson Lakes National Park. Follow
the Wairau River northeast to the vineyards
of Marlborough and Blenheim. Everything
you've heard about Marlborough
sauvignon blanc is true, but also make sure
you taste Framingham's riesling.
Start // Nelson
End // Blenheim
Distance // 182 miles (293km)

THE GREAT OCEAN ROAD

Australia's most famous road hugs the rugged Victorian coast west of Melbourne, revealing beach towns, national parks and the Twelve Apostles.

'Twice a century the ocean lets us know how small we really are. A storm comes out of Antarctica, tearing up the Pacific and it sends a huge swell north. And when it hits Bells Beach it'll turn into the biggest surf this planet has ever seen.' At the climax of the film *Point Break*, fugitive Bodhi is standing on a beach pleading with the FBI agent played by Keanu Reeves for one last wave. No matter that the scene was filmed on Indian Beach, Oregon: *Point Break* brought Bells Beach on the southern coast of Victoria, Australia, to a wider audience. The beach and its surf town of Torquay stand at the start of Australia's Great Ocean Road, so

we started our drive along the Surf Coast by detouring down to the cliffs overlooking Bells. It was a grey, windswept day without much swell but there were still a few black-clad figures bobbing on the waves, waiting for the right one.

Having paid homage to the 1990s' classic, we hopped in our hire car and set out on the Great Ocean Road. We'd planned to drive from Melbourne all the way east to the 12 Apostles, a group of limestone sea stacks just before Port Campbell, about 175 miles (280km) from Melbourne, passing through seaside towns and the Great Otway National Park. It's a classic sightseeing trip from Melbourne but there's much more to the road than just being a

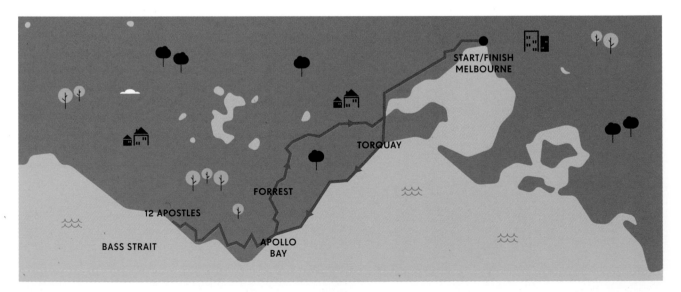

conduit for campervans and cars on the tourist trail. The Great Ocean Road is actually a war memorial, built by 3000 Australian servicemen recently returned from WWI as a tribute to their fallen mates. Work began in 1919 and the road was hewn by pick and shovel, whatever the weather. The full route, from Torquay to Allansford in western Victoria, was opened in 1932, 10 years after the first section from Torquay was finished. It was the first time that the tiny communities along the coast, such as Lorne, were connected.

The tale of the road's construction is told (with extraordinary photographs) in the Great Ocean Road Heritage Centre in Lorne. As you might imagine, working in remote Australia almost 100 years ago, at the mercy of the elements, had its ups and downs. One stormy day in October 1924, at Kennett River, the SS Casino ran aground. The crew had to jettison 500 barrels of beer, which found their way to the workforce. The road is still beset by storms and fires; landslips and washouts are not uncommon.

After Lorne, a beachside town that attracts a lot of weekending urbanites, the driving experience begins in earnest. The road follows every twist, turn, rise and fall of the shore. Where it passes through patches of eucalyptus forest, look out for koalas in the crook of a gum tree's branches. One thing is certain: passengers will enjoy the views out to sea more than the driver, who will need to keep their eyes fixed on the road. This is not a road to rush, not least because you will find yourself stuck behind a slower vehicle.

The route then passes through smaller communities such as Wye River and Kennett River before the next large town, Apollo Bay. With an appointment with some Apostles ahead, we keep on driving. The

TURTON'S TRACK

Between Skenes Creek and Forrest, look out for a left turn onto a single-lane road called Turton's Track. This road wriggles through the fern-filled forest glades and gullies of the Great Otway National Park for eight miles (12km). It's designed to be a slow drive and you can pull off to see the giant messmate eucalypts more closely. If you continue for another 30 minutes or so you'll see signs for the Otway Fly Treetop Walk.

Clockwise from top: walk through the forest canopy at the Otway Fly Treetop Walk; stop to savour the sea air; the Twelce Apostles (note that there aren't Twelve of them now)

road cuts across Cape Otway as it passes through the Great Otway National Park, sending us into a forest of giant trees before rejoining the coast at the Twelve Apostles Visitor Centre. We walk down to the viewing platform, the wind whipping our hair about our faces and snatching our breath away, to see the Twelve Apostles. It's not our first glimpse of these sea stacks – they're in every postcard rack in the state. But it is impressive to see the wind blowing a waterfall back up a cliff face and the gunmetal-grey storm clouds on the horizon.

Some drivers continue to Port Fairy to spend the night, or even press on to Adelaide. But we turn the car around and head back to Apollo Bay. To Sydneysiders, the town could be called 'daggy' (translation: comfortably unfashionable) but others appreciate its unpretentious air, with shops selling boogie boards behind the broad crescent of sand that lends the town its name. There's a pub, a fish-and-chip shop at the harbour and an excellent YHA.

The next day, rather than return to Melbourne along the Great Ocean Road, we turn left and uphill at Skenes Creek into the Otways. Our goal is a town called Forrest, 45-minutes from Apollo Bay. Forrest is a former logging town but since the local logging stopped and mills closed the town has turned to tourism and is starting to thrive. Emma Ashton and husband Pete opened their guesthouse in 2013 and they have expanded it to include an exciting restaurant, Bespoke Harvest, where chef Simon Stewart uses to local ingredients (many from the guesthouse's garden) to create delicious and healthy dishes such as daikon radish and pickled octopus salad.

The town is also known for its brewery, Forrest Brewing Company, and the network of mountain bike trails through the eucalyptus forest. Put the two together and you have a fun day of cycling (rent a bike from The Corner Store) followed by a local ale or two. The next day we continue north and follow the Cape Otway Road to the Princes Hwy and back to Melbourne. **RB**

"This is not a road to rush. Savour the sea views, stop to paddle on a beach, and always keep your eyes on the road."

DIRECTIONS

Start / End // Melbourne (the Great Ocean Road itself starts from Torquay)

Distance // 340 miles (550km) for this loop from Melbourne

When to drive // The road is open all year but spring, summer and autumn (October to May) are the best months for enjoying the beaches. As a consolation for a winter trip, whale-watching season runs between May and September.

Where to stay // The Apollo Bay Eco YHA (www.yha.com. au) is regularly rated one of the best hostels in Australia; it's clean, modern and in a great location behind the beach. In Forrest, Emma Ashton's Guesthouse (http:// forrestaccommodation.com.au) has attractive boutique rooms overlooking a garden, with breakfast included.

Where to eat // Lorne has lots of restaurants, such as the Greek venue Ipsos. In Apollo Bay, scoff fish and chips from the Fisherman's Co-op at the harbour. Wind down with a beer at Forrest Brewing Co. (https://forrestbrewing.com.au).

Opposite: the Triana Bridge over the Guadalquivir River in Seville, Spain

MORE LIKE THIS
CITY-TO-CITY DRIVES

MELBOURNE TO SYDNEY, AUSTRALIA

The Great Ocean Road is an unforgettable start to the 620 mile (1000km) coastal drive between Melbourne and Adelaide, but there is a similarly scenic route between Melbourne and Sydney in the opposite direction. Eschew the straight-as-an-arrow Hume Hwy and take the longer route around the eastern edge of Victoria and up the Sapphire Coast of southern New South Wales. Take a few days for the journey and you can overnight in low-key beach communities and arrive in Sydney relaxed rather than with a 1000-kilometre stare. There are several ways of reaching the east coast from Melbourne – a favourite is to head through Gippsland's green hills before skirting remote Croajingolong National Park, home to wild beaches. If you've got the kit, camping overnight here is a magical experience. Crossing the border into New South Wales, brings you to the Sapphire Coast and its calm bays, secluded surf spots, beach towns and whale-watching vantage points. Overnight options range from motels to B&Bs and upscale resorts.
Start // Melbourne
End // Sydney
Distance // 620 miles (1000km)

DENVER TO SAN FRANCISCO, USA

Friday night, Denver. Delivery driver Kowalski receives the keys to a 1970 Dodge Challenger R/T 440 Magnum and vows to deliver it to an address in San Francisco on Saturday morning. It's a drive of 1200 miles (1900km) across Colorado, Utah, Nevada and California. The film is *Vanishing Point*, a cult classic from 1971 and while we're not suggesting readers self-medicate or break speed limits like Kowalski in order to attempt it in two days, it is a great route across the West that has become something of a pilgrimage. The film itself is not much assistance in planning a route – many of the scenes are shot in wildly different locations – but it is possible to plot a route that avoids Interstate 80 and shares some of the movie's huge horizons. Kowalski heads west on I-70; stop in the ghost town of Cisco in Utah to discover one of the few filming locations along the route. You should also try to find a soul radio station on the dial to add to the atmosphere for an accurate recreation of Kowalski's epic drive.
Start // Denver
End // San Francisco
Distance // 1200 miles (1900km)

MÁLAGA TO SEVILLE, SPAIN

The history of Spain's sunny southern region of Andalucia is replete with extraordinary events that took place in the dramatic settings of mountains, gorges and pirate-plagued coast. The region has changed hands countless times over the centuries, being ruled by Romans, Vandals and Islamic invaders, among others. It was the Moors that left some of the most amazing mementos of their Islamic civilisation here, with cities such as Granada and Córdoba displaying their rich architectural legacies. This drive, from the tourist centre and main regional airport of Málaga to the Andalucian capital of Seville takes in one of the region's most famous *pueblos blancos* (white villages), Arcos de la Frontera, and the clifftop city of Ronda. Established in the 9th century BC, Ronda is one of Spain's oldest settlements and its attractions range from its 18th-century bridge and bullring to the old town, which dates from the Moorish period. The drive (and history lesson) concludes in marvellous Seville, where the Moorish Alcázar was built during the 1300s.
Start // Málaga
End // Seville
Distance // 140 miles (225km)

NORTHLAND & THE BAY OF ISLANDS

Head up from cosmopolitan Auckland for this diverse journey combining spectacular coastal detours, Maori art and culture, and echoes of New Zealand's colonial past.

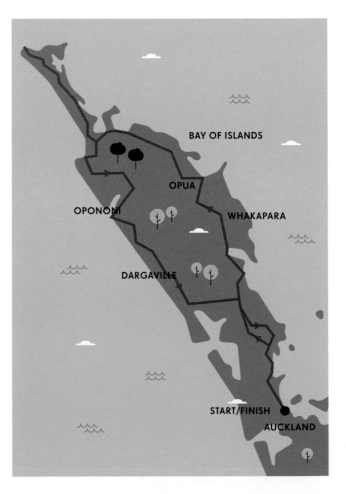

Crossing the graceful arc of Auckland's Harbour Bridge, I'm heading north to warmer climes to revisit a place packed with personal memories of earlier New Zealand road trips with family and friends. Northland – with its epithet 'the winterless north' imbued with Kiwi irony – is usually warmer than the rest of the country. As spring sunshine guides my car along SH1 I've got every reason to concur.

At the riverine town of Warkworth, I make a mental note to return in summer for the beaches, vineyards and markets of nearby Matakana, before pushing on through the tight, bush-clad turns of the Dome Valley, heading east to Mangawhai Heads to continue along a coastal backroad to stunning Waipu and its underground limestone caves. In summer, this winding route via Lang's Beach and Waipu Cove will be enlivened by the crimson splash of the pohutukawa tree and the surf beaches will be packed.

Whereas I would once feed coins into the juke box at the Waipu pub to fuel raucous New Year's Eve celebrations with university friends, this lunchtime I'm dining on wood-fired pizza and craft beer with the friendly brewer at McLeod's Brewery. I must admit that my uneducated palate probably wasn't ready for McLeod's bold hop-fuelled IPAs back then anyway.

From Waipu, I continue north on SH1 with sprawling Bream Bay on the eastern horizon. At Whakapara, 37 miles (60km) from Waipu, it's time to leave the main road and continue along the Old Russell Rd, a 40 mile (64km) route that negotiates forested hills and remote beach settlements dotted with the *marae* (meeting houses) of local Maori, New Zealand's indigenous people. High above Helena Bay a caffeine pit-stop at a local art gallery includes a goofily friendly welcome from three gentle Newfoundland dogs.

The day's final push into Russell skirts the oyster farms at Orongo Bay. In the early 19th century Russell was a raffish haven for boozing and brawling whalers and sailors, but tonight's action in this seaside town is limited to a pub quiz at the local tavern. The following morning I catch one of New Zealand's shortest car ferries to nearby Opua, and continue into the holiday town of Paihia.

The Bay of Islands can be explored by jetboats, helicopter or on dolphin-watching trips, but I'm eager to rediscover the heritage of nearby Kerikeri. Vineyard restaurants, craft shops and citrus orchards all beckon. I decide to explore the colonial history of the Stone Store – built in 1836 and New Zealand's oldest surviving building – before catching up with local artist friends at the lush Wharepuke Subtropical Gardens.

Kerikeri to Mangonui is usually a straightforward 31 miles (50km) blast along SH10, but I detour east again to incorporate another stunning coastal loop that's 24 miles (40km) longer. The Pacific's cobalt expanse segues to the far horizon high above Matauri Bay, before the road drops to prescribe a careful route past the compact coves of Wainui to sleepy Whangaroa Harbour.

I've got family history here – my great uncle and aunt used to manage Whangaroa's Marlin Hotel, and the historic pub is still a favourite watering hole of big game fishing fans. Meandering back to join SH10, I end the day with fish and chips and a cold beer at Mangonui's own heritage hotel built in 1905.

From Mangonui, I head for the far northern tip of New Zealand, and, buffeted by swirling winds, walk the final rolling mile to the Cape Reinga lighthouse. Known as Te Rerenga Wairua to the

THE WAITANGI TREATY

Explore Maori and colonial history at the Waitangi Treaty Grounds (www. waitangi.org.nz) in the Bay of Islands. In 1840, 43 Maori chiefs signed the Treaty of Waitangi with the British Crown. Admission to the waterfront location includes entrance to the Museum of Waitangi, a modern showcase of the role the Treaty has played in New Zealand's past, present and future. A Maori cultural performance is included.

Clockwise from above: scaling the Northland dunes; Waipu Caves; Cape Reinga lighthouse, New Zealand's northernmost point. Previous page: Waewaetorea in the Bay of Islands

Maori, the cape is the departure point for souls making the journey to their spiritual homeland in Polynesia. Beneath the lighthouse, the Tasman Sea and Pacific Ocean merge furiously. The waves rolling in further south at the small settlement of Ahipara are equally tempestuous.

After breakfast at Ahipara's laid-back surfer-run North Drift Cafe, my Northland journey continues down the region's less-visited and sleepier West Coast. Waiting at Kohukohu for a ferry across the Hokianga harbour, I chat with artists at a local gallery before making the short hop across to Rawene.

There's a thriving arts scene among this sleepy collection of heritage 19th-century buildings. The cosmopolitan No 1 Parnell gallery combines big city Auckland smarts with regular exhibitions of Far North artists, while Tupo Art showcases regular pop-up exhibitions often featuring local Maori artists.

My onward route south to Opononi is slowed by a local farmer and his dogs carefully steering a flock of sheep around rural roads. Later, I overnight at the local pub with views across the Hokianga harbour to the towering sand dunes of nearby Omapere. A local Maori family is gearing up for a wedding reception, and as the strummed guitars and easygoing harmonies blend I know I could only be in the northern reaches of New Zealand.

A 30-minute drive south of Opononi, the Waipoua State Forest is also quintessentially Kiwi. I've been here before with my parents and older brother – I was probably bleating 'Are we there yet?' from the back seat – but seeing the Tane Mahuta kauri tree is always an impressive experience. Named for the Maori god of the forest, this mighty tree soars 50 metres high with a girth of almost 14 metres. It's believed that Tane Mahuta was a tiny sapling even before Maori completed the ocean-crossing journeys from their Polynesian homeland 13 centuries ago. **BA**

"As the strummed guitars and easygoing harmonies blend, I could only be in the northern reaches of New Zealand."

DIRECTIONS

Start/End // Auckland
Distance // 613 miles (986 km)
Getting there // Fly in and out of Auckland.
When to drive // February to April offers the warmest and most settled weather, and also avoids New Zealand's busy school holiday period over the new year.
Where to stay // Northland offers everything from motels to luxury lodges. This drive would also be good in a campervan staying in holiday parks or Department of Conservation campsites.
Where to eat // Beyond Auckland's cosmopolitan dining scene, the best restaurants in the north are in Paihia, Russell and at the vineyards, cafes and markets around Kerikeri.
Detour // Foodies should include Matakana's vineyards, craft beer and Saturday morning farmers' market. Matakana also makes a good day trip from Auckland.
More info // See www.northlandnz.com.

*Opposite: Napier, an Art Deco
hotspot on Hawke's Bay*

MORE LIKE THIS
THE NORTH ISLAND

PACIFIC COAST HIGHWAY

New Zealand's indigenous Maori culture, coastal scenery and Art Deco design combine in this off-the-beaten track journey around the country's Pacific Ocean coastline. Start at Whakatane, one of NZ's sunniest cities and the departure point for boat trips to Whakaari (White Island), a sulfurous active volcano off the coast. Nearby Ohope is close to the protected wildlife refuge of Moutuhora (Whale Island). The remote region beyond Opotoki around NZ's easternmost point is steeped in the traditional ways of the Ngati Porou *iwi* (tribe), with local *marae* (Maori meeting houses) displaying beautiful wooden carvings. Further south, Gisborne is blessed with excellent beaches and fine chardonnay wine, while the Hawke's Bay cities of Napier and Hastings combine excellent vineyards with a thriving artisan food scene. Following a city rebuild after an earthquake in 1931, the streets of Napier host one of the world's finest collections of Art Deco architecture.
Start // Whakatane
End // Napier
Distance // 364 miles (586km)

THERMAL HOT SPOTS

Coursing through the North Island's geothermal region, this diverse drive bubbles over with spectacular geysers, steaming hot pools and soaring forests. Along the way there are opportunities to discover Maori culture; challenge yourself in the great outdoors adventure playground around Rotorua; and pay homage to the Middle Earth imaginations of J.R.R. Tolkien and Sir Peter Jackson. From Hamilton en route to Rotorua, stop in Matamata for one of New Zealand's most popular attractions, Hobbiton. Next, Rotorua's geothermal landscapes are actively on display at Hell's Gate, Lake Tarawera and the Waimangu Thermal Valley, while Whakarewarewa also incorporates Maori culture and food. Mountain biking, ziplining and zorbing are all popular in the forests around Rotorua. Further south around Lake Taupo – a huge caldera formed after one of history's greatest ever volcanic eruptions – the steaming geothermal area of Wairakei combines a thermal health spa and more mountain biking.
Start // Hamilton
End // Taupo
Distance // 146 miles (235km)

TARANAKI'S SURF HIGHWAY

Another off-the-beaten-track experience, this short drive begins in New Plymouth where you'll find the leafy Pukekura Park, one of NZ's best urban green spaces (also the venue for the eclectic rhythms of the Womad in March). Check out the spectacular Len Lye Centre exhibiting the thrilling kinetic sculptures of NZ-born artist Len Lye before heading south on SH45. With the comforting presence of Mt Taranaki always on your left, the road meanders through prime dairy farming country with sleepy side roads diverting to surf beaches made famous by intrepid boardriders seeking the perfect wave. Look out for the occasional shipwreck and lighthouse as you explore. Towns like Oakura and Opunake combine good cafes with an authentic Kiwi welcome, and Hawera's excellent Tawhiti Museum showcases the history of the settlers who shaped Taranaki alongside local Maori.
Start // New Plymouth
End // Hawera
Distance // 65 miles (105km)

A SHORT HOP FROM HOBART TO QUEENSTOWN

Delve into World Heritage-listed wilderness on this short drive of immense variety, discovering Tasmania's mountains, rivers and the historical attempts to tame them.

It's the story of a river as much as a road. In Hobart, Tasmania's capital city, the Derwent River flares wide – an estuary reaching its conclusion in the icy Southern Ocean – but in less than three hours I will be parked up beside its source, high in the Tasmanian mountains as it trickles from the deepest lake in Australia.

Rivers will yield to mountains; mountains will split into rivers. The road will carve through forest so thick as to be otherwise impenetrable, and then there will be no forest – a desert landscape created by humans.

I'm driving from Hobart to Queenstown on Tasmania's west coast, a straight-line journey of just over 100 miles (160km), but one that feels like a portal between worlds.

Out of Hobart the drive is all river, with the road running hard against the Derwent's banks – long, flat patches of mirror-still water broken by the occasional gurgle of rapids. In New Norfolk, where the road crosses the river, poplars and willows sparkle with autumn, stencilling colour onto the mist that lingers through the morning. As I drive onwards, the mist spreads like tentacles through the farmland that rolls north. One moment I'm above cloud, then in it, and then under it – it's a game of meteorological hide and seek at 60mph (100kmh).

The climb towards Tasmania's wild mountains begins past the town of Ouse, as the Lyell Highway squiggles skyward through tall forest. An echidna ambles across the highway, its body seeming to roll like a Slinky, and the land is criss-crossed with the canals that form the capillaries of Tasmania's hydroelectric network. For a time, the ground seems as much water as earth as I rise onto

Tasmania's Central Plateau, which is a high, barren tableland covered in untold numbers of lakes.

The most famous of the lakes is Lake St Clair, the first major stop of my drive, about two-and-a-half hours from Hobart. The lake is some three miles (5km) off the highway and, as I turn, I'm reunited with the Derwent River. Here it's in its infancy, flowing out from Lake St Clair as no more than a bubbling mountain stream.

Plunging to a depth of 167 metres and wrapped in magically shaped mountains, Lake St Clair is Australia's deepest lake. It's best known as the southern finish of Australia's most famous

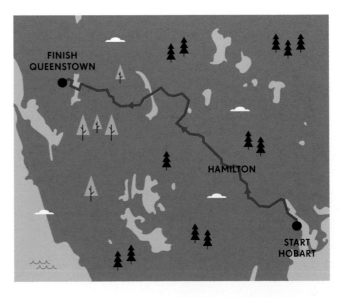

"Some of the tallest, oldest trees on Earth grow in dense rainforest and the land bristles with spectacular mountains"

bushwalking trail, the Overland Track. Stand at its edge long enough and a platypus may peep from the water, but this day there's just a large tiger snake sliding along the shore.

At Lake St Clair, I finally leave the Derwent River – farewell, wet friend – but the real grandeur of the drive is only now about to begin. Past Lake St Clair, as the highway cuts across the grain of the land, the road enters the Tasmanian Wilderness World Heritage Area, an unruly and mostly untouched swath of land that covers almost one fifth of the state.

It's a place where some of the tallest and the oldest trees on Earth grow among dense rainforest, and where the land bristles with the most spectacular and dramatic mountains in Australia. Driving through it on the Lyell Highway is like a wild date with Tasmania, for out here are places of natural legend.

From King William Saddle, just beyond Lake St Clair, the road snakes down to cross the Franklin River and then the Collingwood River where, beside the bridge, rafts are being packed in readiness for one of the world's great white-water trips: down the Collingwood and out into the Franklin River for a week of rapids and remote, wild camping.

I've also come to see the Franklin, but not right here. I drive on, stopping finally at a car park at the start of the hiking trail into a grand mountain named Frenchmans Cap. The walk to the mountain takes days, but it's just a few minutes down the track to the Franklin River, where a swing bridge crosses its famous waters. In the early 1980s there were plans to dam this most gorgeous of rivers. The blockade that ensued remains the most famous act of protest in Australia's history, stopping the dam's construction and helping turn the result of a federal election.

I climb down the banks to the river, slipping off my shoes and stepping into its ice-cold flow. The tannin-stained waters look almost psychedelically yellow as they flow over the pale river pebbles and my equally pale feet.

I'm nearing the end of the drive, but it will be a slow, halting journey from here on, with a series of enticing stops to slow my approach. Briefly there's a view of Frenchmans Cap, with its colossal quartzite summit appearing so white it looks permanently snowcapped. There are Nelson Falls, fanning down a cliff face a short walk from the highway, and large Lake Burbury, so still and reflective this day that the mountains around it seem to be doing headstands in the water.

Most memorable of all, though, is the final section of road into Queenstown. Known locally as the 99 Bend Road, it's my favourite section of driving in Tasmania, curling off the mountains into town through a horrifyingly fascinating landscape. On Tasmania's wet west coast, dense rainforest predominates, but here barely a tree grows, with the slopes denuded and poisoned by the copper mines that were once Queenstown's livelihood.

The bare earth is coloured by the minerals beneath, and it's a true moonscape, made all the more striking for the hours of green and clean wilderness that's brought me here. **AB**

TOWN FOR SALE

As you drive into Tarraleah on the way to Lake St Clair, it may strike you as an ordinary country town. But not all is at seems. Purpose-built to house hundreds of hydroelectricity workers in the 1930s, the town was abandoned in the noughties before being bought wholesale and turned into a town-wide hotel. In 2016 the entire town was again placed on the market, so if you have $11 million rattling around and the 'For Sale' signs are still out...

Clockwise from left: the Q Bank Gallery in revitalised Queenstown; Crater Lake on the Overland Track; rafting down the Franklin River. Previous page: Tasmanian snow gums in Cradle Mountain-Lake St Clair National Park

DIRECTIONS

Start // Hobart
End // Queenstown
Distance // 162 miles (260km)
Getting there // Hobart has direct flights to Melbourne, Sydney and Brisbane. Car hire is available at the airport.
Where to stay // Lake St Clair is one of the premier natural tourist attractions in Tasmania, and a great place to break the journey for a night. Poised at the end of a 250-metre-long jetty, Pumphouse Point (www.pumphousepoint.com.au) provides a quiet piece of luxury, sleeping atop the lake. Enticing lounges sit like a captain's bridge over the lake – grab a wine and hope a platypus pops into view. In Queenstown, the Q Bank Gallery (www.qbankgallery.com.au) offers Airbnb accommodation above an art gallery, all set in a handsome former bank building.

Opposite: the unmistakable profile of Cradle Mountain; the Enchanted Walk track at Cradle Mountain-Lake St Clair National Park; a Tasmanian devil, now a rare sight in the wild

MORE LIKE THIS
TASMANIAN DRIVES

WEST COAST

If you're just getting revved up by the time you reach Queenstown, simply keep driving. Tasmania's west coast keeps giving, with small fishing towns, giant sand dunes and the most recognisable mountain in Australia. From Queenstown, make for the coast at Strahan, the fishing town once described by a US newspaper as the 'best little town in the world'. Swing back past the wind-brushed Henty Dunes to join the Murchison Highway near Zeehan, passing through the small mining towns of Rosebery and Tullah before ducking in to admire the distinctive shape of Cradle Mountain – stretch your legs here with a gentle hike around Dove Lake at its foot. Plunge off the high plains to pass beneath the equally spectacular Mt Roland before joining the Bass Highway at Deloraine for the final stretch of the drive into Launceston.

Start // Hobart
End // Launceston
Distance // 310 miles (500km)

EAST COAST

The gentle counterpoint to the wild west coast is Tasmania's beach-lined east coast. The Tasman Highway climbs through dry hills (with perplexing names such as Break-Me-Neck Hill and Bust-Me-Gall Hill) to reach the coast at Orford. North from here is a succession of often-empty beaches as fine as any coastline in Australia... albeit with chillier water. Turn off onto Freycinet Peninsula to visit the geometrically perfect Wineglass Bay or climb onto the Hazards mountains, and then branch away again into the extraordinary colours – white sands, blue waters, orange lichens – of the Bay of Fires. From St Helens it's a hilly inland run to Launceston. If you're carrying a bike, you can break it out at the world-class mountain biking trails at Derby; or if you have a taste for cheese, duck into the Pyengana Dairy Company, just off the highway out of St Helens.

Start // Hobart
End // Launceston
Distance // 255 miles (410km)
More info // greateasterndrive.com.au

COCKLE CREEK

From Hobart, this drive culminates at the southernmost road in Australia – next stop south from here is Antarctica. For the most scenic route, head out of Hobart on Sandy Bay Rd, passing the Shot Tower in Taroona and then clinging to the coast through Kettering and Woodbridge to reach the laid-back and likeable town of Cygnet. Join the Huon Highway at Huonville – if you've set out early enough you may find that the wide Huon River is mirror flat as you pass through Franklin. From Geeveston, you can briefly detour inland to walk among the treetops at the Tahune AirWalk, or you can do the opposite – burrow underground – with a stop about 25 miles (40km) ahead at the Hastings Caves. The road turns to gravel past the caves, eventually running close to the shores of beautiful Recherche Bay and finally into Cockle Creek with its numerous campsites.

Start // Hobart
End // Cockle Creek
Distance // 112 miles (180km)
More info // www.southerntrove.com.au

ACROSS THE KIMBERLEY: THE GIBB RIVER ROAD

The far northwest Kimberley Region is AUSTRALIA written in capitals and the Gibb River Road is the outback track that takes you there.

Making its complete circuit-of-the-country, Highway 1, in its Great Northern Highway guise, skirts along the southern boundary of the Kimberley region. Between Derby and Kununurra the road runs through Fitzroy Crossing and Halls Creek, but if you want to really get to grips with what is arguably the country's most authentically 'Australian' region then you have to abandon that comfortably smooth thoroughfare and tackle the Gibb River Road. It runs through the heart of the Kimberley and is 125 miles (200km) shorter, but way slower. It can be a car-breaker. Tackle the Gibb River Road in wet conditions and you can be stuck

there waiting for a river to subside. Tackle it in the dry after a long spell without a grader coming through and the notorious corrugations can shake the fillings out of your teeth and rattle your car down to its component parts.

Assorted early explorers touched on the convoluted, inlet-cut, island-dotted coastline of the Kimberley, and today a convoy of adventure travel boats shuttle along this spectacular shoreline. Inland, the Kimberley is something of an open-air gallery of amazing Aboriginal rock art, whether it's the comparatively recent Wandjina paintings or the much older and still puzzling Bradshaw works. The English name comes from Joseph

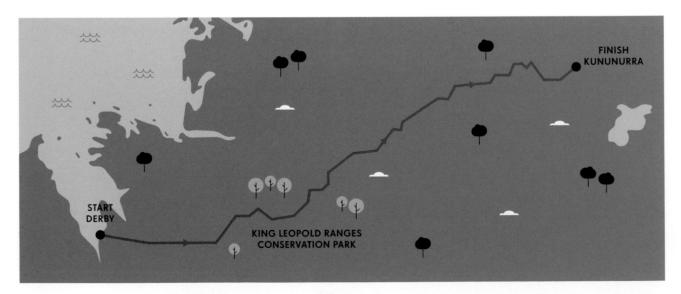

Bradshaw, a late 1800s pastoralist turned rock-art hunter who first categorised and labelled the paintings.

Today they're called Gwion Gwion paintings, but it's uncertain how old they are or even who did them – today's Aboriginals sometimes comment that they're 'not by our mob'. Bradshaw paintings are usually in 'galleries', often rock faces protected by overhangs, while the Wandjina works may be in everyday living areas. The later Wandjina figures are more varied in their subject matter, their design and their colours, but lack the subdued, calm elegance of the Bradshaw figures.

The secret of a successful foray along the Gibb River Road is to take your time, not to hurry. Drive too fast and those corrugations, loose stones, unexpected potholes and sharp edges can shred a tyre in seconds. This is a route where a second spare can be a very good idea. It's not just travelling slowly that can stretch the time, lots of the Gibb River Road attractions are excursions off the main route. You can add days to the trip if you plan to turn off south to the Mornington Camp, or if you head north up the road towards Kalumburu and then decide to divert to the Mitchell Falls.

Close to the Kununurra end of the road is El Questro, with its magnificent gorges and places to stay that range all the way from budget campsites to the luxurious Homestead, which is dramatically perched on a cliff edge above the Chamberlain Gorge. El Questro started out as a Kimberley cattle station and although today it's the best example of combining four-legged

"Tumbling down from one pool to another, the Mitchell Falls are the most spectacular waterfalls in Australia"

and two-legged business, for a number of the Gibb River Road cattle stations tourists are today just as important as 'beasts'.

Travelling east, Derby on the coast is the place to stock up, fuel up, admire the boabs – the Kimberley's signature tree – and enjoy the last stretch of bitumen before the rough stuff starts. Ninety miles (144km) from Derby is the turn-off to the dazzling Windjana Gorge and then Tunnel Creek, you can follow this track all the way to the Great Northern Highway, intersecting it not far west of Fitzroy Crossing. Don't plan to visit these sites in the wet season, but in the dry they're a vital diversion.

There's a campsite at Windjana Gorge and more places to stay at Mt Hart Wilderness Lodge and Charnley River, but many Gibb River Road travellers turn south to visit the Australian Wildlife Conservancy's Mornington Camp near the Fitzroy River. The camp makes a great base to explore over a thousand square miles (3000 square km) of stunning gorges, creeks and waterholes. In between paddling canoes along Annie Creek, visitors can dine under the stars or front the outback bar for a refreshing cold beer. As ever, Australia's outback night sky can offer an extravagant backdrop, while birdwatchers can add

their ticks to the checklist of more than 200 bird species which have been spotted in the sanctuary.

The halfway point comes up soon after the Mt Barnett Roadhouse, followed by the turn-off north to the Drysdale River Station and, almost up at the coast, the Kalumburu Aboriginal community. Another turn from that road takes you down an often very rough track past the Mitchell Plateau airstrip to the Mitchell Falls. They are worth the effort. Tumbling down from one pool to another, these are the most spectacular waterfalls in Australia. There are also swimming opportunities in the pools, as there are at other gorges and waterholes throughout the Kimberley. Of course, you have to keep an eye out for crocodiles at certain locations, but usually it's the reasonably friendly freshwater variety. Only on the way down towards the coast, well away from the Gibb River Road, do you encounter the distinctly less friendly saltwater crocodiles.

In the dry season there's usually a helicopter or two waiting to offer flightseeing trips over the Mitchell Falls. Helicopters also run from the Mitchell Plateau airstrip to the Kimberley Coastal Camp, one of the most remote Kimberley outposts which, if you can afford the entry cost, attracts near fanatical enthusiasts. Finally, there's Ellenbrae and assorted rivers – including the Durack River and the Pentecost River – to ford just before you reach El Questro. Soon after this final taste of the Kimberleys there's bitumen road to signal that it's not far to go to civilisation once again at the town of Kununurra. **TW**

STEP OUT OF THE CAR

It's a Gibb River Road surprise that you often find excuses to abandon your car for alternative transport. This could be your feet on the many interesting walking tracks; exploring the gorges by canoe, kayak or boat at Mornington Camp or El Questro (where horses are also on offer); or, if your credit card will stretch far enough, helicopters. Banking down those Kimberley gorges around El Questro in a chopper is simply mind-blowing.

Clockwise from left: Aboriginal rock art in El Questro Gorge; Outback scenery on the Gibb River Road; a destroyed tyre on Tony Wheeler's 4WD. Previous page: fording Pentecost River; a snorkel helps on deeper rivers

DIRECTIONS

Start // Derby, Western Australia
End // Kununurra, Western Australia
Distance // 440 miles (704km)
Getting there // Broome (138 miles, 220km from Derby) and Darwin (517 miles, 827km from Kununurra) are the major gateways to the region, though there are flights to Kununurra.
When to drive // Not when the wet season kicks in around November, unless you've got the experience to ford deep rivers and the patience to wait if they really are too deep. The road dries out by April.
Where to stay // Bring your camping gear. However, some places offer more permanent accommodation, including real luxury at El Questro (www.elquestro.com.au).
What to take // A 4WD, though when the road is good a rugged car can tackle it with enough ground clearance.

Opposite: tackling the Canning Stock Route requires some serious planning

MORE LIKE THIS
OUTBACK AUSTRALIA

THE SIMPSON DESERT

It's simple: you drive up to Birdsville, Australia's most remote town, just across the South Australia border into Queensland. The Birdsville Track or the Strzelecki Track will take you there. Way back in 1963, the Page family – mum, dad and three kids – ran out of fuel on the Birdsville and died of thirst before anybody came by. Relax, these days a lot more vehicles travel the outback. At Birdsville you turn left and 25 miles (40km) later you come to Big Red. Let down your tyres to get through the soft sand, and charge over this first and biggest sand dune, because if you can't top Big Red you're not going to be able to cross the next 1100 sand dunes from Birdsville to Dalhousie Springs and Mt Dare Homestead. Get over Big Red and you'll have a wonderful time crossing endless empty desert and encountering astonishing scenery, just make sure you've got enough food, enough water and enough fuel. En route you can stop at Poeppel Corner, where South Australia, the Northern Territory and Queensland meet.
Start // Birdsville, Queensland
End // Dalhousie Springs, South Australia
Distance // 315 miles (500km)

THE GUNBARREL HIGHWAY

There's the Gunbarrel, the original Gunbarrel, the real Gunbarrel... oh, never mind, just drive up from Kalgoorlie via Meekathara to Wiluna in Western Australia (where the Canning Stock Route starts). Then head east via Carnegie Homestead, Warburton, the Giles Meteorological Station and Docker River until you find yourself at Katu Tjuta (The Olgas), Uluru (Ayers Rock) and the modern visitor base of Yulara, just like countless thousands of tourists. Except they've all got there the easy, civilised way, from the east – you're today's only arrival from the west. You've travelled along a classic Len Beadell track. Back in the 1950s and early 1960s, Len, with a handful of fellow road builders and a big bulldozer, set out to cut 4000 miles (6000km) of tracks across central Australia so rockets could be launched from Woomera and British atomic bombs could be tested at Maralinga. He made his Gunbarrel Highway really straight, 'to keep Australia looking tidy and neat'.
Start // Wiluna, Western Australia
End // Yulara, Northern Territory
Distance // 850 miles (1350km)

THE CANNING STOCK ROUTE

Once you've done all those other Australian outback tracks it's time to point your 4WD at the really big one, the Canning Stock Route. The trouble is, it's a long way from Wiluna to Halls Creek, all of it in Western Australia. Count on two to three weeks driving and no matter how many long range tanks your 4WD sports, and how many extra containers of fuel you can stack on board, you simply can't cover that distance. The Canning Stock Route is marked by wells, 48 of them put in for the cattle that were, once upon a time, going to be driven down the route. Several times a year a truck drives in to Well 23 and, if you've arranged it, leaves a 50 gallon drum of fuel beside the route with your name on it. So drive north from Wiluna, stop to refuel from your own fuel dump at Well 23 and carry on until on the last day you intersect the Tanami Track, coming in westbound from Alice Springs. Soon after the junction, don't forget to make the little detour to check out the gigantic Wolfe Creek meteorite crater. Easy.
Start // Wiluna, Western Australia
End // Halls Creek, Western Australia
Distance // 1150 miles (1850km)

FOLLOWING THE CAPTAIN COOK HIGHWAY

Cruise the coastal cusp of Far North Queensland, on a shimmering hot strip of twisting tarmac separating the tropical rainforest from the iridescent Coral Sea.

O n the outskirts of Cairns, in the clammy embrace of high noon in the wet tropical north of Australia, great globs of sweat drip from my face onto the searing surface of the highway. On such a sunsoaked cloudless Queensland day, only an idiot would be running towards the city, away from the beaches, along a road made for air-conditioned cars, 4WD utes with windows wide and muscle-vest–clad motorcyclists.

I've drawn the running leg of the Cairns triathlon. It's not the short straw – that went to teammate Dale, who survived swimming the city's crocodile-populated waters – but it's Jeff we're jealous of. He swerved the curves of the Captain Cook Highway on a bike, while it was shut to traffic. As far as anyone can remember, the highway – built in the 1930s – hasn't been closed to cars since it was revamped in the 1980s. And judging by the reaction of some livid locals in this ultra-Australian corner of the antipodes, it may not happen again.

So, I may never taste exhaust-free salt air while cycling the shore-hugging road that slinks from the suburbs of Cairns to the door of the Daintree rainforest. But I will drive it. Tomorrow. And contemplating this keeps me going, across the finish-line.

Cairns might be the rough-and-ready relative of its latte-sipping cousins – Sydney, Adelaide, Melbourne, even Perth and Darwin – but it is busy and modern. And after motoring to Mossman along the Captain Cook Highway, first-time travellers will find themselves somewhere dramatically different – where the terrain has altered little since the eponymous British explorer crash-landed in 1770.

Flanked by dense rainforest on one side and tropical sea on the other; North Queensland is a place where some snakes are capable of swallowing kangaroos whole, and tiny jellyfish pack a punch 1000 times more powerful than a tarantula bite.

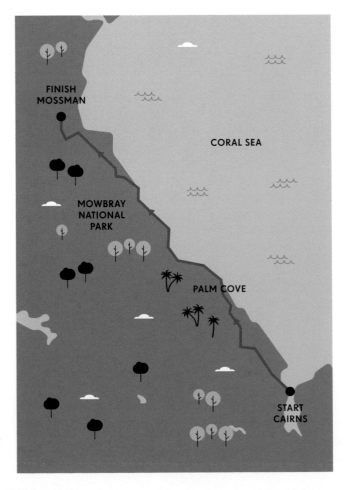

FINISH
MOSSMAN

CORAL SEA

MOWBRAY
NATIONAL
PARK

PALM COVE

START
CAIRNS

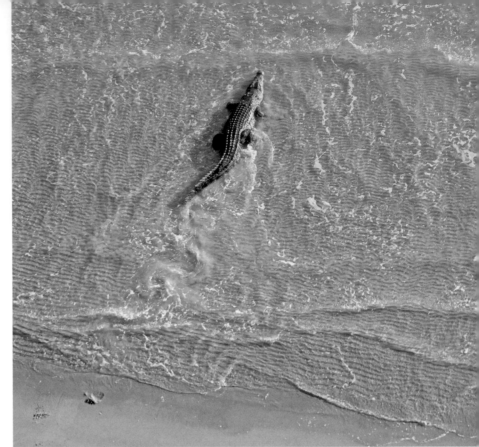

"Drivers are regularly reminded about the killer crocodiles in the creeks that dissect the road, and even on the beaches"

Drivers are regularly reminded about the presence of killer crocodiles in the creeks that dissect the road, and even on the beaches that fringe it – particularly galling, since the sandy oases that punctuate the drive are otherwise paradisaical. These warning signs start before I've escaped Cairns. They seem so incongruous with the suburban setting, as quintessential Queenslander houses cling to the ribbon of road well beyond Barron River bridge.

Approaching Smithfield, Skyrail gondolas float through the hot air, bound for the Tablelands that tower to my left, while roads peel right, leading to several beachy 'burbs and the posing princess of the posse, Palm Cove. Here, locals, blow-ins and backpackers swim, paddle, kitesurf and cavort in the long lagoon of the Coral Sea, becalmed by the Great Barrier Reef that runs parallel to the coast.

As the buxom profile of Palm Cove's Double Island disappears from the rear-view mirror, the road takes on a much more remote feel, as it sidles past the lush leafy face of Kuranda and Mowbray national parks. Below the peering pyramid of Black Mountain, the eucalyptus of these fecund forests are home to a menagerie of odd endemic animals, from tree kangaroos to flightless dinosaur-sized ducks called cassowaries, capable of stamping people to bits.

The road here shadows a super-scenic but little-explored section of seaside, whizzing past Wangetti, where hang-gliders hover on thermals above a lonely 2$\frac{1}{2}$ mile (4km)-long, palm-fringed patch of sand that would be a tropical tourist hotspot anywhere else on Earth.

I continue north, skimming the shoreline between the verdant expanse of Macalister Range National Park and the quiet crescent-shaped cove at Oak Beach, before turning off to Port Douglas, for a two-day diversion involving very different dips into the aquatic environments I've been driving past.

The first sees me stand-up paddleboarding and snorkelling around the Low Isles, a coral cay surrounded by 22 hectares of reef, just nine miles (15km) from Port Douglas. The second involves snorkelling too, but this time in the freshwater of the Mossman River, where a guide explains the relationship between the rainforest and the reef. The former feeds the latter, I learn, sending nutrients out to sea via creeks that sustain the kaleidoscopic coral.

Back on the road, I make it to Mossman, where the highway's bends end, but my learning curve continues, after I go the extra three miles (5km) to the famous gorge. My journey concludes in similar circumstances to the way it started: out of the car and on my feet. But I'm now wandering back through time on a tree-lined trail towards an ancient swimming hole deep in Mossman Gorge, a valley sculpted by the river I earlier snorkelled.

This has been home for the Kuku Yalanji for tens of millennia, as I've just absorbed on a tour led by an Indigenous elder. The peoples' knowledge of the land is immense, their connection to it intense, but their culture has been pushed closer to the edge of the existential abyss every year since Cook came along. This is a disquieting, but appropriate way to conclude a driving experience that's been educational at every turn, along a road named after an explorer who ushered in such seismic change across this continent. **PK**

CAPE YORK

The Captain Cook Highway terminates in Mossman, but continue along the Mossman–Daintree Road to drive into the hot heart of the rainforest. Hang a right on Cape Tribulation Road and ride the car-carrying cable ferry across the Daintree River to continue to Cape Trib for jungle surfing and other adventures, or go further up Cape York Peninsular, to Cooktown and beyond, to explore wild terrain as tarmac turns to dirt (4WD only).

Clockwise from left: a rainforest road on the Captain Cook Hwy; watch for saltwater crocs; Mossman Gorge in Queensland's Daintree National Park

DIRECTIONS

Start // Cairns
End // Mossman
Distance // 46 miles (75km)
What to drive // You don't need a 4WD to negotiate the Captain Cook Highway route, which is a sealed four-season road, but strong aircon will save whatever relationship you have with your travel companion. Alternatively, if you prefer the wind in your hair, it's a cracking trip in a convertible or on a motorbike.
When to drive // Unless you enjoy dressing up like a ninja to go swimming, avoid jelly season, which isn't half as much fun as it sounds, and refers to the period from October through May, when Queensland's tropical coast is plagued by marine 'stingers', including the potentially deadly Irukandji box jellyfish.

Opposite: Le Morne Brabant, Mauritius

MORE LIKE THIS
TROPICAL TRIPS

B9 ROAD, MAURITIUS

Skirting the Indian Ocean–facing Mauritius shoreline, the B9 belies its boring name. From Grande Riviere Noire, the road rounds sheer-faced Unesco World Heritage-listed Le Morne Brabant, a stunning monolith with a poignant memorial to the island's *Maroons* (escaped slaves). Threading through Baie-du-Cap, it then wends around an eye-popping U-bend, past a famous viewpoint at Macondé Rock, before reaching sandy Saint Martin and Bel Ombre's beaches. Passing Jacotet Bay, where a reef break has created a hot surfing spot with a rich history involving invasions and lost pirate loot, drivers reach Mauritius' best beaches – St Félix (snorkelling), Riambel (beachcombing) and dramatic (and dangerous) Gris Gris, with ocean-overlooking clifftop trails – before arriving at Souillac. Driving habits reflect the island's colonial history (Dutch, French, British), which is as colourful and confused as the country's flag. Traffic should keep left – a hangover of British rule – but many cars, clearly conflicted, cruise the middle.

Start // Le Morne
End // Souillac
Distance // 25 miles (40km)

CORAL COAST ROAD, FIJI

Think of Fiji and you'll inevitably picture palm-fringed beaches on perfect islets, a long way from roads and vehicles. But virtually every visitor to this Island nation arrives via Viti Levu – the country's biggest chunk of terra firma – and there's plenty to explore here, including a cracking coastal drive between the rainforest and the deep blue southern sea. Queens Road runs right along Viti Levu's South Pacific-stroked southern flank between its main cities, and from Korotogo, 44 miles (71km) south of Nadi, and Pacific Harbour, 31 miles (50km) west of Suva, the tarmac traces a reef that protects several beautiful beaches, facing out onto an iridescent seascape. Travelling east from Korotogo, the road runs alongside the lagoon for 21 miles (35km), passing a series of beaches, villages and resorts, including sensational Sovi Bay (one of the island's best swimming beaches, though beware strong currents) and the traditional-style Vatukarasa village. In theory, traffic drives on the left, though rules are loose outside the cities.

Start // Korotogo
End // Pacific Harbour
Distance // 45 miles (73km)

SHEK O ROAD, HONG KONG

Although not immediately associated with pleasurable driving, Hong Kong actually offers some sublime sections of subtropical road once you escape Central's chronically congested arteries. One of the best twists to the top of Tai Mo Shan, the territory's tallest peak, along a series of serpentine switchbacks. A very different drive, though, traverses the undulating island, beneath the Peak and Mt Cameron, before cruising the South China Sea coastline around Repulse Bay and crossing the Dragon's Back to Shek O, a lovely little fishing village, and Big Wave Bay Beach. Take Peak Road through Wong Nai Chung Gap, between Mt Nicholson and Jardine's Lookout, before following Repulse Bay Road to skirt the coquettish cove with an ugly name that no one can explain. Take Tai Tam Road across the peninsular and harbour, turn right onto Shek O Road, clamber over the Dragon's Back into Shek O Country Park and continue to the coast. Although most of China is RHT, in the former British territory of Hong Kong, traffic drives on the left.

Start // Central Hong Kong
End // Shek O
Distance // 14.5 miles (23.5km)

THE GREAT ALPINE ROAD

Hit Victoria's High Country for an action-packed Australian road trip that features hiking, biking, swimming and some very good beer.

The best thing about the Great Alpine Road, according to Ben Kraus at Beechworth's Bridge Road Brewery, is that there is so much to do outside the car. Australia's highest paved highway runs southeast from Wangaratta in northern Victoria through the High Country and pitches up at Gippsland's lakes on the edge of the cold Southern Ocean. On the way it passes by Beechworth, where I'm having a beer with its brewer, through the beautiful alpine towns of Bright and Harrietville, up some of the highest mountains in Australia and then descends into the more pastoral landscape of Gippsland. If you're interested in hiking, biking or horse-riding, and tasting some superb beers or wines, this is Australia's ultimate (and very thoroughly signposted) road trip.

I begin the journey with a detour. About half an hour out of Wangaratta, I sidle off the Great Alpine Road and make my first overnight stop in Beechworth (Wangaratta itself is about three hours from Melbourne so it's a sensible place for a pitstop). Beechworth

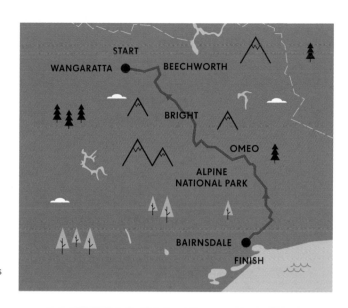

is one of Australia's most historic towns with more than 30 National Trust-classifed buildings and is itself part of Victoria's Golden Heritage Drive, which circles through the state's gold-mining history. If you squint your eyes, the town's crossroads could have stepped straight out of the 19th century, with the bushranger Ned Kelly on his way to settle a score or face justice at the courthouse. But I've stopped for another reason: a lap of the Beechworth Mountain Bike Park followed by a beer at Bridge Road Brewery. The bike park is the first of several in the region – Bright, Mount Beauty, Falls Creek and Mount Hotham have also all embraced the knobbly tyre, with bike rentals available in all but Beechworth. After a morning behind the wheel, it's refreshing to be on two wheels, watching out for echidnas and wallabies on the trails.

Beechworth charms another day out of my trip. It's a hot day but there are waterfalls and lakes to swim in, and the Beechworth Ice Creamery beckons – the intense raspberry ice cream is made with berries grown in Stanley, six miles (10km) up the road, alongside walnut groves and apple orchards.

After a relaxing sojourn, I rejoin the Great Alpine Road, next stop Bright. The road now runs parallel to the Murray to the Mountains Rail Trail, which is another great way of exploring Victoria's High Country. Soon signs of winter snowsports appear: ski hire and chalet rentals. This is a highly seasonal drive: spring is when the fruit trees are in blossom, summer sees dry heat and lazy days dabbling around in the rivers, autumn is the most colourful time of year, attracting leaf-peepers from across the state and winter is when snow falls on the higher stretches of road, to the extent that snow chains are compulsory.

Arriving in Bright an hour later, I park the car at the Bright on Track motel and grab my bicycle for another ride – there are world-class routes off the Great Alpine Road so it's hard to skip an opportunity. This time I pedal up Mount Buffalo. With 1120m of elevation it's one of the country's classic cycling climbs and is definitely a challenge so driving up to the top might suit some. My destination is the Mount Buffalo chalet, Australia's first ski resort. It was built in 1910 by the state government and generations of Victorians have had their first taste of skiing and tobogganing here. Now preserved for its architectural, historical and social importance, it retains an air of *The Shining* about it.

Fantastic hikes, as long or short as you like, fan out along the road into Mount Buffalo National Park. As you climb, whether on foot, by bicycle or in a car, the views along the Ovens Valley open up and the vegetation changes from lush ferns at the foot of the mountain to gnarled little beech trees higher up, and then there's just a bare plateau and The Horn, a granite peak whose shape suggested the mountain's name. Up here, at 1723m, scarlet-breasted robins flutter from rock to rock and the wind whips around the boulders.

Back down in the valley there's more wildlife-spotting to be done, this time in Bright's town centre. Amazingly, at least one family of platypus has set up home in the Ovens river that flows through the centre of town. It's testament to the purity of the mountain waters that these elusive creatures live in such close proximity to people. There's an art to spotting one: wait until just before dusk (unless you prefer a pre-dawn alarm call) and look for a V of ripples that appears to be going the wrong way up the river. The platypus uses its duck-like bill to sift for food such as larvae and shrimp. They nest and lay their eggs in burrows along river banks (yes, trust Australia to have the two egg-laying species of mammal in the world).

Bright, like Beechworth, merits an extended stay. The river-side hikes – whether or not the platypus come out to play – are wonderful. Local cyclists have also built mountain bike trails in the hills behind the town and the town hosts regular cycling events. But at the next stop on the Great Alpine Road, the high mountains are calling.

On the road to Harrietville, it's the wrong time of year for the avenue of trees to usher drivers into the town with a display of red, yellow and gold (arrive in April not November for that). But on higher ground there's still snow. I discover this for myself when I hike the seven miles (12km) from Harrietville to the peak of Mt Feathertop, Victoria's second highest mountain at 1922m. Several routes follow ridge lines to the summit but the quickest and most popular is the Bungalow Spur track. From the top, the Australian Alps disappear into the distance. The mountains were formed not by collision, like many ranges, but separation, as the ancient continent of Gondwana pulled apart. Then 60 million years of ice, frost, wind and water smoothed and eroded the landscape into the valleys and rounded peaks of today.

Once in these higher hills the Great Alpine Road becomes more of a drivers' road, with staggering views and sweeping corners. Approaching Mount Hotham, the steep and twisting road is at its most challenging, before it begins its descent to Dinner Plain and Omeo. The third act of this performance is a winding down from the crescendos of hiking, biking and driving, as the end of the Great Alpine Road returns to sea level in Gippsland. **RB**

GIPPSLAND'S LAKES

On a drive of many epic detours, it's easy to postpone the end of this road trip in Gippsland. Equidistant from Bairnsdale or Metung, where the Great Alpine Road concludes, the heritage town of Bruthen is the start of the signed Gippsland Lakes Drive. This takes in Lakes Entrance and Ninety-Mile Beach, a fitting location for a final stroll. Then it's back in the car for the return trip to Melbourne, about three hours west.

Left: camping on Mt Feathertop. Previous page: a hiking track on Mt Buffalo; driving the Great Alpine Road near Mt Hotham

DIRECTIONS

Start // Wangaratta
End // Bairnsdale
Distance // 195 miles (312km) not including driving the freeway to and from Melbourne (about 3hrs either way).
When to drive // Autumn is the prettiest time, with autumn leaves around Harrietville. Snow chains must be carried from the Queen's Birthday public holiday (early June).
Where to stay // In Beechworth, the Armour Motor Inn (www.armourmotorinn.com.au) offers good value accommodation. In Bright, try Bright on Track (www.brightontrack.com.au), with smart and spacious rooms. In Omeo, try the quiet Omeo Motel (www.omeomotel.com.au).
Where to eat // Two great breweries in Beechworth and Bright offer end-of-drive refreshment. The Commercial Hotel in Beechworth and Ginger Baker in Bright are solid options.

Opposite: a river boat on the Murray

MORE LIKE THIS
GREAT VICTORIAN DRIVES

THE BLACK SPUR

Whether you're on a motorbike or in a nimble sports car, there's a stretch of road in Victoria that gets drivers' pulses racing: the Black Spur, a twisty section of tarmac between Healesville and Marysville that features corner after sweeping corner. It's only 18-miles (30km) in length but your attention will be tightly focused for every second and your arms will get a workout. What elevates this road to be arguably one of the best in Australia is the way it weaves through stands of colossal Mountain Ash eucalypts and giant ferns. It's a mesmerising experience and best experienced away from the weekend traffic. Pick an out-of-season weekday morning and you'll have it to yourself (almost). Healesville, surrounded by vineyards, is a hugely popular destination for weekending Melburnians and Marysville, gateway to the mountains, is returning to its former vibrancy after devastating bush fires. Continue from Marysville up to Lake Mountain for another superb drive.
Start // Healesville
End // Marysville
Distance // 18 miles (30km)

ALONG THE MURRAY RIVER

If your perfect drive is more about places to stop and savour along the way then the slow pace of this roadtrip in northern Victoria is for you. Your slow-swirling companion is the mighty Murray River, an Australian icon. The waterway is lined by river red gum trees and plied by grand old steamboats. In previous centuries the river, Australia's longest at 1500 miles (2500km), was an essential thoroughfare, rising in the snow-capped Australian Alps and flowing along the border between Victoria and New South Wales before reaching its mouth in South Australia. It retains something of that frontier allure with towns such as the main port Echuca still featuring horse-drawn carts, riverboats and historic buildings, if only for the benefit of sightseers not settlers these days. The drive starts in Albury-Wodonga, on the Hume Hwy, passes through the renowned Rutherglen wine region before stopping in Echuca. The next leg runs from Echuca to Swan Hill, as the landscape becomes desert-like before ending in Mildura.
Start // Albury-Wodonga
End // Mildura
Distance // 412 miles (660km)

MANSFIELD TO MARYSVILLE

This collection wouldn't be complete without a taste of Victoria's gravel (unsealed) roads. Unlike the epic drives elsewhere in this chapter, many of Victoria's enviable range of gravel roads run through forests and mountain ranges. They're not generally difficult to drive (although a bit of extra clearance from a soft-roader or 4WD is preferred) but because they venture into more remote parts of the start they do require a little extra planning for fuel stops. East to west, there are hundreds of gravel roads to explore (check out the Otways, the Dandenongs and beyond). One of our favourites is the section between the High Country town of Mansfield and Marysville, closer to Melbourne. This road goes through Woods Point, a tiny town in the middle of a forest that has become a hub for off-road drivers and trail bikers who test their skills and vehicles in the steep surrounding hills. You can do this drive in a few hours, but you get a sense of being a bit further from civilisation than usual.
Start // Mansfield
End // Marysville
Distance // 108 miles (175km)

THE TRACK: ALICE SPRINGS TO DARWIN

Encounter otherworldly rock formations, wild watering holes, grand gorges, monsters and aliens on a long lonely road to the top end of a sunburnt country.

The sign outside Alice claims 1,500km (932 miles) of road stretches between the rental wagon's windscreen and our destination. And we're already 24 hours behind schedule.

We're driving The Track – the section of the Stuart Highway (AKA the Explorers Highway) between Alice Springs and Darwin. Until the 1980s, it was exactly that – a lumpy bumpy dirt track – but now the surface is smooth and flatter than road-train roadkill, and you can legally gallop along at 80mph (130kmh), if your vehicle has the horsepower. I'm not sure our house-on-wheels does, but I'll give it a nudge, now we're running late.

At least the lost day was well spent. By accident, our intended departure for the half-a-continent-crossing clashed with Alice's Henley-on-Todd Regatta, where homemade 'boats' race along an arid riverbed, awash with beer and sweat rather than water. The riotous regatta has only been cancelled once, in 1993, when a flash flood filled the Todd River, rendering the bottomless boats useless. For this, you change your itinerary.

Plans, like pants, are best worn loose on the Explorers Highway, anyway. Not because surprises lie around every bend (there are no bends, you basically aim at the horizon and keep going) but because when something appears on the skyline, it's always worth checking out. Luckily, this route across an agoraphobia-inducing expanse of outback is regularly punctuated by leftfield landmarks.

In its 1761 mile (2834km) entirety, the Stuart Highway cuts a vertical line through the rusty red middle of Australia, from Adelaide to Darwin. It's named after the Scottish explorer John McDouall Stuart, who crossed the colossal country south to north in 1861-62.

Bidding Alice adieu, we drive through a cleavage in the ruddy MacDonnell Range, go past historic Telegraph Hill and cross the

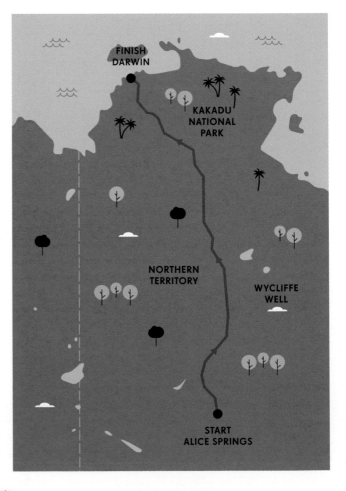

"Little (and large) green men and women populate the campground. Wycliffe claims to be the UFO capital of the country"

train tracks of the Ghan, which roughly chuffs along parallel to the highway. Passing a posse of feral camels (descendents of the Afghan animals brought over to build the railway), we enter the Tropic of Capricorn and hit the open road, to tango with the road trains (immense multi-trailer-trawling trucks) that patrol it.

Pulling into Wycliffe Well hours later, the youngest member of the campervan crew – Ivy, a four-year-old – nearly explodes with excitement. The place is full of alien figures. Little (and large) green men (and women) populate this campground, where a sign stresses that humans are also welcome.

Wycliffe claims to be the UFO capital of the country, a reputation mostly based on accounts of unexplained celestial activity made by bored WWII servicemen. Plenty of people have reported strange sights since, suggesting something extra-terrestrially extraordinary is going on here – or a not-so-mysterious marketing plan is working hard – but either way, this is a quirky and convenient place to stop for a beer and a bite, and to crash for the night, especially with kids.

Just up the road, in relative terms, is Karlu Karlu/Devils Marbles Conservation Reserve. We roll into this genuinely enigmatic spot on a bluebird dawn to find behemoth boulders lying strewn across the outback. Many are split clean in half, presenting perfect photo ops, while others are precariously balanced on top of one another.

Stuart's expeditions were funded by people planning a telegraph route across Australia, and the Track still has a buzzing communication system, with travellers sharing advice in campgrounds along its length. "Don't miss the butchers in Tennant Creek," a grey nomad had croaked over a schooner of NT Draught in one such place. "Best snags [Australian for sausage] in the bloody country." And she wasn't wrong. We stocked up on outback bangers on the way through this much-maligned mining town, and had a cracking roadside barbecue.

For early explorers, sighting the Katherine River – the first free-flowing fresh water since Alice – was cause for celebration, and it's a welcome oasis for modern drivers, too. The area demands several days' diversion on stunning trails through Nitmiluck National Park, walking to plunge pools beneath waterfalls and the gorgeous gorge.

On a canoe trip, just after a dip, we spy slide marks on the banks – the telltale tracks of a crocodile. The resident reptiles here are the supposedly harmless freshwater variety, but we keep our feet dry for the rest of the paddle. After passing through Humpty Doo and turning right onto the Arnhem Highway to Adelaide River Bridge, we meet a few of our friendly freshies' fearsome family members, on a Jumping Crocodile Cruise. Estuarine crocs are Earth's last genuine dinosaurs, and here we're close enough to smell the beasts' breath.

Hours later, munching a barramundi burger in the tropically moist ambiance of Darwin's Mindil Beach Sunset Market, the Track's red dust feels far distant, and Alice Springs could be on another planet.

Darwin's boats have real water to race across, although the tepid Timor Sea and creeks here come with crocs. Soon we'll seek out safe swimming holes in Kakadu's wetlands, back along the Arnhem Highway. But not yet. We've done enough driving for now. **PK**

ARNHEM LAND ART ADVENTURE

Arnhem Land, where the Indigenous population maintain a traditional lifestyle, is typically off-limits to travellers, but you can visit Injalak Art and Culture Centre with a day permit from the Northern Land Council in Jabiru. The trip involves fording the East Alligator River at Cahill's Crossing (possible only at low tide), where saltwater crocs lurk on either side, and driving alongside the amazing Arnhem escarpment, along a bone-shaking road.

Clockwise from left: the little green men of Wycliffe Well; Mindil Beach in Darwin; the Devil's Marbles. Previous page: you risk hitting a roo driving after dark on the Stuart Hwy.

DIRECTIONS

Start // Alice Springs
End // Darwin
Distance // 930 miles (1500km)
Getting there // Fly into Alice Springs Airport, 9 miles (15km) outside town, from most major Australian cities.
When to drive // The Australian winter, from June to August, is the ideal time to do this drive, depositing you in Darwin during the Dry, when the heat is bearable
What to drive // The Stuart Highway is a good-quality, sealed road for its entire length, suitable for pretty much any vehicle. The road is well trafficked, but distances are epic, so be sure to carry spare tyres and plenty of water. Campervans are ideal, providing accommodation (in areas where options are very limited) and transport. To explore areas either side of the road, a 4WD is recommended.

Opposite: the beguiling sand dunes
of Oman's Empty Quarter

MORE LIKE THIS
DRY AND DUSTY DRIVES

MUSCAT TO SALALAH, OMAN

The inland route between Muscat and Salalah is a classic desert drive with epic skyscapes. But stay alert. Recently renovated, Highway 31 is infamous for the carcasses of cars that line it, detritus of disasters caused by high-speed meetings between potholes and motorists stupefied by the relentless immenseness of the 360-degree desert views, including into the Rub' al Khali (Empty Quarter) that stretches into Saudi Arabia. The road also touches terrific highland terrain, however, and during the monsoonal *Khareef* (June-September), delivers drivers to Dhofar during a period of spectacular greenness. Take Highway 15 from Muscat to Nizwa, gateway to Jebel Shams and Jebel Akhdar mountains. From here, doable-in-a-day Highway 31 stretches to the Arabian Seaside in eight bite-size bits, via Adam, Al Ghabah, Hayma, Al Ghaftayn, Muqshin, Qatbit and Thumrayt, from where the road roller-coasters through the Dhofar Mountains to arrive at sensational Salalah and Arabia's finest beaches.
Start // Muscat
End // Salalah
Distance // 646 miles (1040km)

SKELETON COAST, NAMIBIA

Skirting Namibia's Atlantic fringe, the Skeleton Coast runs 410 miles (660km) from Swakopmund to the Angolan border. Despite its seaside setting, this bleached bones and shipwreck-strewn stretch is ultra desolate, like the set of a post-apocalyptic film. However, the C34 salt-and-gravel coastal road from the old German colonial outpost of Swakopmund to the end-of-the-world settlement of Terrace Bay is a brilliantly dramatic desert drive. Travel north through Swakopmund saltworks, a twitcher's paradise, and Henties Bay, gateway to the Cape Cross Seal Reserve. Traverse the Skeleton Coast National Park between the Ugabmund and Springbokwasser gates, looking out for signposted shipwrecks, victims of Africa's version of the Bermuda Triangle (seafog caused by desert heat meeting ocean chills causes the carnage). The road evaporates just beyond Torra Bay at Seal Beach – to go further, you need a charter flight.
Start // Swakopmund
End // Terrace Bay
Distance // 225 miles (363km)
Note // Motorbikes are not allowed to drive the coast.

SANTIAGO TO SAN PEDRO DE ATACAMA, CHILE

Polar regions aside, Chile's Atacama Desert is Earth's highest and driest desert, and a stunning region to drive. Sandwiched between the ocean and the Andes, parts of this place haven't felt rain for over 400 years (possibly ever), yet sometimes snowflakes fall. A place of exquisite extremes, it is possible to drive from the capital in a week via the Pacific Coast, stopping at Chile's chaotic culture capital Valparaíso, plus Viña del Mar, La Serena and Copiapó. The desert drive proper begins after turning away from the coast at Antofagasta to reach the gateway town of Calama. From here, head to San Pedro de Atacama, once the epicentre of a Palaeolithic culture and now a brilliant base for exploring the desert's jewels, including the Salar de Atacama salt flat, stunning Valle de la Luna (Moon Valley) and the extraordinary El Tatio geyser field. From here, continue into Argentina through Reserva Nacional Los Flamencos, or venture into Bolivia via Eduardo Avaroa National Reserve.
Start // Santiago
End // San Pedro de Atacama
Distance // 1060 miles (1705km)

INDEX

Epic Drives of the World
August 2017
Published by Lonely Planet Global Limited
CRN 554153
www.lonelyplanet.com
10 9 8 7 6 5 4 3 2 1

Printed in Malaysia
ISBN 978 17865 7864 8
© Lonely Planet 2017
© photographers as indicated 2017

Managing Director, Publishing Piers Pickard
Associate Publisher & Commissioning Editor Robin Barton
Art Director Daniel Di Paolo
Designer Callum Lewis
Editors Dora Whitaker, Tasmin Waby, Nick Mee
Print Production Larissa Frost, Nigel Longuet

Lonely Planet Offices

Australia
The Malt Store, Level 3,
551 Swanston St, Carlton, Victoria 3053
T: 03 8379 8000

USA
124 Linden St, Oakland,
CA 94607
T: 510 250 6400

Ireland
Unit E, Digital Court,
The Digital Hub,
Rainsford St, Dublin 8

Europe
240 Blackfriars Rd,
London SE1 8NW
T: 020 3771 5100

STAY IN TOUCH lonelyplanet.com/contact

Authors Alex Crevar (**AC**); Amanda Canning (**AC**); Amy Balfour (**AB**); Andrea Sachs (**AS**); Andrew Bain (**AB**); Anita Isalska (**AI**); Anna
Kaminski (**AK**), Anthony Ham (**AH**); Becky Ohlsen (**BO**); Brandon Presser (**BP**); Brett Atkinson (**BA**); Chris Colin (**CC**), Christa Larwood
(**CL**), Duncan Garwood (**DG**); Etain O'Carroll (**EOC**), Garth Cartwright (**GC**); Grant Roff (**GR**); Greg Bloom (**GB**), Joe Bindloss (**JB**); Kate
Armstrong (**KA**); Kerry Christiani (**KC**); Kevin Raub (**KR**), Lucy Corne (**LC**); Mark Johanson (**MJ**); Marcel Theroux (**MT**), Oliver Berry (**OB**),
Oliver Smith (**OS**), Pat Kinsella (**PK**); Paul Rees (**PR**); Peter Thoeming (**PT**); Robin Barton (**RB**); Tim Moore (**TM**); Tony Wheeler (**TW**)

Cover and illustrations by Ross Murray (www.rossmurray.com) **Maps** by Callum Lewis (www.callum-lewis.com)

Paper in this book is certified against the
Forest Stewardship Council™ standards.
FSC™ promotes environmentally responsible,
socially beneficial and economically viable
management of the world's forests.